PRAISE FOR *Be the People*

"*Be the People* is a courageous analysis of today's most pressing issues, exposing the deceptions by the cultural elite and urging 'We the People' to restore America's faith and values."

—SEAN HANNITY
NEW YORK TIMES BEST-SELLING AUTHOR; SYNDICATED RADIO HOST,
THE SEAN HANNITY SHOW; FOX NEWS CHANNEL HOST, *HANNITY*

"Dr. Swain's *Be the People* is an excellent piece of work—a thorough and honest examination of how politics and America's history intertwine in the real world. Dr. Swain explores many public policy topics. I strongly recommend her chapter on immigration policy and politics; she provides a thoughtful examination of a complex topic that often generates strong feelings."

—REPRESENTATIVE LAMAR SMITH (R-TX-21)
CHAIR, COMMITTEE ON THE JUDICIARY, U.S. HOUSE OF REPRESENTATIVES

"In *Be the People* Professor Carol Swain thoughtfully examines the biblical roots and religious significance of today's most pressing issues. Professor Swain shows how to make your voice heard and how to reclaim America's faith and values."

—LOU DOBBS
HOST, FOX BUSINESS NETWORK'S *LOU DOBBS TONIGHT*; NATIONALLY SYNDICATED
RADIO HOST, *LOU DOBBS SHOW* AND *LOU DOBBS FINANCIAL REPORTS*

"There are many good books but only a few really important ones. Dr. Carol Swain's *Be the People* is one of the latter. Brave, informed, candid, and thoughtful, she brings her fine academic mind to bear on the most pressing needs facing our country. She calls on 'We the People' to be the people our nation's founders envisioned, a people united around a common set of moral convictions who have the courage to live them out. Dr. Swain proves that Christian faith and deep patriotism are alive and well and offers a recipe of hope for America's future."

—TONY PERKINS
PRESIDENT, FAMILY RESEARCH COUNCIL

"Carol Swain is that rarest of rare things: a distinguished university professor and prominent public intellectual who is willing to stand up and speak out for God and country. Far from considering herself to be superior to her fellow citizens for whom religious faith, old-fashioned virtues, and a spirit of patriotism are cherished values, she encourages—and, indeed, challenges—the people of the United States to be *more* intensely devoted to what Lincoln referred to at Gettysburg as 'this nation, under God.' *Be the People* is a ringing affirmation of the central principles of the American republic and the traditions of faith and thought that brought it into being. Professor Swain does not turn a blind eye to America's failings, be they the enslavement of her fellow African-Americans earlier in our history or the abandonment of the unborn to abortion, but she reminds us that the key to reform is—as it always has been—renewed fidelity to the principles of liberty and justice on which this great and good nation was founded."

—ROBERT P. GEORGE
MCCORMICK PROFESSOR OF JURISPRUDENCE, PRINCETON UNIVERSITY

"In *Be the People* Dr. Swain offers a vigorous defense of the founding values so many of us hold dear. She exposes the insidious misperceptions, even lies that elites in this country have perpetuated to justify the growth of government and the dilution of our core values. Professor Swain's inspirational book is important for Americans who hope and pray for a better nation."

—REPRESENTATIVE MARSHA BLACKBURN (R-TN-7)
VICE-CHAIR, SUBCOMMITTEE ON COMMERCE, MANUFACTURING, AND TRADE,
US HOUSE OF REPRESENTATIVES

"Carol Swain is simply a *truth teller*. She makes no apologies for her conservative, pro-American stances. *Be the People* will illuminate you to the real truth about the social, fiscal, and godless nosedive our country is experiencing right now. This book will challenge you to stand up and do something about it. God bless Dr. Swain!"

—JOHN RICH
COUNTRY MUSIC SINGER, SONGWRITER, AND PRODUCER

"A courageous, challenging, and controversial call to Americans of all colors to return to their Creator and to come to their Judeo-Christian senses."

—DR. PETER A. LILLBACK
PRESIDENT, THE PROVIDENCE FORUM; AUTHOR, *GEORGE WASHINGTON'S SACRED FIRE*

"I applaud Carol's labor. Everyone should read this work, immediately commit to the action points at the end of each chapter, and recommend this book to someone else. Be a nation-changer! Together, we can reclaim both America's faith and the vision our forefathers carried as they established this great nation."

—Bishop Harry R. Jackson, Jr.
Senior pastor, Hope Christian Church; president and founder,
High Impact Leadership Coalition

"In *Be the People* Carol Swain unflinchingly takes on the cultural elites that disdain America's religious and political traditions. I don't always agree with her, but I am grateful for her voice in the debate."

—James Taranto
Wall Street Journal editor, OpinionJournal.com,
and author, *Best of the Web Today*

"If you desire to be further empowered in taking a meaningful and right stand concerning issues that will shape our future freedoms and the release of God's blessings, if you want a solid resource to aid and enlighten your political position while supporting your beliefs, read *Be the People*.

"Ignorance is not bliss: clearly we must stand united for America with a clear and informed voice at such a time as this."

—Jennifer O'Neill
Actress, author, speaker

"This dynamic and insightful book is a must read for every American as Dr. Swain pulls back the veil and powerfully reveals the truth about those who are actively engaged in the attempt to destroy our nation from within."

—Dr. Richard Lee
Editor, *The American Patriot's Bible*; speaker, There's Hope America

"Carol Swain has written one of the best apologetics for the conservative Christian worldview that I've ever come across. Everyone concerned about the direction this country seems to be going in of late should read this excellent call to action."

—John Rosemond
Family psychologist, author, *The Diseasing of America's Children*

"In *Be the People* Carol Swain does a masterful job of describing the plight of America in 2011. While making no attempt to sugar-coat the reality of the problems we face as a nation, Dr. Swain nonetheless offers practical and time-tested ideas for public policy initiatives that will bring back the blessing of God to America.

"But beyond the insightful analysis of where we are as a nation and the steps to find healing, there is the incredible human story of how, through God, Carol overcame impossible odds to become the accomplished woman she is today. I am left with a sense of awe about the power of Christ to transform a life and then use that life to touch others."

—RANDY HEKMAN
CANDIDATE FOR US SENATE IN MICHIGAN; AUTHOR, *JUSTICE FOR THE UNBORN*

"*Be the People* is a courageous, carefully researched, comprehensive, insightful, and timely gift to the American people. Dr. Carol Swain . . . writes with the sober conviction of one who well understands the risks of speaking up but who has also measured them as carrying far less weight than the risk of silence or compromise. God bless her."

—REV. JESSE LEE PETERSON
FOUNDER AND PRESIDENT, BOND (BROTHERHOOD ORGANIZATION
OF A NEW DESTINY); NATIONAL RADIO TALK SHOW HOST

BE THE PEOPLE

BE THE PEOPLE

A Call to Reclaim America's Faith and Promise

Carol M. Swain

THOMAS NELSON
Since 1798

NASHVILLE   DALLAS   MEXICO CITY   RIO DE JANEIRO

Published in Nashville, Tennessee, by Thomas Nelson. Thomas Nelson is a registered trademark of Thomas Nelson, Inc.

Thomas Nelson, Inc. titles may be purchased in bulk for educational, business, fund-raising, or sales promotional use. For information, please e-mail SpecialMarkets@ThomasNelson.com.

Unless otherwise marked, Scripture quotations are taken from the English Standard Version. © 2001 by Crossway Bibles, a division of Good News Publishers.

Scripture quotations marked KJV are taken from the King James Version of the Bible.

Scripture quotations marked NKJV are taken from the New King James Version®. © 1982 by Thomas Nelson, Inc. Used by permission. All rights reserved.

Scripture quotations marked NIV are taken from the Holy Bible, New International Version®, NIV®. © 1973, 1978, 1984 by Biblica, Inc.™ Used by permission of Zondervan. All rights reserved worldwide. www.zondervan.com

Scripture quotations marked AMP are taken from the Amplified® Bible, © 1954, 1958, 1962, 1964, 1965, 1987 by The Lockman Foundation. Used by permission. (www.Lockman.org)

Library of Congress Cataloging-in-Publication Data

Swain, Carol M. (Carol Miller)
  Be the people: a call to reclaim America's faith and promise / Carol M. Swain.
    p. cm.
  Includes bibliographical references (pp. 261–301) and index.
  ISBN 978-0-8499-4828-2 (hardcover)
  1. Christianity and politics—United States. 2. United States—Moral conditions. I. Title.
  BR526.S93 2011
  261.70973—dc22

                                                                                    2011006168

Printed in the United States of America
11 12 13 14 QG 9 8 7 6 5 4 3 2 1

To fellow Americans who hope and pray
for a reawakening of our nation

We are often told that we live in secular, even postmodern times. The old pieties, not only about God or morality but even about truth itself, no longer command our unqualified allegiance. We are too sophisticated to believe in absolute right or wrong or to make confident moral judgments. We are too worldly to submit to the genius of tradition. We are too enamored with our rights to take our bearings from what we once thought to be our duties. With science and technology pointing the way, the race for health, pleasure, and prosperity is rapidly becoming the only successful game in town. Such, at least, is the conventional wisdom about life in the modern world.

—LEON R. KASS, *The Beginning of Wisdom*[1]

Murder is no better than cards if cards can do the trick. Indeed the safest road to Hell is the gradual one—the gentle slope, soft underfoot, without sudden turnings, without milestones, without signposts.

—C. S. LEWIS, *The Screwtape Letters*[2]

CONTENTS

CONTENTS

ACKNOWLEDGMENTS

I WOULD LIKE TO THANK THOSE WHO PLANTED THE IDEA OF MY WRITING A book about the implications of America's abandonment of its Judeo-Christian roots and provided encouragement for what seemed to be a daunting venture. Foremost among these is Gary Fine, pastor of King of Glory Church, who told me he believed that I would one day write an important book about America.

Friend and colleague Gerry McDermott of Roanoke College read chapter drafts and encouraged me when my ideas were in their rudimentary stages. Others who stood by me at the inception of this project include my agent, Tim Beals, and my friend and colleague Mary Poplin of Claremont Graduate School, who opened her home to me during the fall of 2009. Alan and Becky McClellan of Roanoke, Virginia, and John and Kate Turbyfill of Bonita Springs, Florida, provided me with places of respite.

Author and friend Shelly Beach prayed for me and helped me make the transition from academic to popular press writing. Stephen Haymore, Alexander Sweet, and Saurabh Sharad worked as research assistants. Jason Husser, Robert P. George, Larry Pierce, William Booth, and Marvin Olasky commented on some chapters. Christie Bishop, my Vanderbilt University Law School assistant, cheerfully rendered whatever services I requested. Bishop Sherman Merritt, Pastors Jeff and Becky Dollar, Pastors Carol and L. H. Hardwick, Betsy and Henry Headden, Tami Heim, Sisse Pfieffer, and Tanya Villani showered me with encouragement. And other people, including Facebook and Twitter friends, who are too numerous to mention.

Lastly, I am indebted to Vanderbilt University for providing me with a sabbatical and to the top-notch team at Thomas Nelson Publishers for their commitment to this project. These include acquisitions editor Debbie Wickwire, copyeditor Jennifer Stair, publicist Stephanie Newton, and Matt Baugher, vice president and publisher of nonfiction trade books.

A RISK WELL
WORTH TAKING

AT THE INCEPTION OF WRITING THIS BOOK, I PLANNED A FOUR-DAY VISIT with Mary Poplin, PhD, a colleague at Claremont Graduate University. However, my stay unexpectedly became a four-week retreat of daily writing marathons that resulted in the rough draft of the manuscript.

Mary and I are both successful academicians who rediscovered our Christian roots in midlife. We met a few years ago at a Christian conference. After reading my rough draft, Mary looked me in the eye one morning and said, "Carol, America needs your book. It can help change the course of our nation. It can help cut through the lies, bring clarity to our thinking, and help end confusion about biblical principles. But I fear there is great risk for you. If you publish this manuscript, your academic career could be over. Too many Christian scholars live in fear. They shy away from the tough issues where biblical truth conflicts with cultural norms."

Mary should know. She has fought her own fair share of battles since 1993, when she became openly Christian, and more recently after the 2008 publication of her book, *Finding Calcutta: What Mother Teresa Taught Me About Meaningful Work and Service*, about her experiences working with Mother Teresa.[1]

Yet publishing this book is a risk well worth taking, because America is a nation well worth restoring.

WHY I WROTE THIS BOOK

I have always had a deep love for my country. As one of twelve children living in the rural South in a four-room shack with no running water, I experienced poverty and racism. Yet even when I was a high school dropout and teenage mother, I still trusted in the American Dream. I believed I could make a better life for my family, so I worked hard, got my GED, and not only put myself through college but earned five graduate degrees and went on to have a successful career in academia. I have seen life in America from the bottom, from the middle, and from the top. Through my experiences I have learned something about what works and what doesn't.

I wrote *Be the People* for the millions of hardworking, honest Americans who, like me, have deep concerns about the direction of our nation. Our country is allowing cultural elites to manipulate the public in harmful ways. With our tax dollars "We the People" support public policies and practices that are harmful to our society and to the nations we influence. And we are frustrated by elected officials who act as if the opinions of their constituents no longer matter once elections are over. We often forget that We the People have a responsibility to stand up and *be the people* because we are ultimately responsible for the policies our elected officials enact on our behalf. Although we sometimes feel powerless, We the People can still make our voices heard through organized protests and strategic efforts to influence our culture.

My hope is that this book will expose the lies and empower this generation of Americans to become skilled at gathering, filtering, and evaluating the information that comes to us shaped by the media, the cultural elite, educational institutions, and other gatekeepers who have set themselves up as change agents. We the People can replace passivity with an energized American spirit willing to fight for the values and principles that helped make our nation one of the greatest the world has known.

A CALL TO ACTION

Be the People is intended for three distinct groups. First, the book is presented as a tribute to the 78 percent of Americans who profess a belief in the Judeo-Christian God and who find themselves increasingly disillusioned with the ethical and moral shifts in our political and social institutions. Second, the book offers points to ponder and debate for conservative scholars, public policy makers, intellectuals of all faiths, and persons interested in public policy, religion, and politics. Lastly, it offers atheists and secular humanists an opportunity to examine closely the values and principles that motivate a segment of the population they disparage as the Christian Right.

This book is a call to action for We the People to reclaim our nation's faith and promise. The chapters that follow will expose the deceptions that have infiltrated our culture, reveal the historical and biblical roots of these bedrock issues, and provide action points to take the next steps. I urge you to read this book carefully, educate yourself on the issues and facts, and then join the thousands of other Americans who are taking the risk to restore our country's faith and values.

The futures of our children and grandchildren depend on the choices we make today.

—Carol M. Swain
Nashville, Tennessee
August 7, 2010

PART ONE

BROKEN VOWS

Forsaking What We Once Knew

CHAPTER 1

RESHAPING OUR NATIONAL IDENTITY

That to secure these rights, Governments are instituted among Men . . . That whenever any Form of Government becomes destructive of these ends, it is the Right of the People to alter or to abolish it, and to institute new Government . . . in such form, as to them shall seem most likely to effect their Safety and Happiness.

—THOMAS JEFFERSON, THE DECLARATION OF INDEPENDENCE[1]

It is good to appear clement, trustworthy, humane, religious, and honest, and also to be so, but always with the mind so deposed that, when the occasion arises not to be so, you can become the opposite . . . Let a prince then concern himself with the acquisition of a state; the means employed will always be considered honorable and praised by all, for the mass of mankind is always swayed by appearances and by the outcome of an enterprise.

—NICCOLÒ MACHIAVELLI, *The Prince*[2]

THE AUDIENCE WAS CLEARLY IMPASSIONED. PANELISTS WERE DIVIDED between supporters of reparations for black slavery and pragmatists, such as myself, who rejected the idea as impractical. At one point in the discussion, a well-dressed, middle-aged black man in the audience stood up, identified himself as a successful Harvard graduate, and proceeded to tell the packed audience that nothing much had changed in America for blacks since slavery. He claimed that the country was as racist as it had ever been and would always be. I nearly choked.

I glanced at the man and then studied the faces of students nodding in gullible agreement. I thought, *How could a man who has obviously enjoyed the fruits of success give America's youth such a dismal message?* Unfortunately, I hear negativity like this dispensed often across America by a rainbow coalition of liberals who seem to disdain the country I hold dear.

As a high school dropout and teenage mother in the 1970s, I could see the promise of a better life glimmering before me. I trusted in the American Dream. I believed that if I worked hard enough and played by the rules, my efforts would be rewarded one day. I was one of twelve children born in extreme rural poverty, but even I could arise and make something of myself.

And I did. I earned a GED, went to a community college, and graduated from a four-year college. I moved on to graduate school, where I earned the academic degrees that allowed me to become a university professor. But when I worked in an Ivy League school, I was a fish out of water. I shouldered the disregard of the arrogant, liberal mind-set that showed little patience for a black conservative woman with a thick Southern accent. Looking back on those early years, I chuckle and say, "God has a sense of humor." Nothing else could explain this journey I'm on.

I was born in 1954 and grew up at a time when patriotism and respect for authority still mattered. Unlike many people I've encountered at elite institutions, I've always loved and been proud of my country. I embrace traditional values. I count myself among the middle-aged nerds who never smoked a joint or quite understood all the protests of the 1960s. Through it all, I developed and have sustained a sense of patriotism that now mixes with faith in God.

Today I am in the uncomfortable yet opportune position of being an African American academic who disapproves of the unbiblical direction my country has taken in recent years. I proudly wear my American flag pin, salute the American flag, and stand while our national anthem is played. I believe that America is still the greatest nation in the world. I have written this book because I care about this nation and the promise it still holds. This book sounds a rallying cry for my fellow Americans to stand up and reclaim the promises of life, liberty, and justice envisioned by our forefathers, many of whom were deeply committed to Judeo-Christian values and principles.

This book sounds a rallying cry for my fellow Americans to stand up and reclaim the promises of life, liberty, and justice envisioned by our forefathers.

COMPLICITY'S PRICE

People find it surprising that I take offense when I hear national leaders end their speeches with "God bless America!" This unsettles me, because a national leader asking a blessing from God assumes two things: first, that America acknowledges God, and second, that America considers itself worthy of blessing. However, we must face foundational problems that lie in these assumptions. First, our government has repeatedly taken actions to alienate itself from God. And second, which actions or attitudes in American society in recent memory would warrant God's blessing? While surveys show that the overwhelming majority of Americans profess to believe in the Judeo-Christian God, our individual actions and government policies often disregard or disdain anything holy or sacred.[3] In recent years, we have allowed politicians, educators, media experts, and cultural leaders to persuade us to embrace behaviors diametrically opposed to biblical teachings.

The cold winds of change sweeping through Washington, D.C., and our nation are damning evidence that even though we say we believe in God, we live like atheists. We consider God to be either nonexistent or irrelevant—and certainly not in the business of distributing rewards and punishments. The solemn vows of faith that once impelled our leaders to bravery and provided the solid principles upon which our country was founded have been broken and abandoned to the wind. The virtues produced by faith in God have been banished from our borders.

For the most part, We the People have met the recent radical shifts in our nation with a collective shrug. Thus we have been complicit in not only the erosion of our constitutional rights but also the spiritual malaise that grips our nation.

Recent grassroots uprisings reflect growing disillusionment and demonstrate that we finally realize something is profoundly wrong in our beloved country. The rules of morality have changed, and we sense that the new moral relativism will ultimately result in harm, not good. A Gallup poll taken in 2010 found that 76 percent of Americans agree that moral values have deteriorated.[4] Similarly, a Rasmussen Reports survey found 65 percent agreeing that the United States is headed in the wrong direction.[5]

For the most part, We the People have met the recent radical shifts in our nation with a collective shrug.

Americans' acceptance of cultural relativism has opened the floodgates for many changes.[6] Cultural relativism rejects absolute right or wrong, teaching that truth is valid only for a particular society at a given point in time. Acceptance of this worldview creates an environment in which tolerance is elevated as the highest virtue. In order to gain control and indoctrinate others, "cultural enforcers" in media, education, and government have seized responsibility to set the standards of behavior for the rest of the American people.[7] Often these efforts are tragically well-intentioned, motivated by a desire to create a better world—a utopian society that replaces old values and norms with a better way of life.

Columnist Chris Hedges argues that a small number of elite educational institutions such as Harvard, Yale, Princeton, Stanford, Oxford, and Cambridge shape a disproportionate number of editors and reporters for the *New York Times, Wall Street Journal,* and *Washington Post.* These institutions also produce many Supreme Court justices, members of Congress, corporate executives, political nominees, and presidential Cabinet members. According to Hedges, who is a product of the institutions he criticizes, these universities mold students from the same "cookie cutter" and socialize them to think and act alike:

> The elite institutions disdain honest intellectual inquiry, which is by its nature distrustful of authority, fiercely independent, and often subversive. They organize learning around minutely specialized disciplines, narrow answers, and rigid structures designed to produce answers. The established corporate hierarchies these institutions service—economic, political, and social—come with clear parameters, such as the primacy of an unfettered free market, and also with a highly specialized vocabulary. This vocabulary, a sign of the "specialist" and, of course, the elitist, thwarts universal understanding. It keeps the uninitiated from asking unpleasant questions.[8]

As a university professor I, too, have observed a strong tendency of people educated at elite institutions to smirk at working-class Americans and those whose dialects and behaviors identify them as outsiders. Cultural enforcers disdain the use of biblical references as explanations for human problems. They act as if the answer to every problem lies in the secular humanist's reasoning. Americans empower this group when we weakly defer to their so-called expert opinions, even when these opinions lack sound judgment.

At less-elite institutions of higher learning, administrators and faculties often forget their unique roles as they strive to mimic the universities of the Northeast. Often I hear of institutions of higher learning seeking to be known as the Harvard of the South or the Harvard of the West, yet this is a problematic quest. Our universities rarely, if ever, challenge politically correct rules that demand religious arguments, texts, and references be off-limits in public debates because of the separation of church and state. Many of us have bowed to the atheistic arguments of cultural enforcers at elite universities, even though an overwhelming majority of Americans describe themselves as Christians and even more as believers in Almighty God.

Also highly disturbing is evidence that our nation is following a path strikingly similar to totalitarian societies. In these societies, government gains control over the media, the economy, and educational and religious institutions.[9] Those in power possess the means to shape and manipulate information. Today in America, cultural enforcers are seeking control and deceiving citizens into supporting policies and practices detrimental to our individual and collective interests. Some Americans have awakened to the cultural forces reshaping society but feel powerless to resist. Most prominent among the people who are successfully fighting back are those within the Tea Party movement, largely composed of first-time activists, which swept the country in 2009 and 2010.

Many of us have bowed to the atheistic arguments of cultural enforcers at elite universities, even though an overwhelming majority of Americans describe themselves as Christians and even more as believers in Almighty God.

One of those fighting back is Matt Moynihan, a thirtyish Vanderbilt University graduate and married father. Moynihan cofounded the Sumner County, Tennessee, Tea Party in February 2009 and writes editorials for a conservative newspaper. The election of Barack Obama catapulted Moynihan into action. "I was never involved in politics until the fall of 2008," he said. "I saw we were losing what was beautiful about the country, what our Founding Fathers envisioned and what has made us the envy of the world . . . Electing a black man fueled a celebration of overcoming racism . . . [and] in the process we failed to look at the values of the individual being elected . . . I don't think the Founding Fathers expected it to be this way."[10]

ORWELLIAN PARALLELS

George Orwell examined the process of systematic cultural change in his riveting novel *Nineteen Eighty-Four*. Sobering—perhaps even chilling—

parallels can be seen between twenty-first-century America and the country of Oceania depicted in Orwell's novel. Oceania is a totalitarian society in which government controls every facet of life, including thought. Citizens of Oceania can never be sure when or where the government is monitoring them. They are not free to create or think beyond the boundaries set by "Big Brother," their ruler. Big Brother exerts control through strategic deception, manipulation of rhetoric and language, and revision of history.

Oceania's four government agencies execute its policies. The Ministry of Love administers law and order, the Ministry of Peace conducts war, the Ministry of Plenty controls the economy and the production of goods, and the Ministry of Truth writes and rewrites the history of the nation by exerting power over the news media, schools, entertainment, and arts— all to strengthen Big Brother's grip on society.

LANGUAGE, REVISIONIST HISTORY, AND THE ROLE OF DECEPTION

In Orwell's world, language controls thought. The government manipulates and controls the context and flow of information, producing an illusion of truth. Words are regularly redefined and given new meanings that contradict what they formerly represented. For instance, the definitions of truth and justice are reinvented: "War Is Peace, Freedom Is Slavery, and Ignorance Is Truth."[11]

Oceania's governmental enforcers use a thought-control technique called "doublethink" to befuddle citizens into accepting government-controlled messages. New messages often contradict previously held directives. Citizens are forbidden from questioning government or holding it accountable for actions. One propaganda slogan encapsulates the government's philosophy of deception: "Who controls the past controls the future: who controls the present controls the past."[12]

BIG BROTHER IS WATCHING YOU

The reality of Oceania is knocking on America's doors in the form of increased surveillance and White House authorization to assassinate

American citizens suspected of terrorist links.[13] Acting on recommendations of the Defense Science Board,[14] the Obama Pentagon in January
2010 pushed for creation of an Office of Strategic Deception to gather
and disseminate information to confuse America's enemies.[15] That idea
fortunately never left the proposal stage. But if an Office of Strategic
Deception does not cause chills, perhaps other American similarities
shared with Oceania produce alarm. In August 2009, West Virginia
senator Jay Rockefeller introduced legislation (S.773) that would give the
president emergency control over the Internet.[16] Rockefeller's bill has
been making its way through Congress.[17]

In February 2010, Americans learned that Google, the world's largest
Internet company, had entered an information-sharing agreement with
the same National Security Agency that would gain control under the
Rockefeller bill. This unusual agreement between the government and
a private company potentially compromises the privacy of millions of
Americans who use Google's search engine on a daily basis.[18]

---

*The reality of Oceania is knocking on America's doors in the form of increased
surveillance and White House authorization to assassinate American citizens
suspected of terrorist links.*

In July 2010, the British Broadcasting Corporation (BBC) published
reports that Consumer Watchdogs, an advocacy group, was asking
Congress to investigate reports that Google was using its roaming
street view to spy on members of Congress.[19] It was reported that Rep.
Jane Harman (D-CA), chair of the House Intelligence Committee, and
eighteen members of the House Energy and Commerce Committee had
their homes pictured on Google's StreetView.[20] For this to have happened suggested that their Wi-Fi networks had been scanned.[21] Google
later acknowledged that it recorded information that came across on
unencrypted Wi-Fi networks.[22] Harman's system was unencrypted.[23]

Furthermore, the Department of Homeland Security now monitors social networking and news sites, blogs, and search engines. Twitter, Facebook, the Drudge Report, the Huffington Post, Google, and the Blotter rank among its targets.[24] Existing government-sanctioned Internet surveillance goes beyond searches for terrorists and allows the government to investigate and apprehend drug dealers, "tax delinquents, copyright infringers and political protesters."[25]

In January 2010, the *Washington Post* reported that President Obama had signed off on documents that would allow the Central Intelligence Agency and the Joint Special Operations Command to assassinate US citizens living abroad if the agencies suspect an al Qaeda connection or a potential threat to other Americans. This action allows assassinations of Americans, even if they are not involved in combat situations. Assassinating an American citizen without a trial seemingly violates the due process clause of the Fourteenth Amendment and the long-held understanding of how the rule of law operates in a democratic republic. In Oceania, the state vaporized its enemies.

RADICAL DREAM FOR THE REDISTRIBUTION OF POWER

In his book *Rules for Radicals*, Saul Alinsky, the founder of modern community organizing, articulates strategies disturbingly similar to those practiced by Orwell's leaders in *Nineteen Eighty-Four*. Based in Chicago, Alinsky influenced legions of conservative and liberal activists.[26] Hillary Clinton wrote her senior thesis at Wellesley College about him, and Barack Obama worked as a Chicago community organizer for a group headed by Alinsky's former students. Alinsky's guide to revolution begins with a tribute to Lucifer—yes, the devil—as "the first radical known to man who rebelled against the establishment and did it so effectively that he at least won his own kingdom."[27]

Alinsky advocated deception, infiltration, and manipulation to destroy systems that he believed work against the interests of the people. The ultimate goal of the community organizer, in Alinsky's scheme, is to create a utopian society that redistributes power from the "haves" to the "have-nots": "We are concerned with how to create mass organizations to seize power and give it to the people; to realize the democratic dream of equality, justice, peace, cooperation, equal and full opportunities for education, health, and the creation of circumstances in which man can have the chance to live by values that give meaning to life. We are talking about a mass power organization which will change the world . . . This means revolution."[28]

To be effective as an organizer, according to Alinsky, a leader needs to "play God." He wrote, "The ego of the organizer is stronger and more monumental than the ego of the leader. The leader is driven by the desire for power, while the organizer is driven by the desire to create. The organizer is in a true sense reaching for the highest level for which men can reach—to create, to be a 'great creator,' to play God."[29]

For Alinsky, the ends justify the means. He advises organizers to spread emotionally charged terms such as *liberty, equality, fraternity, common welfare*, and *pursuit of happiness*. To succeed, organizers must "get people pregnant with hope and a desire for change and to identify you as the person most qualified for this purpose."[30] Alinsky's book is popular with the Left. The National Educational Association lists it among its recommended reading for would-be leaders.[31]

DROWNING OUT THE OPPOSITION

Cries for "progress" have drowned out many voices of truth and morality in American society. Increasingly, our leaders are willing to manipulate the facts and use fear to foster uniformity and attack the concept of objective truth. Dissenters who oppose cultural elites can expect attacks like those launched against former vice-presidential candidate Sarah Palin.

We have allowed people in the media, politics, and education to define what is acceptable. We are dazzled by rhetoric, credentials, and titles at elite institutions, where people consider themselves the best and brightest, even if they lack sound judgment. They proclaim that all opinions, cultures, lifestyles, and forms of artistic expression are equal, and only bigots dare say otherwise. Those who question the agendas of cultural elites or defend traditional values, the rule of law, or belief in God are labeled Neanderthal! Nativist! Birther! Fundamentalist! Homophobe! Racist! Xenophobe!

In response, many of us have allowed pressure to silence our voices. We've questioned our own values, hung our heads in shame, and suspended our common sense. Like the citizens of Oceania, we watch passively as government takes control and eradicates liberties from us and our children.

FOUNDATIONAL QUESTIONS

America's foundation is shifting. It is time to think clearly. Who have we been historically, and what kind of nation are we becoming?

The Declaration of Independence declares our national sovereignty by appealing to the rights guaranteed by "the Laws of Nature and of Nature's God."[32] Many of America's founders recognized that the nation was ultimately beholden to God and God alone. Christianity's virtues and principles anchored our nation with a system of ethics, values, and shared vision that helped make us the greatest nation in the world. We are the nation that formed a republic where power lies in the hands of the people whose duties include the election of representatives who are held accountable through the electoral process. The electoral process is our protection against governmental tyranny. Our government runs on a system of checks and balances among the executive, legislative, and judicial branches and shares power among levels of authority. But is America still a sovereign nation under the rule of law?

America's foundation is shifting. It is time to think clearly. Who have we been historically, and what kind of nation are we becoming?

For most of its history, America has presented itself to the world as a Judeo-Christian nation. But times are changing; we have broken the vows made by our Founding Fathers and banished our foundational beliefs.

Revisionist thinking has swept the nation under the presidency of Barack Obama, who stated, "Whatever we once were, we are no longer a Christian nation—at least, not just. We are also a Jewish nation, a Muslim nation, a Buddhist nation, and a Hindu nation, and a nation of nonbelievers."[33] In a statement that earned *Polifact*'s "Pants on Fire" rating for telling a blatant lie while he was in Cairo, Egypt,[34] President Obama repeated a statement he has made in various parts of the world: "If you actually took the number of Muslims Americans [*sic*], we'd be one of the largest Muslim countries in the world."[35] However, this statement is false. According to the CIA's *World Factbook*, America ranks near the bottom of the list of nations in Muslim population, with "less than 1 percent—0.6 percent to be precise—of the 307 million residents identified as Muslim. That means the United States has only 1.8 million Muslims."[36]

Although the United States adheres to a separation of church and state, few people would deny the seminal role of Christianity in shaping the nation's political and social institutions. In 2009, a Gallup poll reported that 78 percent of Americans identify themselves as Christians[37] and a significant percentage respect the Judeo-Christian Bible. While only one-third of Americans believe that the Bible is literally true, a solid majority of college graduates (53 percent) and the postgraduate-educated (57 percent) accept the Bible as the "inspired word of God,"[38] and only 19 percent consider it to be a book of fables. Nevertheless, trends in the American political climate demonstrate that we are discarding biblical morals, ideals, and our Judeo-Christian heritage and are exporting our immorality to other nations.[39]

Over time we have made bad choices that have broken our ancestors' vows of faith to the God of the Bible. We have banished virtues we no longer find relevant. We have educated a generation that does not understand its nation's unique destiny. Today many of our citizens regard our country as unexceptional, and some Americans despise the remarkable heritage that was once highly valued. Because we no longer appreciate our distinctiveness as a nation, we risk accepting the restructuring of our national boundaries and sovereignty.

President Barack Obama has told the world, "I believe in American exceptionalism, just as I suspect that the Brits believe in British exceptionalism, and the Greeks believe in Greek exceptionalism."[40] Furthermore, he has told the UN General Assembly, "It is my deeply held belief that in the year 2009—more than any point in human history—the interests of nations and peoples are shared. In an era when our destiny is shared, power is no longer a zero sum game. No one nation can or should try to dominate another nation. No world order that elevates one nation or group of people over another will succeed. No balance of power among nations will hold."[41]

Over time we have made bad choices that have broken our ancestors' vows of faith to the God of the Bible. We have banished virtues we no longer find relevant. We have educated a generation that does not understand its nation's unique destiny.

Without a doubt, America as a nation stands at a crossroads.

THE CHALLENGE

Without a distinct national identity, we are a nation adrift. Yet as we have become entangled in dubious international agreements, our nation's leaders have convinced us that we are just like the other nations of the world—even though these nations share neither our heritage nor our value system. Our historical position as a world leader has weakened. Today as we struggle with once-unimaginable problems that affect every sector of society; the familiar phrase *God bless America* no longer rings with power. The question Americans must now face is whether we can again infuse these words with purpose and meaning.

To do so, we must take a long, hard look at our choices as a nation and do whatever is necessary to redirect and reclaim our unique American vision.

ACTION POINTS

1. Arm yourself with information about how closely the actions and events we see happening in this nation coincide with life depicted in George Orwell's *Nineteen Eighty-Four: A Novel* (1949).[42] Set up a reading group to read and discuss *Nineteen Eighty-Four* and Saul Alinsky's *Rules for Radicals: A Pragmatic Primer for Realistic Radicals* (New York: Random House, 1971). The latter book has played a powerful role in the shaping of the liberal left agenda and some of that movement's brightest lights.

2. If you are comfortable doing so, write out a prayer to the omniscient, omnipotent, and omnipresent Creator God, thanking him for having the situation under control. Isaiah 40:15 reads, "Behold, the nations are like a drop from a bucket, and are accounted as the dust on the scales; behold, [God] takes up the coastlands like fine dust." Consider what the issues facing America are like from God's perspective.

3. Read and discuss the *Be the People* questions for chapter 1, posted at www.CarolMSwain.com.

CHAPTER 2

AMERICA'S RELIGIOUS ROOTS

God and Christianity are nowhere to be found in the Constitution, a reality that infuriated many at the time. The U.S. Constitution drafted in 1787 and ratified in 1788, is a godless document. Its utter neglect of religion was no oversight; it was apparent to all.

—ISAAC KRAMNICK AND R. LAURENCE MOORE, *The Godless Constitution*[1]

America has not been lucky; she has been blessed. She is the product of the determination of our forefathers to forge a nation built on biblical principles. As they labored to create a Christian nation, God looked with affection and favor upon their efforts and gave them supernatural guidance that enabled them to author foundational documents unlike any the world had ever seen before. The wisdom of our Declaration of Independence and Constitution can only be described as inspired. Truly the hand of God was driving the thoughts and decisions of those men.

—RICK SCARBOROUGH, *Enough Is Enough*[2]

SOON AFTER I JOINED THE FACEBOOK COMMUNITY, I ADOPTED THE MOTTO "Let's debate and not hate." As a public intellectual, political scientist, and law professor—and a conservative Christian—I am well aware of the debates that rage over the faith of our Founding Fathers and other issues related to the role of religion in America. Out of my desire for respectful and honest investigation and interaction, I set ground rules for the way I hoped people on my page would engage one another.

On one hand, Christian conservatives frequently insist that America was founded to be a Christian nation. Conversely, liberal intellectuals point out that the words *Christian* and *Jesus Christ* do not appear in either the US Constitution or the Declaration of Independence. Thus, liberals argue, America's Founding Fathers deliberately established a nation that would be secular and godless in its governmental operation. Conservatives respond by cheerfully pointing out that the men who signed the Constitution chose to reference Christ when they signed the historical document "in the year of our Lord."[3]

However, liberals and conservatives are often reluctant to admit that the historical record provides support for both perspectives.

ROOTS OF COVENANT CULTURE AND COMMITMENT

The American republic was the invention of religious-minded men and women who fled from Europe to birth a nation where people could worship as they pleased. They wanted a land where citizenship would not be predicated on blood lines. The Puritans who landed at Plymouth Rock in 1620 deliberately and purposefully entered into a covenant with God and with each other. The Mayflower Compact bound them to a civil government that would honor the Christian God.[4] Stronger than a contract, a covenant is a solemn pact freely entered into between trusting parties that stipulates the obligations of each side and spells out the consequences for broken vows.

In the Bible, God made a binding covenant with the nation of Israel. Daniel Elazar, a political scientist and specialist on Jewish Studies at Temple University, describes the far-reaching effects of this covenant: "God's covenant with Israel established the Jewish people and founded it as a body politic while at the same time creating the religious framework which gave that polity its raison d'être, its norms, and its constitution, as well as the guidelines for developing a political order based upon proper, that is to say, covenantal, relationships."[5]

Stronger than a contract, a covenant is a solemn pact freely entered into between trusting parties that stipulates the obligations of each side and spells out the consequences for broken vows.

God made his expectations very clear to the Israelites. Through the prophet Moses, the Israelites received the Ten Commandments (Appendix A) and an elaborate set of written hygienic, ceremonial, and moral laws and instructions describing how to live prosperous lives in their interactions with God, each other, and the foreigners who dwelled among them. Israel was to distinguish itself from pagan nations and to seize the land those nations had violated with child sacrifice and other abominations. As the Pentateuch (Torah) and Prophets (Nevi'im) reveal, the Israelites repeatedly broke their covenant with God by engaging in disobedience. As a consequence, and as promised by the prophets, God withdrew his blessings and protection from the Israelites, leading to their defeat in battle and exile into heathen nations.

UNDERSTANDING COVENANT

Through the establishment of ceremonies, constitutions, and pacts, some of the earliest settlers to the New World forged a covenant. Their intention was to define a special destiny for what evolved into the United States of America. In this new land, diverse individuals could become one people under one God. In 1776, at the birth of the nation, the motto *E pluribus unum*, Latin for "Out of many, one," was selected and, six years later, adopted as part of the seal of the United States. Our Founding Fathers risked their lives drafting and signing the Declaration of Independence and took steps that would lead to the formation of our Constitution. We have every reason to believe they saw themselves as nation-builders, making decisions that would bind their progeny.

Unlike contracts, covenants are not easily broken. Elazar argues

that most covenants are "meant to be of unlimited duration, if not perpetual . . . they are political in that their bonds are used principally to
establish bodies political and social."[6]

Many Christians believe the Bible to be the inspired Word of God.
Logically, we believe that scriptures such as Malachi 3:6, which says that
God does not change, indicate that God relates to nations and people today
as he did in the past. In Hebrews 13:8, the apostle Paul said that Jesus
Christ is "the same yesterday and today and forever." From beginning to
end, Scripture indicates that God relates to humanity today as he has done
in the past and that he takes vows seriously. Deuteronomy 23:21–23 says,
"If you make a vow to the LORD your God, you shall not delay fulfilling it,
for the LORD your God will surely require it of you, and you will be guilty
of sin. But if you refrain from vowing, you will not be guilty of sin. You
shall be careful to do what has passed your lips, for you have voluntarily
vowed to the LORD your God what you have promised with your mouth."
Likewise, we read in James 5:12, "But above all, my brothers, do not swear,
either by heaven or by earth or by any other oath, but let your 'yes' be yes
and your 'no' be no, so that you may not fall under condemnation."

The idea of perpetual covenants raises the question whether the vows
and pacts made by nation-builders in the past hold lasting spiritual significance for today. The principle of free will and the individual's ability
to choose suggests that nations and peoples can chart their own courses,
even if it means freedom to break vows and banish virtues once dear to
their ancestors.

---

*The idea of perpetual covenants raises the question whether the vows and pacts
made by nation-builders in the past hold lasting spiritual significance for today.*

God's covenant with Israel inspired some of our forefathers to seek a
similar covenant for the new nation they were founding. The Mayflower
Compact reveals the intent of the earliest settlers to bind themselves in covenant with each other and with the God of the Israelites. Signed in 1620

by forty-one of the Pilgrims who landed at Plymouth Rock in what is now
Massachusetts, the Mayflower Compact established a civil government
and affirmed our forebears' desire to practice their Christian faith:

> Having undertaken, for the Glory of God, and advancements of the
> Christian faith, and the honor of our King and Country, a voyage to
> plant the first colony in the Northern parts of Virginia; do by these
> presents, solemnly and mutually, in the presence of God, and one
> another; covenant and combine ourselves together into a civil body
> politic; for our better ordering, and preservation and furtherance of
> the ends aforesaid; and by virtue hereof to enact, constitute, and frame,
> such just and equal laws, ordinances, acts, constitutions, and offices,
> from time to time, as shall be thought most meet and convenient for the
> general good of the colony; unto which we promise all due submission
> and obedience.[7]

Documents demonstrate that many of our forefathers regarded America
as a new Israel. The people of this nation would share the rewards for obedience or punishments for sins promised to the ancient Israelites. Comments
by John Winthrop, leader of the English Puritans, about the punishments
awaiting them for breaking the divine covenant reflect the view that was
widely held at the time. In 1630, Winthrop declared, "The Lord will be our
God, and delight to dwell among us . . . *for we must consider that we shall be as
a city upon a hill. The eyes of all people are upon us.* So that if we shall deal falsely
with our God in this work we have undertaken . . . we shall be made a story
and a by-word throughout the world."[8]

*The Mayflower Compact reveals the intent of the earliest settlers to bind
themselves in covenant with each other and with the God of the Israelites.*

In 1736, theologian Jonathan Edwards, one of America's greatest
intellectuals, continued the tradition of invoking the national covenant.

Edwards often blamed the sins of the people for the harsh conditions of the land. Theologian and historian Gerald R. McDermott, a preeminent scholar on Jonathan Edwards, notes that Edwards's characterization of the national covenant was "standard fare in New England's Reformed orthodoxy. In a tradition stretching back to pre-Reformation days, God was conceived as entering into covenant with a people or a nation and blessing or punishing that people in proportion to their fidelity to the terms of the covenant."[9] This widely shared belief in a national covenant seemed to flow from the people's understanding of the practical operation of God's sovereignty and his providence. McDermott writes, "One cannot engage in even a cursory examination of the Bible without noting that it repeatedly offers promises of blessings and punishment and it shows God dealing with whole societies and using particular nations."[10]

Originally given to the ancient Israelites, these promises were claimed by the Pilgrims, Puritans, and other Christian groups for their new land: "And if you faithfully obey the voice of the LORD your God, being careful to do all his commandments that I command you today, the LORD your God will set you high above all the nations of the earth" (Deuteronomy 28:1).

Biblical history shows that the ancient Israelites quickly broke their covenant with God and began worshipping the false gods of pagan nations. Some parents even engaged in human sacrifice—killing their own sons and daughters as offerings to Molech, the Ammonite god. Jeremiah, known as the crying prophet, repeatedly spoke God's warning to the Israelites of the consequences of their disobedience: "Hear the words of this covenant and do them. For I solemnly warned your fathers when I brought them up out of the land of Egypt, warning them persistently, even to this day, saying, Obey my voice. Yet they did not obey or incline their ear, but everyone walked in the stubbornness of his evil heart. Therefore I brought upon them all the words of this covenant, which I commanded them to do, but they did not" (Jeremiah 11:6–8).

Finally, Jeremiah announced God's judgment for the apostates: "They have turned back to the iniquities of their forefathers, who refused to hear my words. They have gone after other gods to serve them. The house of Israel and the house of Judah have broken my covenant that I made with their fathers. Therefore, thus says the LORD, Behold, I am bringing disaster upon them that they cannot escape. *Though they cry to me, I will not listen to them*" (vv. 10–11; emphasis added).

Not only did God reject Israel's prayers, but he told Jeremiah to abandon the people: "Do not pray for this people, or lift up a cry or prayer on their behalf, for I will not listen when they call to me in the time of their trouble. What right has my beloved in my house, when she has done many vile deeds?" (vv. 14–15).

In the New World, the covenant-minded settlers entered into their vows and pledges with their eyes wide open. The Pilgrims, Puritans, and other Christians of the day had copies of the complete Bible in their possession and were well aware of God's judgments on ancient Israel. With a keen understanding of both the positive and negative aspects of covenantal relationships, they sought to establish a covenant with the God who allowed his beloved Israel, his chosen nation, to suffer the consequences of willful disobedience. Israel's people had been defeated, humiliated, and exiled—absorbed by the pagan nations God had warned them against emulating.

University of California at Berkeley sociologist Robert Bellah has argued that no one can understand American society without examining the nation's religious history and moral underpinnings. Our Founding Fathers were covenant-makers—demonstrated by their identification with ancient Israel and the best ideals of the Roman Republic. They hoped to "construct a republic on principles so sound that it might avoid . . . [the fate of Israel and Rome]." The founders were certain that "piety and public virtue" would help their new nation avoid decline and fall as prior societies had not.[11] However, in contrast to the vision of many of the Founding Fathers, unprecedented numbers of today's Americans have traded piety and virtue for unfettered irreverence as they have emulated the immorality practiced by the fallen Greco-Roman nations and the Ammonites.

CHRISTIAN, DEIST, AND ATHEIST
FOUNDING FATHERS

In 1775, Patrick Henry, a Virginia statesman, addressed the House of Burgesses about the need to declare independence from England. Henry acknowledged the existence of a just God who controlled the destiny of nations and who had the ability to raise supporters for the rebellion. Henry's words are still among the most recognizable to Americans today: "Gentlemen may cry, Peace, Peace—but there is no peace . . . Why stand we here idle? What is it that gentlemen wish? What would they have? Is life so dear, or peace so sweet, as to be purchased at the price of chains and slavery? Forbid it, Almighty God! I know not what course others may take; but as for me, give me liberty or give me death!"[12]

Although many members of America's founding generation were devout Christians, some understood God in more deistic terms. *Deism* comes from the Latin word for God, *deus*, and connotes belief in the existence of God on purely rational grounds rather than through supernatural revelation. Deists compare God to a divine watchmaker who designed the universe but later disassociated himself from it. Some eighteenth-century deists, however, did believe that God intervened in world affairs and that events such as the American Revolution could be providential.

Perhaps nowhere are the religious views of our nation's framers more clearly stated than in the Declaration of Independence (Appendix B). The July 4, 1776, document officially declared the birth of the nation and the decision of its leaders to honor the rule of law:

> When, in the course of human events, it becomes necessary for one people to dissolve the political bonds which have connected them with another, and to assume among the powers of the earth, the separate and equal station to which the laws of nature and of nature's God entitle them, a decent respect to the opinions of mankind requires that they should declare the causes which impel them to the separation.
>
> We hold these truths to be self-evident, that all men are created

equal, that they are endowed by their Creator with certain unalienable rights, that among these are life, liberty and the pursuit of happiness. That to secure these rights, governments are instituted among men, deriving their just powers from the consent of the governed.[13]

The Declaration of Independence refers to nature and nature's God—acknowledgments of what some people today call "natural law." At the core of natural law is the belief that a law written on the heart provides an internal standard of right and wrong for every human being. Thirteenth-century philosopher and theologian Thomas Aquinas taught that natural law is the part of God's law that individuals can know on their own simply by applying reason. Philosopher C. S. Lewis famously challenged his readers to "think of a country where people were admired for running away in battle, or where a man felt proud for double-crossing all the people who had been kindest to him. You might as well try to imagine a country where two and two made five."[14]

University of Texas at Austin philosopher J. Budziszewski argues that because of natural law, some moral truths are impossible to evade.[15] Our moral intellect is woven into our minds (Romans 2:14–15). Evidence for the existence of natural law includes the human conscience, the complementary design of male and female bodies for procreation, and the consequences—both for good and bad—flowing from our actions. In other words, a law of the harvest exists in which one reaps what one sows.[16]

Natural law was a belief system that deists and Christians could hold in common. Duke University professor George Marsden notes that our nation's founders "strictly maintained the religious formalities of the day, including laws requiring church attendance . . . but the England from which the settlers came was itself a mix of the religious and the secular. This after all, was the age of William Shakespeare, whose plays reflected the sophisticated, Renaissance, this-worldly humanism of the day."[17]

Thomas Paine, a deist, is a hero to modern-day atheists because he freely denigrated Christians and Christianity. In *The Age of Reason*, he wrote:

> Of all the systems of religion that ever were invented, there is no more
> derogatory to the Almighty, more unedifying to man, more repug-
> nant to reason, and more contradictory to itself than this thing called
> Christianity. Too absurd for belief, too impossible to convince, and too
> inconsistent for practice, it renders the heart torpid or produces only
> atheists or fanatics. As an engine of power, it serves the purpose of
> despotism, and as a means of wealth, the avarice of priests, but so far as
> respects the good of man in general it leads to nothing here or hereafter.[18]

Although Thomas Paine criticized Scripture, he "quoted it relentlessly, showing the enduring power of the Bible, even for deists. In *Common
Sense* he cites Gideon, Samuel, and David to show how the Bible argues
against kingship. And he calls King George III a pharaoh."[19]

John Adams, Benjamin Franklin, and Thomas Jefferson (the latter
two deists) pushed for an American seal that would include a depiction of
Moses. A draft of Franklin's proposal, with the words in brackets crossed
out, reads: "Moses [in the Dress of High Priest] standing on the Shore,
and extending his Hand over the Sea, thereby causing the same to over-
whelm Pharaoh who is sitting in open chariot, a Crown on his Head and
Sword in his Hand. Rays from a Pillar of Fire in the Clouds reaching to
Moses, to express that he acts by [the] command of Deity."[20]

Jefferson proposed a version picturing the "children of Israel in the wil-
derness, led by a cloud by day, and a pillar of fire by night." For the back of
the seal, Jefferson proposed an image of Saxon rulers Hengist and Horsa.[21]

One cannot read the works of historians Nathan Hatch and Mark
Noll without conceding that Christianity, generally, and Protestantism,
specifically, shaped American culture profoundly. Hatch, president of
Wake Forest University, argues that Christianity and its church denominations facilitated the embrace of democratic ideals. The Christian idea
of equality provided opportunities for ordinary men to attain leadership
positions rather than defer to cultured elites.[22]

In his detailed history of Christianity in the United States and Canada,
Notre Dame University's Mark Noll argues that the Puritans, the Great

Awakenings, the American Revolution, and the Civil War helped integrate American Christianity into the wider culture.[23] Many of our state, local, and national laws and statutes, including Blue Laws mandating store closings and banning alcohol sales on Sunday, were rooted in biblical principles.

Christianity generally, and Protestantism specifically, shaped American culture profoundly.

Moreover, Christian purposes were planted deeply in the founding of the nation's first colleges and universities. "Of our 119 first colleges and universities, 104 were founded to teach biblical values. The original seal of Harvard read, 'Truth for the Church and for Christ,' and part of its original reason for being founded was to 'let every student be plainly instructed . . . to know God and Jesus Christ, which is eternal life.' Even public universities commonly had Christian roots. A prominent building at Miami University in Oxford, Ohio, a public university, features the motto, 'Ye shall know the truth and the truth shall make you free,' John 8:32."[24]

THE CONSTITUTION AND
THE FIRST AMENDMENT

The Constitution of the United States of America is a secular document that makes no reference to God or to Christians (other than Article VII's reference to "in the year of our Lord"). The framers made a decision to keep religion and politics in separate spheres. Isaac Kramnick and R. Laurence Moore note that the omission of God was not an oversight, but rather the outcome of a long debate between Christians who wanted God referenced and those who opted to keep politics and religion separate.[25] Nevertheless, the authors concede that the "political convictions of the men who struggled to ratify a godless Constitution were not products of personal godlessness. Far from it. Almost everyone who participated in the debates about the Constitution shared a concern about the health of religion."[26]

Roger Williams, a devout Puritan, played a key role in persuading others to adopt a document that would maintain a healthy separation between spiritual and worldly matters.[27] The bloody conflicts that surrounded the Protestant Reformation, Martin Luther's effort to reform the Catholic Church, and the birth of the Anglican Church (Church of England) were fresh on the minds of many of the founders.

The Constitution includes the First Amendment, which states, "Congress shall make no law respecting an establishment of religion, or prohibiting the free exercise thereof; or abridging the freedom of speech, or of the press; or the right of the people peaceably to assemble, and to petition the Government for a redress of grievances."[28]

The so-called establishment clause of the First Amendment ("Congress shall make no law respecting an establishment of religion") was aimed at ending the conflict among Christian denominations, especially the outright persecution of minority sects such as Baptists. The amendment ensured that America would never have an established church, like the Church of England. Although the founders made certain there would never be a national church, scholars like Hatch and Noll argue that the founders understood from the very beginning that the new country was to be a Christian nation. Christianity, in its various denominational forms, became the unofficial religion of the nation.

The founders understood from the very beginning that the new country was to be a Christian nation. Christianity, in its various denominational forms, became the unofficial religion of the nation.

In 1883, Supreme Court Justice Joseph Story III offered his understanding of the First Amendment's prohibition against the establishment of a national religion. In Section 1871 of his *Commentaries on the U.S. Constitution*, Story said:

> The real object of the amendment was, not to countenance, much less
> to advance Mahometanism, or Judaism, or infidelity, by prostrating

Christianity; but to exclude all rivalry among Christian sects, and to prevent any national ecclesiastical establishment, which should give to a hierarchy the exclusive patronage of the national government. It thus cut off the means of religious persecution (the vice and pest of former ages) and of the subversion of the rights of conscience in matters of religion, which had been trampled upon almost from the days of the Apostles to the present age.[29]

Certainly Justice Story's understanding of the purpose of the First Amendment was a much closer rendering than (and superior to) that of groups such as the Secular Coalition of America or the Americans United for the Separation of Church and State, which maintain that the Constitution requires a strict separation of religion and politics necessary to ensure religious freedom for all faiths.

Justice Story's interpretation of the First Amendment should have been enough to end the debate, but the issue of America's identity as a covenant nation remained unsettled. Since the nineteenth century, America has drifted from her identity as a Christian nation and developed a "civil religion" that, while retaining certain Christian elements, is not explicitly or exclusively Christian. Borrowing the idea from the French philosopher Jean-Jacques Rousseau, American civil religion includes the following beliefs we associate with Christianity: "the existence of God, the life to come, the reward of virtue and the punishment of vice, and the exclusion of religious intolerance."[30] According to Berkeley sociologist Robert N. Bellah, "Words and acts of the founding fathers, especially the first few presidents, shaped the form and tone of the civil religion as it has been maintained ever since."[31]

Although most of our Founding Fathers believed major Christian denominations and religions contained important elements of moral and religious truth that were universally valid and worthy of propagation, their positive views of religion were tempered by an acute awareness that potentially harmful elements of religion needed to be pruned. Among these were intolerance of other religions and the coercive imposition of one's religion on outsiders. Consequently, America's forefathers drafted a constitution that ensured the nation would never create an established church at the national level. The religion clauses of the First Amendment guaranteed that America would never name an official national religious orthodoxy or national church (the establishment clause) but also guaranteed that all Americans would have the right to believe and worship as they chose without hindrance from the national government (the free exercise clause).

Constitutional scholar Philip Hamburger, a professor at the Columbia University School of Law, has written a definitive study on how the principle of separation of church and state became enshrined in American constitutional law.[32] Hamburger provides support for the view that the Constitution is a document carefully crafted to prevent a national church. He explores how the Constitution's framers sought to protect the separation of church and state with the First Amendment, then shows how the rise of American anti-Catholicism during the nineteenth century led to demands for separation of the church and judicial decisions against religion in the public square, particularly against the Christian religion.

Hamburger believes, however, it would have been inconceivable to the framers that the First Amendment would one day be invoked to support bans against prayer in schools and public displays of the Ten Commandments. But the First Amendment was used as a basis for the removal of the following simple prayer from public schools: "Almighty God, we acknowledge our dependence upon Thee, and beg Thy blessings upon us, our parents, teachers and our country. Amen."[33]

The 1962 *Engel v. Vitale* US Supreme Court decision broke a two-hundred-year tradition of public school systems across America beginning their days with prayer and asking for God's blessings, provision, and protection on their students, themselves, and our nation. Throughout our nation's history, the Bible and the Pledge of Allegiance provided cornerstones for generations of children who learned principles and values such as morality, virtue, piety, and patriotism—the founding roots of American government. The expulsion of God from public schools was a blow to civil religion and a clear repudiation of what Jesus proclaimed to be the greatest commandment.

It would have been inconceivable to the framers that the First Amendment would one day be invoked to support bans against prayer in schools and public displays of the Ten Commandments.

In Matthew 22:36–40, we read of a young lawyer who approached Jesus and asked, "'Teacher, which is the great commandment in the Law?' And [Jesus] said to him, 'You shall love the Lord your God with all your heart and with all your soul and with all your mind. This is the great and first commandment. And a second is like it: You shall love your neighbor as yourself. On these two commandments depend all the Law and the Prophets.'"

The removal of prayer from public classrooms across the nation censored the name of God in America's educational institutions and eroded an important foundation for teaching virtue and morality to America's youth. This is the same God whose name was emblazoned on our public buildings and our nation's currency and who continued to be publicly invoked for blessing by our nation's politicians.

MANIFEST DESTINY, IMPERIALISM, SLAVERY, AND GENOCIDE

Jeremiah 17:9 states, "The heart is deceitful above all things, and desperately sick; who can understand it?" At the core of Christianity is the belief that man lives in a fallen state of imperfection and cannot fix himself without a savior. Consequently, those who look for perfection or near perfection in themselves or others are always disappointed. America, like ancient Israel, has certainly been imperfect, abusing its covenant with God. Politicans have used Christianity and the covenant relationship to justify the subjugation, and even the extermination, of human beings.

For example, America's covenant relationship provided justification for the concept of Manifest Destiny, the nineteenth-century belief that America was divinely ordained to extend its borders from the Atlantic Ocean to the Pacific Ocean. Just as the Israelites had to rid themselves of the Canaanites before they could claim their lands, some of our ancestors felt entitled to rid themselves of the pagan occupants of their land.[34] This empire-building imperialism led America into transactions that resulted in the Louisiana Purchase, the Spanish-American War, the displacement of Native Americans, and the acquisition of territories including Puerto Rico, Guam, the Virgin Islands, the Northern Mariana Islands, and American Samoa. Inherent to US imperialism was the belief that "civilized people" were responsible to civilize and Christianize the non-Christian world.

Nevertheless, Christians were also involved in heroic causes. Among these leaders was Britain's William Wilberforce, who was instrumental in helping end slavery in his nation. In America, Harriet Beecher Stowe's novel *Uncle Tom's Cabin* was the first to present a black man as a Christlike figure, and it helped turn the tide against slavery.[35] The biblical principle that all of humanity possesses a moral sensitivity paved the way for the abolition of slavery, establishment of women's rights, protection of children, and pursuit of justice around the world.

Slavery itself troubled some Americans, who scorned holding other human beings in bondage. In 1944, Swedish economist and Nobel laureate Gunnar Myrdal, author of *An American Dilemma: The Negro Problem and Modern Democracy*, pointed out contradictions between the principles embodied in the Declaration of Independence, a statement adopted by the US House of Representatives in 1917 called American's Creed, and the behavioral patterns of many white Christian Americans toward nonwhites, especially the black descendants of slaves.[36] Decades later, black religion scholar C. Eric Lincoln argued that the "dilemma is still with us . . . [It is] the same dilemma that produced the Black Church, which shared the birth of our nation; and it continues as the dilemma that plagues church and society alike today."[37]

Despite slavery and the Jim Crow racism that followed, America's ethos allowed the nation to attain higher levels of justice, prosperity, and security for its people than most nations of the world. "This great 'irony of history,' as Christian theologian Reinhold Niebuhr calls it, extends to Africans in Africa as well. Given conditions in most African countries, the sale and transport of black slaves to America carries all the hallmarks of divine providence."[38] African Americans and other racial and ethnic minorities prosper when the nation as a whole prospers.

In 1995, journalist Keith Richburg, the *Washington Post*'s Africa Bureau chief from 1991 to 1994, witnessed the horrors of the Somalian and Rwandan civil wars. Richburg recounts the experience of standing on a bridge, watching the bodies float by like logs:

> Somewhere, sometime, maybe 400 years ago, an ancestor of mine whose name I'll never know was shackled in leg irons, kept in a dark pit, possibly at Goree Island off the coast of Senegal, and then put with thousands of other Africans into the crowded, filthy cargo hold of a ship for the long and treacherous journey across the Atlantic. Many of them died along the way, of disease, of hunger. But my ancestor survived, maybe because he was strong, maybe stubborn enough to want to live, or maybe just lucky . . . Then one of his descendants somehow made it up to South Carolina, and one of those descendants, my father, made it to Detroit . . . and there I was born . . . And if that original ancestor hadn't been forced to make that horrific voyage, I would not have been standing there that day on the Rusumo Falls bridge, a journalist—a mere spectator—watching the bodies glide past me like river logs. No, I might have instead been one of them . . . And so I thank God my ancestor made that voyage.[39]

Strong parallels exist between the experiences of black descendants of slaves and the four-hundred-year bondage and redemption of the Israelites in Egypt that begins with the story of Joseph. One of Jacob's twelve sons, Joseph was sold by his half brothers into slavery as part of

God's plan to save the nation during a prolonged famine. Despite hardship, Joseph became a powerful Egyptian leader. When the opportunity came to reveal himself to his terrified brothers, he said:

> And now do not be distressed or angry with yourselves because you sold me here, for God sent me before you to preserve life. For the famine has been in the land these two years, and there are yet five years in which there will be neither plowing nor harvest. And God sent me before you to preserve for you a remnant on earth, and to keep alive for you many survivors. So it was not you who sent me here, but God. He has made me a father to Pharaoh, and lord of all his house and ruler over all the land of Egypt. (Genesis 45:5–8)

"Using their influence in America, black religious and political leaders can help their African brethren as Joseph helped the Israelites. Whatever challenges Africans face today, they could be much worse without the voices of African Americans, influential and powerful enough to speak and act on behalf of the continent."[40]

IS THERE A GOD WHO JUDGES NATIONS?

President Abraham Lincoln believed in a God fully capable of inflicting punishment for national sins. In 1863, he declared a national fast, imploring the people with these words: "inso much as we know that, by His divine law, nations like individuals are subjected to punishments and chastisements in this world, may we justly fear that the awful calamity of civil war, which now desolates the land, may be a punishment, inflicted upon us, for our presumptuous sins, to the needful end of our national reformation of the whole People?"[41]

In his second inaugural address, Lincoln declared, "Fervently do we pray that this mighty scourge of war may speedily pass away. Yet, if God wills that it continue until all the wealth piled by the bondsman's two hundred and fifty years of unrequited toil shall be sunk, and until every drop of blood drawn with the lash shall be paid by another drawn with the sword, as was said three thousand years ago, so still it must be said 'the judgments of the Lord are true and righteous altogether.'"[42]

In 1820, Thomas Jefferson labeled the division of America over slavery as a "momentous question, [that] like a fireball in the night, awakened and filled me with terror."[43] More than six hundred thousand American soldiers, as well as many civilians, died during the Civil War in what remains the nation's bloodiest conflict.

Historian Stephen Keillor, who has written about God's judgment of nations, points out that much of the Old Testament describes God's judgment of nations, and there is nothing in the New Testament that indicates that God has ended this practice.[44] Among the people destroyed because of their sins were those in Sodom and Gomorrah, Nineveh, Tyre, and Sidon. God stripped the Canaanite people of their lands because of their detestable behaviors, which he forbade Israel to emulate.

Keillor raises the possibility that the 9/11 attack that killed nearly three thousand Americans might be an act of judgment against the United States.[45] Mark Noll's foreword provides an excellent summary and analysis of Keillor's thesis.[46] Keillor points out that it is well established that Islamic terrorists have given the following reasons for their *jihad* against America: US support for globalization and free trade, which enriched the West while harming less-developed nations; the exportation from the United States of morally decadent values and perverted notions of sexuality; and America's foreign policy toward the Middle East, with its long record of supporting Israel. Keillor reasons that if God is holy, he is angered by America's exploitation of the poor and our promotion of values and behaviors the Bible condemns. When American leaders endorse behaviors condemned by the Judeo-Christian Bible, they stand as representatives of a Christian nation. Members of other nations equate their attitudes with Christianity and with the attitudes of missionaries working around the world to spread the Christian gospel.

> *Much of the Old Testament describes God's judgment of nations, and there is nothing in the New Testament that indicates that God has ended this practice.*

America often appears to thumb its nose at biblical teachings while remaining under the guise of being a Christian nation. This practice seemingly invites God's judgment. Pagan nations became the instruments of God's judgment of ancient Israel; therefore, Keillor raises the question, "Why wouldn't God use Islamic terrorists to remind Westerners of the gospel's high moral standards? In other words, apostasy in Scripture is a communal as well as personal problem and the West, in Christian terms, looks apostate."[47]

THE PRINCIPLE OF SOWING AND REAPING

The Old Testament book of Deuteronomy guaranteed that the Israelites would receive blessings for obedience and curses for disobedience. Many "prosperity preachers" and televangelists enthrall audiences by focusing on the blessings. However, Scripture clearly presents curses for willful disobedience. Deuteronomy 28:15–22 states:

> But if you will not obey the voice of the LORD your God or be careful to do all his commandments and his statutes that I command you today, then all these curses shall come upon you and overtake you. . . . The LORD will send on you curses, confusion, and frustration in all that you undertake to do, until you are destroyed and perish quickly on account of the evil of your deeds, because you have forsaken me. The LORD will make the pestilence stick to you until he has consumed you off the land that you are entering to take possession of it. The LORD will strike you with wasting disease and with fever, inflammation and fiery heat, and with drought and with blight and with mildew. They shall pursue you until you perish.

According to the passage in Deuteronomy, a nation that rebels against God will not thrive. Its people will suffer ill health, and natural disasters will strike the land. Its ventures will not prosper. Until recent decades, America has prospered. But the twenty-first century finds us dealing with incurable diseases such as HIV/AIDS, deadly cancers, the reemergence of tuberculosis and leprosy, Ebola, swine flu, and penicillin-resistant sexual diseases. We are being confronted with numerous natural disasters and freak weather patterns. Could some of these occurrences be related to our decision to reject biblical injunctions against abortion, greed, homosexuality, fornication, and adultery?

Has our behavior brought God's judgment upon America in the form of the curses spelled out in Deuteronomy 28? While the words of this passage were originally spoken to ancient Israel, they are still significant for a nation that portrays itself as Christian and whose Founding Fathers included men seeking a lasting covenant that would bring blessings to themselves and future generations.

Today, politically correct Americans—both leaders and citizens—mock and turn their backs on the God of the Bible. Christians have allowed nonbelievers and secularists to persuade them to place their God on an equal status with the gods of other nations and to blend religious practices with interfaith chapels and retreat symbols, a practice that runs counter to biblical warnings about apostasy and the worship of other deities. This takes place at retreat centers and functions where non-Christian religious leaders share the same worship space as Christians. The God of the Bible would no doubt reject the argument of one-God-many-paths associated most prominently with the new age movement.

Deuteronomy 28:43–44 seemingly speaks to our financial dependence on foreign nations and our failure to control our borders: "The sojourner [foreigner] who is among you shall rise higher and higher above you, and you shall come down lower and lower. He shall lend to you, and you shall not lend to him. He shall be the head, and you shall be the tail."

As of March 10, 2011, the US government owed more than $14 trillion and, of course, the clock is ticking.[48] The national debt consists of

the direct liabilities of the United States government. Foreign governments and investors own or control a significant proportion of the US
economy and infrastructure, and China has become our biggest lender.
Our dependence has become so great that our leaders have been reluctant to press China about its horrible human rights record. China has
the power to destroy our struggling economy. Secretary of state Hillary
Clinton has said that China's human rights record is a secondary concern
to the United States.[49] Signaling to the world that China was on equal
footing with the United States, in January 2011 President Obama hosted
a state dinner for China's president Hu Jintao and allowed the US flag to
fly alongside the flag of communist China.[50]

A 2006 *USA Today* article illustrates the enormous influence of foreign investment. According to the article, "more than half of US debt
available for public purchase . . . [was] held by foreigners, according to
the Treasury Department."[51] In 2005, foreigners owned $2.2 trillion in
US Treasury securities out of a total of $4 trillion of privately held US
debt. The biggest holders were the Japanese, who owned $685 billion
of Treasury securities. Airlines, energy sources, toll roads, telecommu-
nications, drinking water, waste services, and rail systems are largely
dependent on foreign investment.[52]

Clearly, we are living in tumultuous times. What impact, if any, could
America's broken vows and forgotten covenants have on our safety at
home and abroad? Could broken vows affect our ability to win wars with
other nations and even put our personal freedoms at risk? Deuteronomy
28:49–50 speaks to these matters as well: "The LORD will bring a nation
against you from far away, from the end of the earth, swooping down like
the eagle, a nation whose language you do not understand, a hard-faced
nation who shall not respect the old or show mercy to the young."

China and Iran are internationally recognized for their appalling
human rights records.[53] Most Americans would be shocked at the idea of
the United States becoming subjugated to one of these nations. Yet, if God
has historically dealt with the sin of nations by allowing subjugation by their
enemies, then we, too, risk punishment at the hands of our adversaries.

What impact, if any, could America's broken vows and forgotten covenants have on our safety at home and abroad?

Finally, Americans could be vulnerable for judgment because of our country's treatment of the Jewish people. Many Christians believe that Israel stands in a unique relationship with God and take seriously God's words in Genesis 12:3, referring to Abraham: "I will bless those who bless you, and him who dishonors you I will curse, and in you all the families of the earth shall be blessed." These Christians believe that Israel is not just another nation; therefore, some argue that a direct correlation exists between America's treatment of Israel and the resulting natural disasters in our country. According to this view, America suffers when we turn our backs on the descendants of Abraham—the modern-day Jews who occupy the biblical Holy Land.[54]

Herein lies a major dilemma for liberal and conservative Christians: if God does not change his Word, then consequences inevitably flow from individual and collective decisions. Either Israel is like any other nation, or it is special. If Israel is special, then how we treat the nation matters. If how we treat Israel matters, then America suffers when it makes the wrong decisions about intervention in affairs in the Middle East. Obviously, we will never know with certainty whether any given terrorist attack or natural disaster is linked to national decisions regarding treatment of Israel. But it is only wise to ponder and ask ourselves, "Is America, like ancient Israel, reaping the consequences of choices our leaders have made on the part of We the People? And what consequences remain to be seen?"

PRESENT REALITIES IN SECULAR BANS AGAINST RELIGIOUS REASONING

A foundational principle of academia is that religion is a private matter, never to be discussed in the public square. Citing Scripture and other religious texts is out of bounds—even though it is permissible for politicians or other public figures to quote their favorite philosophers, educational experts, rock stars, or new age gurus. In 1984, Richard John Neuhaus wrote about this troubling trend in his seminal book *The Naked Public Square*.[55] Of course, this taboo against Scripture advantages the cultural elite, connoting by its very existence the correctness of their ideas and the backwardness of ours. This view is exemplified in an opinion piece that US labor secretary Robert Reich published before the 2004 elections:

> The underlying battle will be between modern civilization and anti-modernist fanatics; between those who believe in the primacy of the individual and those who believe human beings owe blind allegiance to a higher authority; between those who give authority to life in this world and those who believe that human life is no more than preparation for an existence beyond life; between those who believe truth is revealed solely through scripture and religious dogma, and those who rely primarily on science, reason, and logic.[56]

As long as the overwhelming majority of Americans define themselves as Christians, the marketplace of public dialogue, opinion, and debate is an appropriate forum for Scripture and religious reasoning, cited alongside scientific, philosophical, and other forms of knowledge. Law professor Steven D. Smith argues that public discourse needs to be freed from the constraints imposed on it by secularists. According to Smith, the demand that arguments avoid religious reasoning results in a secular vocabulary "too truncated to express the full range of values, intuitions, commitments or convictions" necessary for addressing common interests.[57] Unable to use religious language and hemmed in by their own rules, Smith argues that secularists smuggle in religious concepts but call them by other names, such as *liberty, freedom*, or *equality*. This, Smith says, creates a "secular cage."

As long as the overwhelming majority of Americans define themselves as Christians, the marketplace of public dialogue, opinion, and debate is an appropriate forum for Scripture and religious reasoning.

In order for genuine public discourse to exist in America, we must create intellectual and political spaces where people can offer religious reasoning and scriptural proofs that undergird their deepest values. These values connect Americans today with the hopes and aspirations held by the Founding Fathers, who envisioned a society with an unswerving commitment to virtue and justice. Our forebears balanced a commitment to virtue and justice with a deep awareness of the moral conflict that lies at the heart of humanity. In doing so, they forged a nation unlike any other—with a deep sense of reverence for the human spirit, yet deferential to the God who weighs the affairs of men.

ACTION POINTS

1. Read the Declaration of Independence and the US
    Constitution (Appendices B and D). What do these
    documents tell us about the wisdom and insights of the
    Founding Fathers?

2. Read Joel J. Miller and Kristen Parrish's *The Portable
    Patriot: Documents, Speeches, and Sermons That Compose the
    Soul of America* (Nashville: Thomas Nelson, 2010).

3. Meet with other Bible believers to discuss specific ways
    and actions that might help return our nation to its
    Judeo-Christian roots.

4. Read and discuss the *Be the People* questions for chapter 2,
    posted at www.CarolMSwain.com.

CHAPTER 3

ABORTION'S FRAGILE FACADE

Abortion is the greatest destroyer of peace, because we are able to destroy the life that is given by God. If a mother can become the murderer of her children, what can we say about other kinds of murders and wars in the world? Abortion is the source of the evils in the world.

—MOTHER TERESA[1]

Abortion is a blessing and our work is not done. Let me hear you say it: abortion is a blessing and our work is not done.

—REV. KATHERINE HANCOCK RAGSDALE,
PRESIDENT OF EPISCOPAL DIVINITY SCHOOL[2]

THE CENTER FOR BIO-ETHICAL REFORM ESTIMATES THAT 43 PERCENT OF *all* women will have at least one abortion by the time they reach forty-five years of age, and of these women, 47 percent will have more than one.[3] Abortion can become an addiction. It certainly did for Irene Vilar, a Latina mother of two who wrote a memoir about having had fifteen abortions in sixteen years, many of them while she was married.[4] In contemporary America, abortion on demand has become an entitlement sometimes subsidized directly or indirectly by state and federal dollars that are often funneled through Planned Parenthood. Because our tax dollars help underwrite the cost of abortions, it behooves us to ponder whether the practice is the source of evil decried by Mother Teresa or the blessing embraced by Rev. Ragsdale.

Mother Teresa is no longer alive to perpetuate and defend her view, but Rev. Ragsdale has the ear of thousands of young people training to become leaders in liberal Christian churches. Millions of people around the world consider Mother Teresa a saint because of her dedication to life and her ministry to Calcutta's poorest of the poor. Rev. Ragsdale views sainthood from a starkly different perspective; she believes that saints are those involved in the advancement of abortion—the ending of life—work she defines as "holy." According to Rev. Ragsdale, abortion is always a blessing and never a sin. It is a blessing, she says, when

> a woman wants a child but can't afford one because she hasn't the education necessary for a sustainable job, or access to health care, or day care, or adequate food . . . And when a woman becomes pregnant within a loving, supportive, respectful relationship; has every option open to her; decides she does not wish to bear a child; and has access to a safe, affordable abortion—there is not a tragedy in sight—only blessing. The ability to enjoy God's good gift of sexuality without compromising one's education, life's work, or ability to put to use God's gifts and call is simply blessing.[5]

Rev. Ragsdale uses the authority of her office to absolve troubled consciences and promote her unorthodox views, which are not limited to abortion. She denounces many tenets of the traditional Christian faith, raising questions about the death, resurrection, and atonement of Jesus Christ, which lie at the heart of the gospel. The head of a Boston-area seminary charged with training the next generation of theologically liberal Episcopalian priests, she is an outspoken and proud lesbian. She states that her sexual orientation was freely chosen: "Who would choose this? Let me answer that with three words, 'Me! Me! Me! In a New York minute! Me!'"[6]

DOGMATICALLY DECEIVED

Rev. Ragsdale embodies the theological decline of America's religious leaders and the distance they have strayed from the biblical understanding of previous generations of educated Americans. Not only is Rev. Ragsdale deceived, but she is positioned to deceive others. Ironically, her pulpit stands in the city where John Winthrop warned his fellow Puritans that the eyes of the world would be watching their "city upon a hill": "We shall be made a story and a by-word throughout the world. We shall open the mouths of enemies to speak evil of the ways of God . . . We shall shame the faces of many of God's worthy servants, and cause their prayers to be turned into curses upon us til we be consumed out of the good land whither we are a-going."[7]

In 2 Timothy 3:6–7, the apostle Paul spoke of "weak women, burdened with sins and led astray by various passions, always learning and never able to arrive at a knowledge of the truth." In Rev. Katherine Ragsdale's words, we see the kind of deceit of many religious leaders across our nation who compromise moral principles and teach theologies directly opposed to the Bible. She is both a victim and a perpetrator of deception.

The apostle Paul prophesied in 1 Timothy 4:1–2 that "in later times some will depart from the faith by devoting themselves to deceitful spirits and teachings of demons, through the insincerity of liars whose consciences are seared." A seared conscience is one that has been violated so many times that the violator can no longer discern right from wrong. Any sensitivity to God's voice and to the standard to which he calls believers is lost. Once a conscience is seared, it is no longer of much use. J. Budziszewski argues, "If the law written on the heart can be repressed, then we cannot count on it to *restrain* us from doing wrong; that much is obvious . . . repressing it hurls us into *further* wrong. Holding conscience down does not deprive us of its force; it merely distorts and redirects that force."[8]

ABORTION PROCEDURES

Abortions can be the result of deliberation and decision, or they can occur spontaneously in miscarriages. A woman who experiences the spontaneous loss of a child through miscarriage might tell friends or family, "I lost my baby." If her pregnancy is developing normally, she will tell someone,

"I'm going to have a baby." However, when an abortion is deliberately induced because of unwanted conception, people dehumanize the life in the womb by referring to it as a "fetus." Interestingly, a pregnant woman who wants her child does not refer to the life in her womb as a fetus. She calls it a baby.

Medical personnel use various techniques to terminate pregnancies, sometimes by the violent removal of a developing baby before the unborn child can survive outside the mother's womb.[9] Several different abortion procedures exist. One of the most common forms of abortion is RU-486, a three-pill prescription regimen administered for two days to several weeks to complete the abortive process.[10] The FDA describes Ella, the most recent abortion pill, as a five-day contraceptive.[11] However, its opponents point out that it can cause the spontaneous abortion of a fertilized egg.[12] Another common abortive method during the first trimester is "manual vacuum aspiration," which uses a syringe or electric vacuum to suck out the contents of the womb. In the second trimester, abortion procedures include "dilation and curettage" (D&C), in which the baby is dismembered and removed limb by limb; injection of drugs or saline solution into the amniotic fluid to cause the woman's body to expel the unborn child; and the most gruesome procedure of all, "partial-birth abortion."

When an abortion is deliberately induced because of unwanted conception, people dehumanize the life in the womb by referring to it as a "fetus." Interestingly, a pregnant woman who wants her child . . . calls it a baby.

Partial-birth abortions are performed after the baby has reached the point of viability, having developed the capacity to live outside the uterus. Doctors deliver the baby just as in a normal birth, except for the baby's head. During the abortive process, the doctor pierces the base of the baby's skull with a sharp instrument, inserts a tube in the base of the skull, and then removes the remainder of the brain using a vacuum suction. Without the brain, the skull collapses, allowing the doctor to pull the dead body from the woman's birth canal.

In 2003, President George W. Bush's administration signed a law criminalizing late-term abortion, but this did not end the procedure. Congress drafted the partial-birth abortion law with wording that left abortion providers with a loophole to circumvent the spirit and intent of the law. In 2007, three Harvard University–affiliated hospitals (Massachusetts General, Brigham and Women's, and Beth Israel Deaconess) acknowledged routinely using lethal drugs to kill babies inside the womb so they would be born dead. This method enables the medical practitioner to circumvent federal law, which states that a person who "knowingly performs a partial-birth abortion and thereby kills a human fetus" can face fines or imprisonment. By killing the unborn baby inside the womb and causing it to emerge as stillborn, doctors can perform abortions well past twenty weeks' gestation, when babies have reached viability.[13]

Coming to terms with the ugly side of abortion procedures can be a slow and painful process for those who deal with the issue personally. In May 2009, Lisa Harris, a University of Michigan assistant professor, published an academic article about her dismaying experience while performing an abortion on a baby at the same stage of development as the one in her womb. Professor Harris wrote:

> When I was a little over 18 weeks pregnant with my now pre-school child, I did a second trimester abortion for a patient who was also a little over 18 weeks pregnant. As I reviewed her chart I realized that I was more interested than usual in seeing the fetal parts when I was done, since they would so closely resemble those of my own fetus . . .
>
> With my first pass of the forceps, I grasped an extremity and began to pull it down. I could see a small foot hanging from the teeth of my forceps. With a quick tug, I separated the leg. Precisely at that moment, I felt a kick—a fluttery "thump, thump" in my own uterus. It was one of the first times I felt fetal movement. There was a leg and foot in my forceps, and a "thump, thump" in my abdomen.

Instantly, tears were streaming from my eyes—without me—
meaning my conscious brain—even being aware of what was going
on. I felt as if my response had come entirely from my body, bypassing
my usual cognitive processing completely. A message seemed to travel
from my hand and my uterus to my tear ducts. It was an overwhelming
feeling—a brutally visceral response—heartfelt and unmediated by my
training or my feminist pro-choice politics.[14]

Harris concluded, "Abortion is different from other surgical procedures. Even when the fetus has no legal status, its moral status is reasonably
the subject of much disagreement. It is disingenuous to argue that removing a fetus from a uterus is no different from removing a fibroid."[15]

ABORTION SURVIVAL

Amazingly, some babies survive the abortion process. To protect these
babies, Congress passed the Born-Alive Infants Protection Act in 2002,[16]
which defines a viable fetus surviving the abortion process as a person
entitled to medical assistance. Before passage of this law, nurses testified
of botched abortions that resulted in the live births of newborn babies
of the same size and condition as those successfully treated in neonatal
units across the country. Popular pro-life speaker Gianna Jessen is an
abortion survivor from Australia who shares her amazing story around
the world.[17]

Jill Stanek, a registered nurse, was instrumental in passage of not only
the federal law but also a law in her home state of Illinois. In July 2000,
Stanek testified before Congress:

When I worked at the hospital, in the event that a baby was aborted
alive, he or she was not given any medical care but is [*sic*] rather given
what the hospital calls comfort care . . . Comfort care is defined as
keeping the baby warm in a blanket until the baby dies, although until
recently even this was not always done . . . It is not uncommon for live

aborted babies to linger for an hour or two or even longer. One of these babies once lived for almost an entire eight-hour shift.[18]

Stanek has become a leading activist and spokesperson for the pro-life movement. In the 2008 presidential contest, she fiercely opposed then candidate Barack Obama because of his staunch opposition to Illinois's Born-Alive Infants Protection Act and other actions she felt made him an enemy of the unborn. The perception of Obama as a strong proponent of abortion was fueled even more when, as a candidate, he told a town hall crowd, "I've got two daughters, nine years old and six years old. I am going to teach them first of all about values and morals. But if they make a mistake, I don't want them punished with a baby."[19] His attitude demonstrates an interesting perspective: few of us would consider our unborn grandchild a punishment.

THE LEGAL STATUS OF ABORTION LAWS

In *Roe v. Wade* (1973),[20] the Supreme Court applied a formula to determine when a woman could terminate her pregnancy. First-trimester terminations posed no problems for the Court. But once the baby reached the point of viability, meaning that the baby could "live outside the mother's womb," the Court imposed further restrictions. The Court indicated that viability occurred at about twenty-eight weeks but acknowledged that it could occur as early as twenty-four weeks. After the point of viability, abortion could take place only when circumstances were deemed necessary to protect a woman's health. Modern neonatal care now makes it possible for infants to survive at twenty weeks of age. Also, we now know that legal abortions can be performed at any stage of gestation if the mother can get documentation from a physician that mental or physical harm might ensue from a live birth.

To reach its decision, the Court unearthed a previously unknown constitutional right to privacy implied in the Fourteenth Amendment's due process clause. Yale Law professor Robert Bork states that the justices "invented a heretofore unheard of Constitutional right to 'personal dignity and autonomy.'"[21] Harvard Law professor Mary Ann Glendon argues that opinion leaders including Justice Sandra Day O'Connor have persistently mischaracterized *Roe v. Wade*, since courts have "permitted no regulation at all in the interest of protecting the unborn child for the first two trimesters."[22]

Modern neonatal care now makes it possible for infants to survive at twenty weeks of age.

DOE V. BOLTON

Glendon points out that on the same day the Supreme Court decided *Roe*, it also issued a decision in a less-cited but ultimately more consequential case named *Doe v. Bolton*.[23] In *Doe*, the Court interpreted a Georgia law in a manner that struck down abortion restrictions in all fifty states. The Court ruled that the life of the mother did not have to be in jeopardy for her to get an abortion for health reasons, effectively nullifying the point of viability restriction in *Roe*. Justice Blackmun, writing for the majority, concluded that determination of medical necessity for an abortion should be between the woman and her doctor. Blackmun wrote, "Medical judgment may be exercised in the light of all factors—physical, emotional, psychological, familial, and the woman's age—relevant to the well-being of the patient. All these factors may relate to health."[24] According to Glendon, "*Roe* got all the attention, [but] it is fair to say that *Doe* . . . was the more ominous of the two decisions. *Doe* was more ominous for two reasons that have never been well understood. First, by striking down a modern statute that attempted to protect both the woman's interests and the life of the unborn child, *Doe* signaled the doom of legislative efforts to provide even modest protection of unborn life."[25]

When it comes to late-term abortions, America has one of the least-restrictive laws in the world. Unlike in countries where legislatures have established the rules, in the United States, the Supreme Court found a constitutional right to privacy as its basis for bypassing the deliberative process. *Roe v. Wade* and *Doe v. Bolton* helped spawn a still-raging cultural war that has split political parties in America into the anti-abortionist Republicans versus the pro-abortionist Democrats.

When it comes to late-term abortions, America has one of the least-restrictive laws in the world.

Political philosopher Robert P. George has argued that *Roe* became the "symbol of judicial usurpation of authority vested in the people and their representatives."[26] The Court's handling of *Roe* "short-circuited the democratic process" by removing a morally charged public policy issue from the political process and the deliberations associated with it.[27] Sociologist Anne Hendershott notes that a decade of intense lobbying at the state level made the 1973 decision inevitable. By the time of *Roe*, nineteen states had already modified their abortion laws in response to growing feminist demands.[28]

PLANNED PARENTHOOD V. CASEY

The next major Supreme Court case dealing with abortion, *Planned Parenthood v. Casey*,[29] came in 1992. In this case, the Court reaffirmed a woman's right to have an abortion without state interference before her unborn child reaches the point of viability. It also upheld the power of the State to restrict abortion after the baby has reached the point of viability, acknowledged the right of the state to create exceptions for pregnancies endangering a woman's life or health, and affirmed the concept that the state has legitimate interests in protecting the health of both the mother and her unborn child throughout the pregnancy.[30] Although in *Planned Parenthood* the Court admitted it might have made a mistake in *Roe*, it reasoned that it would not be prudent or practical to overturn *Roe*:

[*Roe*'s] limitation on state power could not be repudiated without serious inequity to people who, for two decades of economic and social developments, have organized intimate relationships and made choices that define their views of themselves and their places in society, in reliance on the availability of abortion in the event that contraception should fail. The ability of women to participate equally in the economic and social life of the Nation has been facilitated by their ability to control their reproductive lives. The Constitution serves human values, and while the effect of reliance on Roe cannot be exactly measured, neither can the certain costs of overruling Roe for people who have ordered their thinking and living around that case be dismissed.[31]

The Court also reaffirmed its position that the constitutional basis for abortion rested in the Fourteenth Amendment's due process clause, which guarantees individuals a right to privacy in certain areas of life.

STERNBERG V. CARHART

Abortion rights were expanded again in 2000 when the Court declared Nebraska's partial-birth abortion law unconstitutional in *Sternberg v. Carhart*.[32] Nebraska's law lacked an exception for women's health and a clear definition of the partial-birth abortion procedure and therefore placed an undue burden on the woman, the Court ruled. But in 2007, the Court upheld President Bush's Partial-Birth Abortion Ban of 2003 in *Gonzales v. Carhart*.[33] In reaching its decision, the Court relied on factors including psychological research revealing the profound regret some women feel after undergoing a partial-birth abortion, and descriptive details about how such an abortion is performed. The Court distinguished the decision reached in *Sternberg*, meaning it showed how the cases differed, but it did not overturn *Sternberg*.

Pro-choice advocates see *Gonzales v. Carhart* as a setback because it was the first time since 1973 that the Court placed restrictions on any form of abortion and because it potentially affected the fifty states. Vanderbilt University Law School dean Chris Guthrie questions how the Court arrived at its decision and argues that the Court misunderstood the psychological literature on the subject. According to Guthrie, the Court failed to consider the overwhelming research indicating that people overestimate the actual amount of regret they feel from significant life events. Guthrie further claims that human beings are able to minimize their regret and then learn from it. Guthrie concluded that the Court inappropriately gave too much sway to the prospect that women would regret their decisions and used this finding to restrict an important constitutional right.[34]

Dr. Bernard Nathanson, cofounder of the National Association for the Repeal of Abortion Laws (NARAL, renamed National Reproductive Rights Action League), worked with activists Lawrence Adler and Betty Friedan (author of *The Feminine Mystique*[35]) to establish NARAL by telling a big lie that helped persuade the public of a critical need to take action. Dr. Nathanson is among the many abortion providers who have switched sides in the abortion debate. He offers an insider's view of converging factors that made legalization of abortion possible:

> We persuaded the media that the cause of permissive abortion was a liberal, enlightened, sophisticated one . . . Knowing that if a true poll were taken, we would be soundly defeated, we simply fabricated the results of fictional polls. We announced to the media that we had taken polls and that 60 percent of Americans were in favor of permissive abortion. This is the tactic of the self-fulfilling lie. Few people care to be in the minority. We aroused enough sympathy to sell our program of permissive abortion by fabricating the number of illegal abortions done annually in the US. The actual figure was approaching 100,000, but the figure we gave to the media repeatedly was 1,000,000.
>
> Repeating the big lie often enough convinces the public. The number of women dying from illegal abortions was around 200–250 annually. The figure we constantly fed to the media was 10,000. These false figures took root in the consciousness of Americans, convincing many that we needed to crack the abortion law.[36]

The implication of Dr. Nathanson's confession is obvious: lies have led our federal government and Supreme Court to enshrine a law into practice that many of our citizens see as reprehensible.

ABORTION'S ADVERSE IMPACT ON WOMEN'S HEALTH

The abortion debate typically focuses on women's reproductive rights versus the unborn child's right to life. But in 2004, a group of professional women raised serious questions about the long-term consequences of abortion on women's health and well-being, and the supposed neutrality of peer-reviewed research. In *The Cost of "Choice,"* editor Erika Bachiochi examines links between abortion and culture, women's health, law, regulation of abortion clinics, and abortion alternatives. Among the distinguished contributors were Mary Ann Glendon, Learned Hand Professor of Law at Harvard University; Dr. Elizabeth Shadigan, clinical professor of obstetrics and gynecology at the University of Michigan Medical School; Dr. Angela Lanfranchi, surgical oncologist and assistant professor of surgery at Robert Wood Johnson Medical School; and Dr. Joanne Angelo, psychiatrist and assistant clinical professor at Tufts Medical School.

Contributors to *The Cost of "Choice"* argue that over the "last three decades, legal abortion has had deleterious effects on women—socially, medically, psychologically and culturally."[37] Few women know about these findings because the powerful abortion industry, which includes the organized medical associations, has worked to hide this information. Consequently, women are deceived about the impact abortion can have on their lives.

Dr. Shadigan argues that much of the research on legalized abortion has focused on short-term surgical complications and that the few commissioned studies on long-term effects have concluded that more research is needed. Shadigan contends that a code of silence exists in the medical community regarding research that documents a history of

induced abortion associated with increased long-term risk of breast cancer, placenta previa,[38] preterm birth, and maternal suicide. She reports,
"The risk of breast cancer increases with induced abortion when: (a) the
induced abortion precedes a first full-term pregnancy; (2) the woman is a
teenager; (c) the woman is over the age of 30; (d) the pregnancy is terminated at more than 12 weeks of gestation; or (e) the woman has a family
history of breast cancer. *All* the pregnant teenagers in one study who had
a family history of breast cancer and aborted their first pregnancy developed breast cancer."[39]

> *The powerful abortion industry . . . has worked to hide this information.*
> *Consequently, women are deceived about the impact abortion can have on*
> *their lives.*

For each area of abortion-related medical risk, Shadigan provides
in-depth documentation of scientific sources. She acknowledges that the
National Cancer Institute and the American College of Obstetricians
have published statements indicating that "induced abortion is not an
independent risk factor for breast cancer" but argues that these groups
did not sufficiently credit research studies that have found such a link.

Dr. Lanfranchi, the Robert Woods Johnson oncologist, also believes
a link exists between induced abortion and breast cancer and that the
medical community is engaged in a conspiracy of silence about this
fact. After reviewing the academic studies and science surrounding the
"abortion–breast cancer" (ABC) link and discussing her professional
experiences with breast cancer patients and colleagues, Dr. Lanfranchi
states, "Published epidemiological studies [about] the physiology of the
breast, and experimental studies in mammals all evince a link between
abortion and breast cancer—called the ABC link."[40] Politics, however,
has led the research community to attribute the results to "poorly conducted research and flawed arguments," she says.

Breast cancer is the only major cancer that continues to rise, particularly among women twenty to forty years old. In fact, 30 percent of her breast cancer patients—those with no family history of breast cancer—have had an induced abortion. Dr. Lanfranchi attributes the lack of support in the medical community to "an intimidating political climate" that has caused doctors to "fear repercussions to their name and their career if they disclose what is already known about the ABC link."[41]

Dr. Lanfranchi has found some support in Dr. Stuart Donnan, editor of the *Journal of Epidemiology and Community Health*, who urged his pro-choice colleagues to become "pro-information" without censorship of data. Dr. Donnan argues, "If these researchers are correct [referencing Brind's 1996 Meta-Analysis], a more open approach to medical research could save thousands of lives."[42] Nevertheless, the American Cancer Society website states, "The topic of abortion and breast cancer highlights many of the most challenging aspects of studies of people and how those studies do or do not translate into public health guidelines. The issue of abortion generates passionate viewpoints in many people. Breast cancer is the most common cancer, and is the second leading cancer killer in women. Still, the public is not well-served by false alarms. At this time, the scientific evidence does not support the notion that abortion of any kind raises the risk of breast cancer."[43]

In summarizing studies on placenta previa, a medical condition that makes Cesarean section necessary, Dr. Shadigan cites three studies and one meta-analysis combining data from several studies that found "induced abortion increased the risk of placenta previa by approximately 50 percent."[44] Other studies have documented linkages between premature births or low-birth-weight babies from women who have had induced abortion, increased risk of suicide, and a higher risk of death compared to women who have not had induced abortions.[45]

Citing data from the Centers for Disease Control and Prevention, Dr. Shadigan reports, "Certain women are at much higher risk of death immediately after an induced abortion. For example, black women and other minorities have 2.5 times the chance of dying as white women, and abortions performed at more than 16 weeks gestation have 15 times the risk of maternal mortality as abortion at 12 weeks. Also, women over 40 years old have 3 times the chance of dying as teenagers."[46]

Dr. Shadigan believes that enough evidence of the long-term health consequences from induced abortion—such as breast cancer, placenta previa, preterm birth, maternal suicide, and a higher likelihood of death in the year after an abortion compared to the year after a live birth for women—exists to justify laws requiring informed consent of the mother.

Still other studies report an adverse effect on mental health. Dr. Angelo of Tufts Medical School, reporting on thirty years of psychological research, says women suffer enormous grief after spontaneous miscarriages and induced abortions, especially late-term abortions, which take longer. She notes that psychiatric literature is beginning to document these results and that organizations such as Project Rachel, started by the Catholic Church, minister to women who suffer psychologically after abortions.[47]

THE POLITICS OF PEER-REVIEWED RESEARCH

The Cost of "Choice" also raises questions about the role of deception in the long-term health consequences of abortion. The consequences of abortion to the health of women are rarely included in debates between pro-life and pro-choice factions. Instead, debates focus on the harm to the unborn child and the reproductive rights of the woman. But this omission does not change the fact that these potentially serious side effects have drastic implications for women, especially for young girls.

Peer review is a process whereby experts determine if research meets scholarly standards for publication. Ideally, the process is blind, but often that standard is impossible to attain because attendance at professional meetings and conferences means that peers know who is conducting research in a given area. The process affords many opportunities for gatekeepers to suppress unpopular ideas or settle scores with actual or imagined competitors. At best, the system is flawed, but it is the only process for maintaining the integrity of research.

The politics of federally funded research grants and the peer-review process create especially interesting problems and conflicts for scientists who consult with private corporations for profit-making ventures involving drugs and similar goods.

Whether the issue is climate change, evolution versus intelligent design, or the long-term consequences of abortion, powerful political interests control the flow of information reaching the public. Increasingly, people have come to doubt the objectivity of "scientific" findings both inside and outside colleges and universities. Scholars have begun to question certain aspects of the peer-review process. They know that each journal represents an ideological stance and typically accepts only articles that support that stance. In the 2009 "Climategate" scandal, the public discovered after Internet leaks that scholars were willing to distort data to fit particular ideologies.[48] Flaws in the peer-review system were exposed. The scientific method was not at fault. Some journal editors, scholars, and politicians who had a financial or personal stake in a particular outcome were willing to lie and manipulate data to support their personal agendas.[49]

In the 2009 "Climategate" scandal, the public discovered that scholars were willing to distort data to fit particular ideologies.

FORTY-FIVE MILLION BABIES KILLED

The most recent estimates of the number of legal abortions in the United States come from the Centers for Disease Control and Prevention and the Guttmacher Institute, a research arm of Planned Parenthood. These statistics indicate that more than forty-five million babies have died from legal abortions since 1973.[50] Reporting an abortion is not mandatory, so the exact number of legal and illegal abortions is not known. But we do know that abortion ends the lives of far more black and Hispanic babies than white or Asian babies.

The Guttmacher Institute estimates that 1.2 million abortions occurred in 2005.[51] Black women were 4.8 times more likely than non-Hispanic white women to abort their babies. Hispanics were 2.7 times more likely. That means 683,000 black babies were aborted, or 56 percent of the American total, despite the fact that blacks represent only 13 percent of the US population. One out of every three black babies is killed before birth, while only one out of every six white babies faces this tragedy.

Although Latina women constitute a smaller percentage than black women, at 14 percent of the population, they undergo 22 percent of America's abortions. High rates of abortion among minority women result primarily from the cumulative choices of poor women who find themselves with an unplanned pregnancy and then succumb to the lure of neighborhood abortion clinics.

Most abortion clinics are located in blighted metropolitan areas in order to pander to minorities. Live Action, an investigative organization, reports that 79 percent of Planned Parenthood clinics are strategically located in minority neighborhoods.[52] In 2009, Planned Parenthood was planning a huge clinic in Houston that is the "second largest abortion facility in the world, next to China." The six-story, 78,000-square-foot building is situated "in the middle of four minority neighborhoods. Three of these neighborhoods have an average 85 percent Hispanic population, and the fourth is 80 percent black American. The third floor was being specially designed as an ambulatory surgical center for the purpose of performing late-term abortions."[53] Walter Hoye, director of community relations at Progressive Missionary Baptist Church in Berkeley, California, and founder of Issues4Life, calls abortion "the Darfur of the African-American community."[54] Although it is a bit much to suggest that these statistics suggest a form of genocide, which involves systematic and purposeful action to eliminate a race, the facts regarding Planned Parenthood and African Americans are especially troubling.[55]

I am counted among the millions of black women who terminated an unplanned pregnancy out of convenience. At the time I was married and had two children. An abortion clinic was nearby. I reasoned that if the procedure was legal, it must be moral. But I have since come to the knowledge that not everything that is legal is right. In my case the law mattered: had abortion been illegal, I would have opted to have my child. It took me more than twenty years to share my experience with others. The guilt of my abortion led me to try to replace my lost child with a planned pregnancy, which I lost to spontaneous miscarriage. I suffered some of the adverse medical and psychological effects discussed in *The Cost of "Choice."*

Live Action, an investigative organization, reports that 79 percent of Planned Parenthood clinics are strategically located in minority neighborhoods.

PLANNED PARENTHOOD FEDERATION OF AMERICA

Planned Parenthood Federation of America is the largest abortion provider in the United States. The organization has chapters in every state, and its international arm has offices in seventeen countries in Africa, Asia, and South America. Under the guise of family planning and reproductive rights, Planned Parenthood extends its work to underdeveloped nations. It works in conjunction with the US government's practice of tying a nation's receipt of federal dollars to its willingness to establish family planning policies that include abortion. Instituted during the Reagan administration, the Mexico City Policy (also called "The Global Gag Rule") prevented organizations that offered abortion counseling in other countries from receiving federal funds. President Bill Clinton reversed the Mexico City Policy shortly after taking office, President George W. Bush restored the policy, and within days of being sworn into office President Obama issued an executive order reversing the policy again. A Planned Parenthood press release states:

Planned Parenthood Federation of America is the nation's leading sexual and reproductive health care advocate and provider. We believe that everyone has the right to choose when or whether to have a child, and that every child should be wanted and loved. Planned Parenthood affiliates operate nearly 880 health centers nationwide, providing medical services and sexuality education for millions of women, men, and teenagers each year. We also work with allies worldwide to ensure that all women and men have the right and the means to meet their sexual and reproductive health care needs.[56]

Planned Parenthood performs some necessary services, including screening for sexually transmitted diseases and providing information about sexuality and forestalling teen pregnancy. It also provides general health-care screening and support for smoking cessation. But disturbing realities exist behind the scenes. For example, Americans may be surprised to learn that their tax dollars are contributing, in large part, to fund Planned Parenthood. Each year, Planned Parenthood Federation of America receives millions of federal dollars to support its activities across the world and in all fifty states. In 2005–2006, the organization took in nearly $1 billion and reported a surplus of $55 million. Approximately one-third of Planned Parenthood's income, $305 million, came from government subsidies.

A 2010 report by the Government Accounting Office[57] revealed that between 2002 and 2008 Planned Parenthood and its programs received $2.3 billion in government grants, while its records indicate expenditures of $657 million; astute citizens are asking what happened to the remaining $1.6 billion.[58] The organization's president receives annual compensation of almost $1 million. At a time when abortions nationwide are declining, Planned Parenthood is performing more abortions than ever: 264,943 in 2005–2006. These abortions bring in at least one-third of the organization's $345 million in clinic income.[59]

It is important to know that Planned Parenthood competes for private and federal dollars with Crisis Pregnancy Centers, which support comprehensive programs for women who desire to keep their unborn children. Although Planned Parenthood does not explicitly prevent such programs from providing assistance, it positions itself to undercut these organizations in their ability to receive funding.

A look behind Planned Parenthood's politically correct facade reveals that certain practices appear suspicious, if not sinister. In November 2009, Abby Johnson, a former director of a Planned Parenthood clinic in Bryan, Texas, quit her job after participating in the procedure room during an abortion.[60] When Johnson began to talk about her experiences with Planned Parenthood during the previous eight years, the organization sued her for breach of confidentiality. Johnson gained national visibility by sharing the inner workings of the organization. She said her superiors pressured her "to increase profits by performing more and more abortions, which cost patients between $505 and $695." According to Johnson, "Every meeting that we had was, 'We don't have enough money, we don't have enough money—we've got to keep these abortions coming . . . It's a very lucrative business, and that's why they want to increase numbers.'"[61]

On December 9, 2009, Live Action released footage of staff members at an Appleton, Wisconsin, Planned Parenthood abortion clinic misleading clients about fetal development and urging a woman to get an abortion by telling her that childbirth can be deadly. However, as world health statistics reveal, childbirth is much less deadly in nations with restrictive abortion laws, such as Ireland, Poland, and the African nation of Mauritius than in the United States, which has virtually unrestricted abortion laws.[62]

ALLEGATIONS OF RACISM

Allegations of racism have repeatedly shadowed Planned Parenthood. No one should be surprised, given that its founder, Margaret Higgins Sanger, was a well-known eugenicist who believed that society would be better off if immigrants, blacks, and people with mental deficiencies or other handicaps stopped reproducing.[63] Her most famous book, *The Pivot of Civilization*,[64] was published three years before Hitler published *Mein*

Kampf.[65] Ethicist Benjamin Wiker, PhD, author of *10 Books That Screwed Up the World*, describes Sanger as "one of the great leaders of the international eugenics movement." He notes that Margaret Sanger "didn't just peddle birth control and also espouse eugenic views, as if these were two unrelated passions. Eugenics was at the very heart of her reasons for pushing birth control."[66]

In a widely quoted letter to Dr. Clarence J. Gamble, Sanger wrote, "the most successful educational approach to the Negro is through a religious appeal. We do not want word to go out that we want to exterminate the Negro population, and the minister is the man who can straighten out that idea if it ever occurs to any of their more rebellious members."[67] Sanger lived long enough to see one of history's greatest black leaders receive Planned Parenthood's Margaret Sanger Award. On May 5, 1966, Martin Luther King Jr. was given the award "for his courageous resistance to bigotry and his lifelong dedication to the advancement of social justice and human dignity."[68] King's acceptance speech was reprinted by Planned Parenthood to advertise its services and praise Sanger. The organization encouraged black families to use family planning as a path to betterment.

> Margaret Sanger "didn't just peddle birth control and also espouse eugenic views, as if these were two unrelated passions. Eugenics was at the very heart of her reasons for pushing birth control."

In 2007, Lila Rose became an instant celebrity after the release of a video and transcript exposing racism at seven Planned Parenthood centers across the nation. At the time, Rose, a UCLA sophomore, worked as a student researcher and editor-in-chief for the pro-life magazine *The Advocate*. Rose hired a professional actor in the summer of 2007 to call Planned Parenthood clinics around the country, offering donations to "lower the number of black people" by targeting black babies for abortion. Planned Parenthood clinics in seven states accepted the proposed contribution. Not one Planned Parenthood employee objected to the call-er's racist remarks or purposes.[69]

THE SABOTAGE OF AMERICA'S SEXUALITY

Other forms of deception are also infiltrating American politics and cul-ture. Most Americans are oblivious to how Planned Parenthood Federation of America (Planned Parenthood) is sexualizing our preteen children. Planned Parenthood has endorsed and disseminated copies of Robie Harris's slick and glossy book *It's Perfectly Normal: Changing Bodies, Growing Up, Sex, and Sexual Health*,[70] which includes graphically illustrated chapters on heterosexual intercourse, homosexuality, masturbation, birth control, and abortion. Planned Parenthood recommends the book for children ages ten and older. Many mothers and fathers don't realize that Planned Parenthood partners with the Girl Scouts of America to distribute literature such as *It's Perfectly Normal* to the young girls who attend Scout meetings.

In March 2010, Planned Parenthood used the Girl Scouts to dis-tribute a shameful brochure titled "Healthy, Happy, and Hot: A Young Person's Guide to Their Rights, Sexuality, and Living with HIV"[71] at its meeting at the United Nations. According to the brochure, "Sharing your HIV status is called disclosure. Your decision about whether to disclose may change with different people and situations. You have the right to decide if, when, and how to disclose your HIV status."[72] The brochure explains:

Many people think sex is just about vaginal or anal intercourse . . . But, there are lots of different ways to have sex and lots of different types of sex. There is no right or wrong way to have sex. Just have fun, explore and be yourself . . . Improve your sex life by getting to know your own body. Play with yourself! Masturbation is a great way to find out more about your body and what you find sexually stimulating. Mix things up by using different kinds of touch from very soft to hard. Talk about or act out your fantasies. Talk dirty to them.[73]

Giving children sex instruction, condoms, and birth control pills is not the way to stop sexually transmitted disease and unwanted pregnancies. Studies show that teens who use birth control have a much higher failure rate than adults and are less likely to use protection consistently.[74] When failure ends in pregnancy, Planned Parenthood stands ready to give your daughter an abortion, in some states without your consent.

EVASION OF RAPE LAWS

Planned Parenthood's confidentiality principles conflict with laws in every state that require health-care workers to report to law enforcers suspected sexual abuse or statutory rape. Investigators have identified a national pattern when it comes to Planned Parenthood's failure to report sex crimes against underage teens. In 2002, the pro-life group Life Dynamics called eight hundred abortion clinics around the country, many of them run by Planned Parenthood. The representative for Life Dynamics claimed she was a thirteen-year-old girl who needed an abortion and stated that her boyfriend was twenty-two. Ninety-one percent of the clinics told the caller they would give her an abortion but warned her not to reveal her boyfriend's age.

Furthermore, Planned Parenthood New York City's confidentiality page for teenagers advertises free services and informs teens of the specifics of state law: "New York state law allows teens to consent to confidential family planning services and reproductive health care, including abortion. This means you can make an appointment and get any of these services at our health centers without asking your parents' permission." Live Action Video has taped Planned Parenthood clinics around the country counseling young women to evade the state's statutory rape laws. For example, in the transcript, the childlike voice of Lila Rose told the intake worker in Memphis, Tennessee, that she was pregnant and wanted an abortion:

"I'm 14."

And what about the man who impregnated her?

"He's 31."

Instead of calling the police or the young woman's parents, the counselor advised the supposed fourteen-year-old: "Just say you have a boyfriend, 17-years-old, whatever."[75]

SHIFTING PUBLIC OPINION

For decades, most Americans have described themselves as "pro-choice" when asked about a woman's right to terminate an unwanted pregnancy. As of 2009, however, that statistic has changed. A May 2009 Gallup Poll found that a majority of Americans identify themselves as pro-life. In response to the question "With respect to the abortion issue, would you consider yourself pro-choice or pro-life?" 51 percent described themselves as pro-life while 42 percent described themselves as pro-choice.[76] A follow-up question about when abortion should be considered legal found "about as many Americans now say the procedure should be illegal in all circumstances (23%) as say it should be legal under any circumstances (22%)."[77] These responses contrast sharply with the previous four years, when Gallup found a "tilt of public attitudes in favor of unrestricted abortion."[78]

In analyzing the shift, Gallup senior editor Lydia Saad wondered whether the public was responding to the election of a liberal pro-choice president who had pushed "the public's understanding of what it means to be 'pro-choice' slightly to the left." Saad noted that President Obama's administration had made or was planning to make changes that further liberalized abortion laws. For example, she cites the president's change of policy on funding overseas abortion (Mexico City Policy) and his backtracking on his support for the Freedom of Choice Act, which would have allowed health-care workers not to participate in abortion without risking their jobs.[79] There is also the real possibility that President Obama might rescind federal job protections for medical workers who refuse to participate in abortion procedures.

Other reasons that might account for the shifting opinion on abortion include high-profile coverage of news stories about abortion and the use of new technologies that enable observation of unborn babies in the womb,[80] including seeing the facial features and acrobatics of babies in 3-D. Technology may be undermining the arguments of those who have long denied the humanity of the unborn. They are also more willing to embrace children with special needs, such as Sarah Palin's son Trig, who has Down syndrome. Vanderbilt University, for example, enrolls students with intellectual challenges into a special two-year program that allows them to take classes with other Vanderbilt students.[81] Whatever the cause, it is clear that more Americans are finding abortion distasteful and are questioning whether the government should permit it.

ETHICAL AND MORAL CONSIDERATIONS

Are human beings special creatures entitled to moral respect and protections that we would not provide other mammals? How we answer this question profoundly affects how we treat people throughout the world we may never meet, but who suffer because of our choices. Our answer also affects how we treat people at the beginning and the end of their lives, including our genetic offspring.

A person does not have to be religious to know that abortion and experimentation with embryonic human stem cells are repugnant. The most ardent secular humanist might easily recoil when confronted with data about the multibillion-dollar biotechnology trade in human fetal tissue obtained from aborted babies. Companies can order fresh tissue harvested to their specifications, including vivisected (cut up while still alive) brains, testes, prostates, eyes, and ovaries. Similar to the law that bans partial-birth abortion, the law against selling fetal tissue comes with loopholes that allow wholesaler employees to rent space in abortion clinics, dissect aborted babies, and ship their parts to laboratories across the country.[82]

Embryological textbooks provide contradictory perspectives about the full humanity of unborn babies. Research summarized by Robert

P. George and Christopher Tollefsen documents the following scientific understanding among biologists:

> The embryo is from the start distinct from any cell of the mother or of the father . . . The embryo is human: it has the genetic makeup characteristic of human beings . . . The embryo is a complete or whole organism, though immature.
>
> The human embryo, from conception onward, is fully programmed and has the active disposition to use that information to develop himself or herself to the mature stage of a human being, and, unless prevented by disease or violence, will actually do so.[83]

Thirteenth-century philosopher and theologian Thomas Aquinas pointed to the existence of a natural law whose core principles are knowable by all people through moral reasoning. University of Texas philosopher J. Budziszewski emphasizes that "not every moral principle is part of the core [of natural law], but all moral principle is derived from it, if not by pure deduction (killing is wrong and poison kills, so poisoning is wrong), then with the help of prudence (wrongdoers should be punished, but the appropriate punishment depends on the circumstances.)"[84] This means that because of the natural wiring of human beings, *all* people can discern right from wrong, and they can learn from wrong decisions.

Robert P. George, professor of jurisprudence at Princeton University, uses moral reasoning rather than religious authorities to challenge his students to think more deeply about abortion. He posits:

> If abortion is wrong, surely it is wrong because it is the unjust taking of the life of a developing human being . . . And if one believes that, then what could possibly justify a regime of law that licenses so grave an injustice? . . . If abortion is not a form of homicide, if the developing embryo or fetus has the moral status of an unwanted growth—such as a tumor—there would be no grounds on which to "personally oppose"

abortion. So the question is this: Is the developing embryo or fetus a human being or a mere unwanted growth?[85]

In the reasoning process, George has transformed the issue from a primarily religious or ethical issue into a question about human embryology and developmental biology.

In speaking of the moral confusion that often surrounds issues like abortion, Budziszewski notes, "Most who call abortion wrong call it killing. Most who call it killing say it kills a baby. Most who call it killing a baby decline to prohibit it altogether. Most who decline to prohibit it think it should be restricted."[86] Getting to the crux of the matter, Budziszewski concludes, "If abortion kills a baby then it ought to be banned to everyone; why allow it? But if it does not kill a baby it is hard to see why we should be uneasy about it; why restrict it?"[87]

Feminist doublespeak masks the horror that is taking place. Like me, professor Mary Poplin of Claremont Graduate University is among the millions of women who regret having an abortion. Looking back at factors influencing her decision, Poplin wrote:

> Now I can see how the radical feminist literature with which I was once enthralled is so contradictory. How can such intellectuals profess that women are more caring than men are, yet simultaneously advocate vociferously for abortion? One feminist scholar even refers to the fetus as "an information speck." Language shapes our attitudes and actions. The postmodernist idea that language can construct reality often belies and obscures the very real spiritual and natural impact of words on our choices, and ultimately on our lives and the lives of everyone around us.[88]

Poplin notes that, as a radical feminist, she "criticized the abstraction of language about women's bodies, but not when it came to abortion. Here the abstraction helped to mask the reality and give me the freedom to do what I wanted to do . . . I believe that the abstract medical terminology surrounding 'pregnancy' is one of the reasons women like me could see abortions in such a disconnected way, and subsequently why it was so easy to choose abortion. After all, it is treated as a medical condition to be alleviated."[89]

THE THREAT OF CARBON-EMITTING BABIES

A chilling new link with environmentalism also threatens the unborn. In July 2009, Paul Murtaugh and Michael G. Schlax, professors in the Department of Statistics at Oregon State University, released a study warning of the huge carbon footprints associated with babies.[90] A carbon footprint measures the impact we have on the environment through the production of greenhouse gases. The authors concluded that the energy savings from reduced human populations far exceeded gains from actions such as recycling and switching to energy-saving devices and greener lifestyles. The article warned that population growth and global consumption rank highest among the world's challenges.

The global warming hypothesis and the desire to reduce the carbon footprint have led to bizarre programs such as the Britain's Optimum Population Trust, which launched Pop*Offsets*, a program that encourages people to invest in reducing the world's population by helping fund abortion and birth control for the world's poor. The website explains why this funding is a good investment. According to Pop*Offsets*, "More people = more emissions. Rapid population growth is a major contributor to global warming."[91] For instance, a person can click on a Pop*Offsets* Calculator to figure the amount of carbon emissions an airline trip might produce. "If you fly round-trip from London to Sydney—which emits ten tons of carbon—you must pay around £40 ($70) and help prevent the birth of one child in Kenya."[92] The group's website states, "One less birth into poverty is not only one less person to suffer poverty and the expected severe impacts of climate change, but also one less to produce more greenhouse gases in (hopefully) escaping poverty."[93]

Abortion certainly prevents the birth of a carbon-emitting child. Of course, the argument in favor of abortion on environmental grounds leads exactly where one might suspect: wealthy first-world nations seeking to reduce the carbon-emitting offspring of women in poor nations.

NATIONAL AND INTERNATIONAL IMPLICATIONS OF ABORTION

Abortion affects more than the men and women who make decisions to terminate unwanted pregnancies. Cumulatively, the demographics of the nation are affected. One need only look at China to see the devastating impact of forced and coerced abortions. As a result of concerns about population growth and their impact on the economy, China adopted a one-child policy in 1979. Because of that nation's cultural preferences for males, the policy resulted in a current imbalance of thirty-two million more males under the age of twenty than females.[94]

Today many Chinese men who want to marry and have children must seek wives outside their nation. By 2005, the imbalance had led to complaints of kidnapping and trafficking of young women.

Abortion affects more than the men and women who make decisions to terminate unwanted pregnancies. Cumulatively, the demographics of the nation are affected.

Interestingly, the US Agency for International Development (USAID) —the federal agency providing economic and humanitarian assistance— has reached across the world with its dollars, encouraging other nations to embrace an agenda that includes abortion.[95]

What would it take to reduce significantly the number of abortions today? Marvin Olasky of *World* magazine argues that only a combination of legislation, prevention, and compassionate care of pregnant women will reduce abortion rates.[96] Compassionate care includes providing women with greater access to prenatal crisis centers that assist women with diapers, baby clothes, counseling, medical care, sex education, and

job training. Women need clear alternatives to the government-funded
Planned Parenthood centers that push abortions on some of the most
vulnerable members of society: teenagers and minorities. It would also be
helpful to streamline the abortion process for families and provide more
group homes and encouragement for women who choose to offer their
babies for adoption.

ABORTION HURTS MEN TOO

Society also needs to acknowledge that women are not the only individuals harmed by abortion. More and more men are turning to counseling
to deal with the trauma associated with the abortion of the child they
wanted or the one they thought they didn't.

Greg Hasek is a licensed marriage and family therapist who lives in
Oregon. He specializes in treating addiction, abuse, and abortion-related
trauma. Hasek reports that more and more men are beginning to talk
about how abortion has affected them as a result of a shift in cultural
acceptance or validation of their pain, combined with an increase in
resources available for these men. "Many of these men come to counseling with other presenting problems such as addictions to pornography . . .
Many of these men have an abortion decision in their history and often
the unresolved grief as a result puts these men at an increased risk of med-
icating the loss through addiction. Until that loss is resolved, often these
men are unable to maintain their recovery from addiction."[97] According
to Hasek:

> Men are more likely to connect to the loss of a role rather than the loss
> of the baby. The loss becomes real for them when they connect the
> abortion to the loss of fatherhood or the role of being a father. They
> also seem to have an omnipotent responsibility in the abortion deci-
> sion, often times more than the woman. They internalize a sense of
> failure as a provider and protector of not only a future child but also
> of their partner. This internalized sense of failure as a man often later.

contributes to relationship difficulties and at times the eventual loss of that relationship.

Men also grieve differently than women. Men are more likely to grieve through thinking and action. The fact that men grieve differently is often perceived in our culture as men are indifferent or don't hurt as a result. This is far from the truth.[98]

Hasek explains that, since the 1970s, our culture has been "stuck in their view of men as the perpetrators of women's pain and only able to experience emotional pain as a soldier coming back from war. Until there is movement in culture's view and understanding of men, millions of men will deny the existence of the pain as a way of conforming to a culture that seems to condition them in the very same way that attracts condemnation."[99]

Phil Holsinger, CEO of Blue Ridge Women's Center in Roanoke, Virginia, shares his own abortion story:

As a young man growing up in a family conspicuously deficient of exemplary fathering, I was left on my own to determine what it meant to be provider and protector as well as what it meant to be a man. In the absence of a good role model, I found myself attempting to prove myself a man through risky behavior and sexual conquest. When a pregnancy resulted from my attempts to prove myself a man, it was easy to suggest abortion. From my perspective at the time, being a man had nothing to do with being a father. But once I became a man, not from behavior but rather from confirmation and affirmation by a real man, fatherhood became the expression of my manhood. It was then that I had to come to grips with my responsibility to be provider and protector. One of the greatest impacts of abortion on the men who participate in that decision is how it impacts our ability to fulfill the role as father for our other children . . . Abortion is a direct assault on fatherhood because it countermands the basic concepts of protection and provision; the very character traits God created me to express.[100]

MORAL REASONING

One does not have to be a Christian to realize that abortion is wrong. Moral reasoning is accessible to all human beings. We live in a world where all major religions teach that abortion is morally wrong. Classical Hindu texts condemn abortion, teach that families have a duty to bear children, and assert that life begins at conception, when the soul fuses with the body, withholding the exception when the life of the mother is at stake.[101] Traditional Buddhism also condemns the destruction of life and teaches that life begins at conception. Diverse schools of Islamic thought exist, although most condemn abortion. According to Muslim scholar Abul Fadl Mohsin Ebrahim:

> The Hanafi school is the most flexible on abortion. It specifies that before the fourth month of pregnancy, an abortion may be induced if a woman's pregnancy poses a threat to the life of her already existing infant. The Maliki position prohibits an abortion after implantation has taken place, while the Shafi'i school maintains that at any stage after fertilization the zygote should not be disturbed, and interference with its development would be a crime. The Hanbali school, by stipulating the payment of blood wit (a monetary compensation) for causing a miscarriage shows that it regards abortion as a sin.[102]

The Qur'an states, "If anyone slays a human being unless it be (in punishment) for murder or for spreading corruption on earth—it shall be as if he had slain the whole of mankind; whereas, if anyone saves a life, it shall be as if he had saved the lives of the whole of mankind."[103]

THE BIBLICAL POSITION ON HUMAN LIFE

The Bible does not explicitly address abortion, despite clear evidence that the practice existed during biblical times. Several scholars have conducted research into why the New Testament is silent about the issue. Historian Gerald McDermott has written that there was no reason to address the issue of abortion, given that most writers of Scripture were Jews:

> In the *Sentences of Pseudo-Phocylides* (50 BC–AD. 50), for instance, we find that "a woman should not destroy the unborn babe in her belly, nor after its birth throw it before the dogs and vultures as prey." The apocalyptic *Sybilline Oracles* includes among the wicked two groups—women who "produce abortions and unlawfully cast their offspring away" and sorcerers who dispense abortifacients. The Hellenistic Jewish philosopher Philo of Alexandria (25 BC–AD 41) rejected the pagan notion that the fetus is part of its mother's body (this idea was not generated in the 20th century!). He said that anyone inducing abortion is to be fined if the fetus is unformed and given the death penalty if the fetus is formed. The silence of the New Testament on abortion simply means that there was widespread agreement on the subject.[104]

According to theologian Michael J. Gorman, associate professor at St. Mary's Seminary and University, early church fathers uniformly condemned the use of abortifacients—drugs or chemicals that cause abortions. Condemnation of abortion is found in the writings of early Christian scholars Clement of Alexandria, Basil the Great, Jerome, Augustine, Origen, and John Chrysostom.[105]

The biblical position on life is implied by scriptures such as Genesis 1:27–28, which states that mankind is created in God's image and that reproduction of the species is part of God's divine plan: "So God created man in his own image, in the image of God he created him; male and female he created them. And God blessed them. And God said to them, 'Be fruitful and multiply and fill the earth and subdue it and have dominion over the fish of the sea and over the birds of the heavens and over every living thing that moves on the earth.'"

Nowhere in the Bible is there evidence that fetuses are anything but human. Throughout the Bible, pregnant women are described as "with child," and frequent references refer to unborn children as sons and daughters. These children were always blessings from God.

The Bible also suggests that each unborn child has a unique identity and destiny. God told Jeremiah, "Before I formed you in the womb I knew you, and before you were born I consecrated you; I appointed you a prophet to the nations" (Jeremiah 1:5). David wrote in Psalm 139:13, "For you formed my inward parts; you knitted me together in my mother's womb." In the cases of Jesus and John the Baptist, an angel names each child before the child is born, giving names that are connected with some aspect of the child's personality (Matthew 1:21; Luke 1:13).

Nowhere in the Bible is there evidence that fetuses are anything but human. Throughout the Bible, pregnant women are described as "with child," and frequent references refer to unborn children as sons and daughters.

Exodus 20:3–17 lists the Ten Commandments that God gave to the Israelites. The sixth commandment states, "You shall not murder" (v. 13). Throughout the Bible, starting with the death of Abel, God distinguishes between murder and other kinds of killing, such as in capital punishment, God-ordained war, and accidents. Murder—the deliberate taking of innocent life—is strongly condemned. The Bible speaks of innocent blood crying out from the ground, and of lands polluted by the shedding of innocent blood. In Genesis 4:10, we read, "And the LORD said [to Cain], "What have you done? The voice of your brother's blood is crying to me from the ground." Proverbs 6:17 tells us that God hates "haughty eyes, a lying tongue, and hands that shed innocent blood."

In Leviticus 18:21, the Israelites are told, "You shall not give any of your children to offer them to Molech, and so profane the name of your God." Likewise, we read in Psalm 106:37–38: "They sacrificed their sons and their daughters to the demons; they poured out innocent blood, the blood of their sons and daughters, whom they sacrificed to the idols of Canaan, and the land was polluted with blood."

These scriptures admonished the Israelites not to follow the detestable practices of the Canaanites and neighboring peoples who sacrificed their children to Baal and Molech.

If God exists and is unchanging, how does he feel about the innocent blood of the preborn so callously shed in the United States on a daily basis? Our blatant national disregard for the value of human life is obvious to religious leaders throughout the world. Mary Poplin, who worked as a volunteer for two months with Mother Teresa and her order, the Missionaries of Charity, in Calcutta, observed that the nuns refused to send children to the United States for adoption because of our nation's high abortion and divorce rates.[106] Mother Teresa pitied our nation for its poverty of spirit, saying, "If abortion is permitted in wealthy countries that have all the means that money can buy, those countries are the poorest among the poor."[107]

Although the majority of Americans today profess Christianity, our lifestyles, lack of biblical knowledge, and unwillingness to honor God's standards about the sanctity of human life contradict our claim.

Mother Teresa pitied our nation for its poverty of spirit, saying, "If abortion is permitted in wealthy countries that have all the means that money can buy, those countries are the poorest among the poor."

Many women, like Mary Poplin and me, had abortions before we came to know Christ. We often suffer in silence. Poplin frequently discusses the deep remorse she felt about her abortion after she started to follow Christ. For two years after her conversion, she repeatedly repented for her two abortions and doubted whether God would truly forgive her for such a grievous sin.[108] She recounted how she finally overcame that doubt:

All at once I heard a male voice in my spirit clearly say, "Who are you not to forgive someone I have forgiven?" I stopped, stunned and confused by the question that had appeared in my spirit . . . [I] said aloud, "Lord, who have I not forgiven?" Into my spirit the Lord spoke, "I forgave you the first time you asked me. I do not want you to ask me again."[109]

We can rest in the knowledge that God forgives the sins and trespasses of those who place their trust in his promises.

ACTION POINTS

1. Visit or volunteer at a local crisis pregnancy center. Some of these centers provide diapers, bottles, formula, and other support until a child is at least a year old. Your donations of goods, services, or dollars would make a difference to a struggling mother.

2. Get on the mailing lists of pro-life organizations. ProlifeAmerica.com maintains a list of organizations that could use your support.[110]

3. Read and discuss the *Be the People* questions for chapter 3, posted at www.CarolMSwain.com.

PART TWO

BANISHED VIRTUES

Reclaiming Truth and Justice in Policy Choices

CHAPTER 4

FAMILY MATTERS

I didn't marry you because you were perfect. I didn't even marry you because I loved you. I married you because you gave me a promise. That promise made up for your faults. And the promise I gave you made up for mine. Two imperfect people got married, and it was the promise that made the marriage. And when our children were growing up, it wasn't a house that protected them, and it wasn't our love that protected them—it was that promise.

—MAGGIE ANTROBUS IN THORNTON WILDER'S *The Skin of Our Teeth* (1942)[1]

The problem lay buried, unspoken, for many years in the minds of American women. It was a strange stirring, a sense of dissatisfaction, a yearning that women suffered in the middle of the 20th century in the United States. Each suburban wife struggled with it alone. As she made the beds, shopped for groceries, matched slipcover material, ate peanut butter sandwiches with her children, chauffeured Cub Scouts and Brownies, lay beside her husband at night—she was afraid to ask even of herself the silent question—"Is this all?"

—BETTY FRIEDAN, *The Feminine Mystique*[2]

THORNTON WILDER'S 1942 PULITZER PRIZE–WINNING PLAY *THE SKIN OF Our Teeth* introduces the struggles of George and Maggie Antrobus, a couple fated to experience eternally the disasters of human history. They survive Noah's flood, the Ice Age, wars, and a direct attack on their marriage. In each instance, the family escapes "by the skin of their teeth." As their story unfolds, Maggie—wife and mother of two— speaks the words quoted above after her husband of five thousand years breaks the news that he wants to divorce her for a younger woman. Maggie's monologue articulates how a promise can anchor a marriage and protect and stabilize family members when the inevitable adversity hits home.

Two decades after Wilder's play opened on Broadway, feminist Betty Friedan's 1963 book *The Feminine Mystique* burst onto the scene. After surveying women who were college graduates, Friedan declared that middle-class American mothers and homemakers were trapped in domestic servitude. Friedan's provocative volume arrived in bookstores just one year after the US Supreme Court removed prayer from public schools and the same year the Supreme Court silenced Bible reading in schools. Friedan, who in 1966 would cofound the National Organization for Women (NOW), envisioned women across the nation abandoning their unfulfilling lives as homemakers for a still-ambiguous promise of "liberation" in the workplace and in politics. The book ignited a revolution as millions of middle-class white women left home, went to work, and explored sexual liberties heretofore associated with men.

Yet not every woman was caught up in the excitement. Many American families remained intact, as marriage partners kept the faith with their first spouses. Many of these partners were white women who married during the 1940s; interestingly, 86 percent of women who married in the 1940s have remained with their husbands until death.[3]

Nevertheless, the women's liberation movement crashed into American homes like a wave. The result was catastrophic for marriages and families. Almost half of the couples who married during the 1960s and 1970s divorced by the 1990s.[4]

The women's liberation movement crashed into American homes like a wave. The result was catastrophic for marriages and families.

I count myself among these numbers. I married in 1970 and filed for divorce in 1975, and my divorce was finalized in 1976. Then I married again in 1978 and filed for divorce again in 1989. In both cases, I married for reasons other than love. Although I married twice,

I did not have weddings, which are not part of the underclass culture I come from.

QUIGLEY AND BRENDA MOYNIHAN: TRADITIONALISTS MARRIED IN THE LATE 1960S

Why do some marriages survive and others fail? Why do some work, even when the partners hardly know each other prior to the wedding? Some people seem to know instantly when they've met their life partners. Such was the case for Quigley Moynihan, who told me his story in December 2009 as I was writing this book.

I boarded a plane in Nashville and found myself sitting beside Quigley. It took only a few moments to notice this gruff, elderly white man wasn't the typical business-class passenger. He was dressed casually, asked for a Budweiser, and drank it from the can. But Quigley and I quickly hit it off as we discussed race, family, America, and social class. His story about his short courtship and ensuing long marriage, despite a lifetime of challenges, fascinated me.

Twenty minutes into their first date, then twenty-one-year-old Quigley Moynihan popped the question to his future bride, Brenda. What's even more remarkable is that she accepted, and six months later, on August 2, 1969, they married at a Catholic church in Fort Wayne, Texas.[5] But serious differences between Quigley and Brenda surfaced early in their relationship.

He told me, "I had to go to counseling classes, because Brenda and her mom were Catholic, and certain rules had to be followed to guard against a Catholic marrying a heathen like me. I jumped all of those hoops and remember being grilled by the priest at the Catholic church where we were going to have the ceremony. When we talked about faith, I said, 'I don't know anything about that, but I know one thing, I know I love Brenda.' For whatever reason, this grumpy old priest married us, and the rest is history."[6]

The first five years of marriage introduced the Moynihans to some of their greatest challenges. Quigley informed Brenda that he didn't want to have children. "My folks had shown me a lot of bad parenting skills, and I didn't want to pass them on to another generation," he explained. Eventually, however, Quigley relented. He fathered twins Matthew and Michael, whom Brenda raised to be devout Catholics. "And to top the year off," Quigley said, "we conceived again in 1973." Melissa Shey Moynihan was born within months of the twins.

"The way the months of birth worked out, we started Melissa in kindergarten the same year as the boys," Quigley recalled. "I did, however, finally figure out what was causing the high birth rate on Driscoll Boulevard, and I had a doctor surgically fix my problem."[7]

Reminiscing about the pressures of early parenthood, Quigley said, "It would have been easy for Brenda or me to just give up and quit working at our marriage . . . the whole thing could have come tumbling down, but it didn't. So 1973 wasn't a year for lightweights in our home. Faith in God got us through, but I don't believe either one of us realized that fully at the time."[8]

Quigley Moynihan's simple statement about faith encapsulates an important truth. Even though the Moynihans' marriage was far from perfect, Brenda and Quigley's promise—their commitment to their vows based on their faith in God—was their anchor in difficult moments when either could have chosen to walk away.

AL AND TIPPER GORE:
AN UNLIKELY COUPLE TO SPLIT

Forty-year-long marriages like the Quigleys' would seem to be secure, wouldn't they? But the notion of faith in long-term marriage was dealt a knockout blow in June 2010 when former vice president Al Gore and his wife, Tipper, announced their separation shortly after their fortieth anniversary. It was a blow to millions of people that the high school sweethearts known to the world as a couple that embodied marital stability had decided to part ways. What was especially troubling was that the announcement of their separation came on the heels of their fortieth wedding anniversary.[9] Many of us have an image seared into our minds of the passionate kiss and embrace that the couple gave each other at the 2000 Democratic National Convention.

Most people would have bet on former president Bill Clinton and his wife, Hillary, as the high-powered Washington couple most likely to divorce within ten years of leaving the White House. Few would have thought that couple would be Al and Tipper Gore.

But perhaps America should have seen the breakup coming. In today's culture, marriage vows are no longer considered unbreakable covenant promises—naturally, more couples are willing to give up and walk away when the going gets tough. Columnist Linda Chavez reminisces about a bygone era: "Not too long ago, it would have been unthinkable for as prominent a couple as the Gores to break up. Divorce not only ended a marriage, it diminished the involved individuals' social standing, career, and certainly their political aspirations. No longer . . . No one blinks an eye at a divorced corporate CEO. And even the clergy's ranks include divorced men and women."[10]

In today's culture, marriage vows are no longer considered unbreakable covenant promises—naturally, more couples are willing to give up and walk away when the going gets tough.

Bemoaning the Gore separation that caused Americans angst, Chavez writes, "The Gores, like most couples, made a vow to remain together—'until death do us part.' Couples make those vows in front of family and friends and with the blessings of religious institutions and the state. They are not private promises; they are public affirmations. So if the Gores decide to break those vows, they've hurt all of us, not just each other, and they've chipped away at the very institution of marriage. Let's hope they don't move from separation to divorce, for all our sakes."[11]

THE MARRIAGE COVENANT

Adherents of Judeo-Christian religions have traditionally viewed marriage as an institution ordained by God for purposes of companionship and procreation. Consequently, it is called "holy matrimony." According to Roman Catholic teaching, "Matrimony gives the graces necessary for those who are to rear children in the love and fear of God."[12] In Genesis 2:24, we read, "Therefore a man shall leave his father and his mother and hold fast to his wife, and they shall become one flesh." In the book *Male and Female He Created Them: On Marriage and the Family*, Cardinal Medina Estévez summarizes his understanding of Old Testament teachings about God's intention for men and women:

- man is an image of God and one of his works;
- the difference between the sexes is God's work;
- the reason for this difference is the propagation of the human race and mutual assistance;
- woman has the same dignity as man;
- the union between man and woman is so deep that it surpasses even the union between parent and child; and finally
- before sin there was no sexual disorder.[13]

Pope John Paul II frequently pointed out the obvious: the bodies of men and women are designed for physical union. "In the mystery of creation, man and woman are a mutual gift . . . they were united by awareness of the gift. They were mutually conscious of the nuptial meaning of their bodies, in which the freedom of the gift is expressed and all the interior riches of the person as subject are manifested."[14]

In most marriages, couples exchange rings and vows before God in the presence of their family and friends. The couple pledges to stay together for better or worse until death do they part.

Roman Catholic tradition has long defended the sacredness of the marriage covenant. Unlike Protestants, Catholics count marriage as a sacrament, or "outward sign of inward grace instituted by Christ for our sanctification."[15] Nevertheless, the Catholic Church grants annulments voiding marriages—even those that have lasted fifteen to twenty-five years and have produced children and grandchildren. Catholics take pains to distinguish civil divorce from an annulment of marriage. An article on the American Catholic website states:

> *A declaration of nullity is a judgment by the Church that what seemed to be a marriage never was in fact a true marriage.* An annulment is not a divorce for it does not dissolve an existing marriage. A declaration of nullity is granted when it can be shown that some essential or juridical defect made a particular marriage invalid from the beginning despite outward appearance, despite even the good faith of the partners or the establishment of a family. It should be underscored that an annulment does not affect the legitimacy of the children of such a marriage.[16]

To Protestants, annulment and divorce look the same. Even Catholics can find it incomprehensible how a marriage blessed by the church in a ceremony witnessed by family and friends can somehow not exist. Yet, although the Catholic Church grants annulments, it still maintains that a "consummated, sacramental marriage bond is lifelong and cannot be broken by civil or Church authority."[17] Annulments can confuse and anger divorced spouses and children. How do you tell your adult children that your marriage was never valid?

Throughout history, societies have viewed marriage in various ways. In the Muslim faith, marriage is a contractual arrangement with terms negotiated for each side. In some Muslim countries, men are allowed to practice polygamy (more than one wife), but women are not allowed to practice polyandry (more than one husband). The Islamic Centre points out that the Qur'an explicitly prohibits men from marrying women who already have a husband.[18]

In former days, cultures leveraged the institution of marriage to form political alliances that established and maintained ruling families.

Couples today usually marry for love and then divorce when the passion grows cold.[19] In some cultures, parents are deeply involved in selecting spouses.

Couples today usually marry for love and then divorce when the passion grows cold.

Whatever the society or cultural setting, strong marriages don't just happen, argues Maggie Gallagher, president of the Institute for Marriage and Public Policy. "Marriage, like a corporation or private property, is an institution that must be supported by law and culture; if it is to exist at all [it] has to be carved from nature by law, faith, custom and society."[20]

MARRIAGE: THE BEST INSURANCE AGAINST POVERTY

Family structure affects academic achievement, tendency to commit crime, mental health, and the likelihood of drug abuse.[21] It includes whether the mothers and fathers are related biologically to the children and whether the parents are married, divorced, or single heads of households. A person's education, employment, and marital status when he or she has a child can determine a poverty statistic.[22] Jennifer Marshall, director of the Devos Center for Religion and Society, calls these factors the golden rules of avoiding poverty.

Race, divorce, and single parenthood can also affect whether a child reaches adulthood and remains in poverty.[23] Pennsylvania State University sociologists David Eggebeen and Daniel Lichter see a significant relationship between child poverty rates, race, and family structures. They argue that child poverty rates would have been reduced by one-third in 1988 had children continued to live in the type of two-parent families common in 1960.[24] Changes in family structure have accounted for nearly 50 percent of the increase in child poverty rates since 1980.

Higher poverty rates among blacks and Hispanics relate directly to higher rates of children in households that are headed by females. Rutgers University sociologist David Popenoe is among researchers who have found evidence of a marriage gap related to education: people with college degrees are more likely to marry and less likely to divorce than those with less education.[25] Having a college education can relieve the economic pressures that less-educated people experience as they work in low-paying, dead-end jobs. Popenoe found that every form of social malady concentrates in the homes of poorer, less-educated families, affecting every aspect of their lives.

TRIAL MARRIAGES

Couples today frequently engage in "trial marriages," cohabiting for a while before entering into traditional marriage. Studies have shown that the marriages of cohabiters are more likely to end in divorce.[26] Black women are more likely to cohabit than white women and less likely to have their relationships result in marriage; when black women do marry after cohabitation, their marriages are likely to end more quickly than the marriages of white women.

Among the reasons researchers give for the failure of cohabiting relationships to result in successful marriages is that individuals involved in nonmarital relationships may have been less committed to the relationship than those who married. Those who make the best transitions from cohabitation into lasting marriages are educated, childless white couples with religious backgrounds from two-parent families.[27]

Studies have shown that the marriages of cohabiters are more likely to end in divorce.

Explaining why some couples cohabit rather than marry, University of Chicago professor of sociology Linda J. Waite and Maggie Gallagher argue, "The difference between marriage and cohabitation in contemporary American culture has to do with the time horizons and commitment. What makes marriage unique among emotional and financial relationships is the vow of permanence. With marriage, partners publicly promise each other that neither will be alone any longer. Whatever else happens in life, someone will care about and take care of you."[28] Waite and Gallagher cite a wealth of information indicating that married people report better outcomes than single people when evaluated on various indicators of well-being.

DIVORCE: A BROKEN COVENANT

Almost 50 percent of marriages in the United States end in broken covenants. Many of these divorces occur within the first five to ten years of marriage. Today marriage is not considered a lifetime commitment. People often say "I do," knowing they can always say "I don't"—that divorce offers an alternative if difficulties arise. In an effort to strengthen marriages, Arizona, Arkansas, and Louisiana have enacted laws giving marrying couples an option to legally bind themselves in "covenant marriages," which are harder to dissolve, or to upgrade their existing marriage contracts to covenant marriages.[29]

Existing data seems to suggest that once individuals break their first marriage contract, they more easily break subsequent marriage agreements. Jennifer Baker of the School of Professional Psychology at Forest Institute in Springfield, Missouri, documents that 50 percent of first marriages, 67 percent of second marriages, and 74 percent of third marriages end in divorce.[30] Retired New Mexico district judge Anne Kass says that stepchildren are cited as a factor in 70 percent of failed second marriages.[31]

Once individuals break their first marriage contract, they more easily break subsequent marriage agreements.

Only 65 percent of married couples reach their tenth anniversary; 52 percent reach their fifteenth anniversary, and 33 percent their twenty-fifth.[32] Divorcées in second marriages are more likely to complain that their most recent spouse was too much like the first or that the presence of stepchildren contributed to their latest divorce.

NO-FAULT DIVORCE LAWS

No-fault divorces make it easier for individuals to break vows and walk away from familial obligations without having to prove wrongdoing on the part of the other spouse. Douglas Allen and Maggie Gallagher of the Institute for Marriage and Public Policy found that divorce rates in America doubled after the passage of no-fault divorce laws. Seventeen of twenty-four states implementing no-fault divorce reported increases in divorce rates of 10 percent to 88 percent.[33] The adverse effects of no-fault divorce laws tended to fade over time for couples with college educations and higher incomes and social status, but couples without these advantages faced a permanent increase in their risk of divorce.

> Under the older fault system, "faultless" divorces could be informally obtained by a couple, but only by mutual consent: that is, a couple who wished to divorce for no particular legally acceptable reason could agree in advance to present to the court an uncontested fault ground, and obtain a divorce . . . Therefore, the most significant practical legal change created by "no-fault" divorce was that it licensed *unilateral divorce*: for the first time, one spouse could successfully petition for divorce over the objections of his or her spouse, without alleging any grounds.[34]

Divorce law is not the major cause of divorce over the past fifty years; other factors also helped drive the divorce rate, Allen and Gallagher concede. Yet they warn scholars, policymakers, and judges to consider the significant impact that divorce and family law have not only on the behavior of couples, but on the likelihood that children will be able to grow up in stable households.[35]

Gallagher would like to end unilateral divorce, in which one partner can divorce the other without his or her consent. She would also like states to impose multiyear waiting periods for contested divorces and to expand covenant agreements.[36]

ARE CHRISTIANS NEGATIVE ROLE MODELS FOR MARRIAGE?

In 1999, George Barna, president of Barna Research Group, published a study that shook the church. Barna showed that divorce rates among born-again Christians were significantly higher than among other faith groups. Born-again Christians were more likely to divorce than other Christians (27 percent to 24 percent) and also experienced more rejection from their faith communities after their divorces.[37] Jews experienced the highest rate of divorce (30 percent), and atheists and agnostics ranked among the lowest rates (21 percent).

Some researchers and organizations denounced the study, pointing to alleged methodological flaws. For example, Barna does not define *born again*. Among Christians, the meaning of "born again" varies widely. Whether the research reflects a methodological flaw or not, the number of divorces among Christians is deeply disturbing. Clearly, something is wrong when Christians have lower success rates in marriage than non-believers. A regional difference might help explain Barna's finding: people in the Bible Belt enter their first marriages at younger ages, with less education, and lower family incomes than those in the Northeast, an area populated by more Catholics and where the divorce rate is lower.[38]

In 2008, Barna reported on a new study that showed Americans are comfortable with divorce.[39] He found that the "groups with the most prolific experience of marriage ending in divorce are downscale adults (39%), Baby Boomers (38%), those aligned with a non-Christian faith (38%), African Americans (36%), and people who consider themselves to be liberal on social and political matters (37%)."[40] There was also some encouraging news for Christians. "Among the population segments with the lowest likelihood of having been divorced subsequent to marriage are Catholics (28%), evangelicals (26%), upscale adults (22%), Asians (20%) and those who deem themselves to be conservative on social and political matters (28%)."[41] Barna found that born-again Christians who were not evangelicals were indistinguishable from non-Christians.

Clearly, something is wrong when so many self-professed Christians have lower success rates in marriage than nonbelievers.

Brad Wilcox, director of the National Marriage Project at the University of Virginia, and Steven Nock, former professor at the University of Virginia, found that a couple's commitment to marriage and their church attendance are associated with higher levels of female marital happiness. Declines in church attendance and liberalized attitudes about sex and divorce have weakened the supports for marital longevity.[42] In *Soft Patriarchs and New Men: How Christianity Shapes Husbands and Fathers*, Wilcox shows that theologically conservative churches produce men who endorse the belief that it is better for the husband to earn a living and for the wife to take care of the children and the home.[43] These attitudes, which are reinforced by church activities and social networks, mean some conservative Protestant men are less helpful around the home.[44]

The impact of religion and the church is significant among young urban couples who attend church. Wilcox argues that the rate of single-parent households would be even higher if not for urban religious institutions that "depict marriage as a sacred institution that is the best context in which to have sex, raise children, and enjoy divine favor for an intimate relationship."[45]

Christian marriages should be stronger than non-Christian marriages. According to the Bible, Christian marriage is a permanent institution between one man and one woman, and the head of the Christian home is the husband. Ephesians 5:23–24 states, "For the husband is the head of the wife even as Christ is the head of the church, his body, and is himself its Savior. Now as the church submits to Christ, so also wives should submit in everything to their husbands."

The influential novelist, Christian writer, and academician C. S. Lewis writes, "The need for some head follows from the idea that marriage is permanent. Of course, as long as the husband and wife are agreed, no question of head should arise . . . But when there is disagreement, what is to happen? Talk it over, of course; but I am assuming they have done that and failed to reach agreement. What do they do next? They cannot decide by majority vote, for in a council of two there can be no majority."[46] Because marriage is intended to be permanent, one individual in the relationship must make final decisions for the relationship to endure.

Unlike rules in the secular culture, rules governing biblical institutions are not arbitrary. God's view of the family does not change based on circumstances or the whims of a culture. Fornication (sex between unmarried people), adultery (sex with another person's spouse), and homosexual sex (sex between two people of the same sex) are all condemned in the Bible. The Bible does not teach that God changes his mind about sin. The Bible teaches that issues of sexual morality are life-and-death sin issues and that our attitudes about sin cannot change regardless of who engages in the behavior. Whether the sinner is a political leader, a church leader, or our own son or daughter, we must speak the truth in love.

BIBLICAL GROUNDS FOR DIVORCE

Biblical teaching on marriage and divorce is clear and direct. In 1 Corinthians 7:10–11, the apostle Paul wrote, "To the married I give this charge (not I, but the Lord): the wife should not separate from her husband (but if she does, she should remain unmarried or else be reconciled to her husband), and the husband should not divorce his wife."

Paul made it clear that being married to a nonbelieving spouse is not a legitimate reason for a Christian to divorce. In 1 Corinthians 7:12–15,

Paul continued, "To the rest I say (I, not the Lord) that if any brother has a wife who is an unbeliever, and she consents to live with him, he should not divorce her. If any woman has a husband who is an unbeliever, and he consents to live with her, she should not divorce him. For the unbelieving husband is made holy because of his wife, and the unbelieving wife is made holy because of her husband. Otherwise your children would be unclean, but as it is, they are holy. But if the unbelieving partner separates, let it be so."

Mark 10:2–9 gives this account of Jesus' position on divorce:

> And Pharisees came up and in order to test him asked, "Is it lawful for a man to divorce his wife?" He answered them, "What did Moses command you?" They said, "Moses allowed a man to write a certificate of divorce and to send her away." And Jesus said to them, "Because of your hardness of heart he wrote you this commandment. But from the beginning of creation, 'God made them male and female.' 'Therefore a man shall leave his father and mother and hold fast to his wife, and the two shall become one flesh.' So they are no longer two but one flesh. What therefore God has joined together, let not man separate."

In Matthew 5:32, Jesus said, "But I say to you that everyone who divorces his wife, except on the ground of sexual immorality, makes her commit adultery, and whoever marries a divorced woman commits adultery." The Greek word translated "sexual immorality" in this passage is *porneia*. Many scholars say that in today's language, the term would include homosexuality, bestiality, pornography, phone sex and cybersex, and other sexual perversions.

SAME-SEX MARRIAGES

In the past two decades, America has embroiled itself in debate over whether two men or two women who affirm love for each other should have the same legal right to marry as heterosexual couples. Most likely the US Supreme Court will be asked to decide if state bans against same-sex marriages violate the due process and equal protection clauses of the Fourteenth Amendment to the US Constitution. According to Professor Robert P. George of Princeton University, "We are in the midst of a show-down over the legal definition of marriage. Though some state courts have interfered, the battle is mainly being fought in referenda around the country, where 'same-sex marriage' has uniformly been rejected, and in legislatures, where some states have adopted it."[47] George is among those who believe that the issue is headed for the Supreme Court, where the nation risks the Court repeating its error in the *Roe v. Wade* abortion case, succumbing to the temptation of trying to "remove a morally charged policy issue from the forums of democratic deliberation and resolve it according to their personal lights."[48]

America's first legal recognition for same-sex marriage came in the case of *Goodridge v. Department of Public Health*, where the Massachusetts Supreme Judicial Court ruled 4–3 that, under the state's constitution, same-sex couples had the right to marry as heterosexuals.[49] The majority argued that, in light of due process and equal protection laws,[50] restricting homosexuals from marrying would serve no reasonable or legitimate state interest.[51]

The ruling in *Goodridge* followed a trend started by the Supreme Court in the case of *Lawrence v. Texas*[52] in which the justices appealed to Canadian law and policy rather than legal precedent.[53] Ironically, the Massachusetts decision came in the same state where, in 1630, John Winthrop preached his sermon "A Model of Christian Charity," laying out arguments for appropriate behavior in the community. Thus the state in which the Pilgrims landed became the first to issue licenses for same-sex marriages. In response, twenty-three states approved constitutional bans against same-sex marriages; four states already had state constitu-tions banning such marriages.[54]

By August 2010, same-sex marriages were legal in New Hampshire, Iowa, Vermont, and the District of Columbia. New York, New Jersey, and Rhode Island granted legal recognition of marriages performed in other states. A few states approved civil unions or comparable arrangements.

Conservatives across the country have fought tooth and nail to prevent same-sex marriages. In fact, many conservatives began mobilizing against same-sex marriages more than a decade ago.

The state in which the Pilgrims landed became the first to issue licenses for same-sex marriages.

In the nation's capital, the Council of the District of Columbia bypassed the conservative electorate and voted 12–1 for a measure recognizing gay marriages.[55] The bill was signed in a Unitarian church with the proud pastor telling his congregation that he was heartened by the role his congregation played in passage of the legislation, which included formation of a coalition of nearly two hundred clergy who supported the bill. "We contributed money, marched on the Mall, called our Council members, and talked with our neighbors. We helped change hearts and minds," the minister said.[56]

As reported at Stateline.org, "The first states to enshrine bans on same-sex marriage in their Constitutions acted before 2004: Alaska, Nebraska and Nevada. Hawaii voters in 1998 also used their Constitution to block gay marriage, though its amendment differs from those now passed in 26 other states. It strips judges of the power of deciding gay-marriage rights but does not define marriage as a union between a man and woman."[57]

In California, the courts struck down two voter-passed propositions. In 2000, voters passed Proposition 22, which changed the Family Code to define marriage as an arrangement between a man and a woman. Eight years later it was struck down in a 4–3 decision. In response, voters quickly passed Proposition 8. Perhaps to close what was seen as a loophole that some thought could lead to polygamous marriages, the new law defined *marriage* as a union between one man and one woman. It was struck down in the August 2010 case of *Perry v. Schwarzenegger.*[58] Vaughn Walker, chief judge of the US District Court for the Northern District of California, argued that Proposition 8 unconstitutionally burdened gays and lesbians and that it placed "the force of law behind stigmas against gays and lesbians."[59] The ban implies that "gays and lesbians do not have intimate relationships similar to heterosexual couples; gays and lesbians are not as good as heterosexuals; and gay and lesbian relationships do not deserve the full recognition of society."[60] Walker's decision landed at the Ninth Circuit Court of Appeals, considered the most liberal in the country. That Court issued a stay, meaning everything is on hold until it issues a decision. Whatever the Ninth Circuit decides, the losing side will appeal to the US Supreme Court for a final determination.[61]

THE DEFENSE OF MARRIAGE ACT (DOMA)

Conservatives who anticipated the arrival of same-sex marriages persuaded Congress to pass legislation ensuring each state's right to ban, allow, or recognize same-sex marriage laws passed in other states.[62] The Defense of Marriage Act (DOMA) codifies the right of individual states to make their own decisions[63] and defines marriage as a "legal union between one man and one woman as husband and wife, stating that the word 'spouse' refers only to a person of the opposite sex who is a husband or a wife."[64]

Opponents have argued that DOMA is unconstitutional because it prevents same-sex couples from receiving federal benefits designated for married heterosexual couples and allows conservative states the option of refusing to recognize the legitimacy of same-sex marriages performed in other jurisdictions.[65] Forty-two states have enacted statutes similar to DOMA. As the California cases indicate, judges can overrule a statutory ban if the statute violates another right guaranteed by the state's constitution.[66] On February 23, 2011, the Obama administration announced that it would enforce but no longer defend DOMA against challenges to its constitutionality.

WHAT'S AT STAKE WITH GAY MARRIAGES?

Professors Robert Benne and Gerald McDermott of Roanoke College are among social commentators who argue that same-sex marriages, if accepted as equivalent to heterosexual marriages, will eventually bring harm to children and society at large.[67] According to Benne and McDermott, the first casualty of same-sex marriages is the definition of marriage itself. He notes that for "thousands of years and in every Western society, marriage has meant the lifelong union of a man and a woman. One effect of gay marriage will be that sexual fidelity will be detached from the commitment of marriage."[68]

To drive home this point, Benne and McDermott quote Troy Perry, gay activist and founder of Metropolitan Community Church, which affirms lesbian, gay, bisexual, and transgender communities. "Monogamy is not a word the gay community uses . . . we talk about fidelity," Perry argues. "That means you are in a loving, caring, honest relationship with your partner . . . Some would say that committed couples could have multiple sex partners as long as there is no deception."[69] Making the same point, political commentator Andrew Sullivan, an outspoken advocate for gay marriages, writes, "There is more likely to be a greater understanding of the need for extramarital outlets between two men than between a man and a woman . . . Something of the gay relationship's necessary honesty, its flexibility, and its equality could undoubtedly help strengthen and inform many heterosexual bonds."[70] Moreover, according to Benne and McDermott, "Researchers found that even among stable homosexual partnerships, men have an average of eight partners per year outside their 'monogamous' relationship."[71]

The first casualty of same-sex marriages is the definition of marriage itself.

Benne and McDermott argue that institutionalized gay marriage will mean that more childern will be raised in homes without their biological parents. They point out that social scientific studies have shown that children raised by their married natural parents on average do significantly better in their schoolwork, are less likely to have children out of wedlock, are more likely to have stable marriages themselves, are less likely to become involved in crime, and are more likely to hold steady jobs as adults. They also point to studies suggesting that "children raised by homosexuals were more dissatisfied with their own gender, suffer a greater rate of molestation within the family, and have homosexual experiences more often."[72]

Lastly, Benne and McDermott argue that while gay marriages do not hurt strong marriages, their acceptance reinforces the idea that marriage does not require sexual fidelity. They note that, in spite of the weight of public opinion against same-sex marriages, judges continue to impose their will regarding homosexual unions, thus altering the culture and mind-set of the American people.

ADVOCATES FOR SAME-SEX MARRIAGE SEE BENEFITS TO SOCIETY

Gay rights advocates frequently liken bans against same-sex marriage to bans in Southern states against interracial marriage that lasted until 1967, when the US Supreme Court declared them unconstitutional in *Loving v. Virginia.*[73] But as Robert P. George of Princeton points out, "The definition of marriage was not at stake in *Loving.* Everyone agreed that interracial marriages were marriages. Racists wanted to ban them as part of the evil regime of white supremacy that the Equal Protection Clause was designed to destroy."[74]

In 2006, the New York State Court of Appeals explicitly rejected the comparison of same-sex marriages with the issues raised in the *Loving* case. In *Hernandez v. Robles*, the Court said:

> The historical background of *Loving* is different from the history underlying this case. Racism has been recognized for centuries—at first by a few people, and later by many more—as a revolting moral evil . . .
>
> But the traditional definition of marriage is not merely a by-product of historical injustice. Its history is of a different kind. The idea

> that same-sex marriage is even possible is a relatively new one. Until
> a few decades ago, it was an accepted truth for almost everyone who
> ever lived, in any society in which marriage existed, that there could
> be marriages only between participants of different sex. A court should
> not lightly conclude that everyone who held this belief was irrational,
> ignorant or bigoted. We do not so conclude.[75]

Proponents of same-sex marriages have written books and articles about why marriage is important to gays and lesbians and how it might prove beneficial to society. They challenge conservatives to demonstrate the harm gay marriages would pose to heterosexual marriages. Conservatives have been slow to respond compellingly. In 2010, the American Bar Association passed a resolution to fight for an end to restrictions on gay marriages.[76]

Yale law professor William Eskridge Jr. has undoubtedly influenced the thinking of many elites with *The Case for Same Sex Marriage: From Sexual Liberty to Civilized Commitment*. Eskridge issued this careful analysis of the history of same-sex relationships, and the benefits that he believes such marriages would bring to society, in 1996.[77] He argues that the modern West stands alone in its condemnation of same-sex unions. He also says that legalizing same-sex relationships would help civilize gay males and provide gays and lesbians with the same rights that heterosexuals enjoy, allowing them to be full participants in all areas of life, including adoption and raising children.

Evidence from the Netherlands, however, suggests the opposite is true. In that country, marriages and stable partnerships have not dramatically reduced promiscuity within homosexual relationships. Opponents of same-sex marriages believe that the redefinition of marriage means a clear abandonment of monogamy. As evidence, Robert P. George cites a 2006 statement titled "Beyond Same-Sex Marriage" in which "over 300 lesbian, gay, and allied activists, educators, lawyers, and community organizers—including Gloria Steinem, Barbara Ehrenreich, and prominent Yale, Columbia, and Georgetown Professors—call for legally recognizing multiple sex partner ('polyamorous') relationships."[78] George says their "logic is unassailable once the historic definition of marriage is overthrown."[79]

Because Scripture and religious reasoning have been marginalized in the public square, opponents of same-sex marriages do not appeal to religious values and virtues. Opponents of religious reasoning consider faith-based opposition as bigoted, homophobic, and ignorant. Their name-calling has silenced many voices rising to protest the vast changes sweeping through the country that have subverted traditional Judeo-Christian values and principles. Yet as long as most Americans profess Christianity, it is appropriate and reasonable for people to refer to the biblical principles that have undergirded the nation.

ARE PUBLIC ATTITUDES ABOUT GAY MARRIAGES SHIFTING?

If one were to believe some polls, opposition to same-sex marriages in the United States has melted away.[80] A May 2010 CNN/Gallup Poll reported that 53 percent of men and 51 percent of women agreed that homosexual relationships were "morally acceptable," and only 46 percent opposed same-sex marriages. But are these polls valid? North Carolina Public Policy Polling tried to duplicate results found in the CNN poll using "robo calls" rather than human callers, but its poll, released on August 13, 2010, produced strikingly different results. North Carolina Public Policy Polling reports:

> Fifty-seven percent of Americans think it [gay marriage] should be illegal while 33 percent think it should be legal and 11 percent have no opinion. Republicans are pretty universal in thinking it should be illegal, at a margin of 81/12, while Democrats only narrowly favor it at 47/40. Independents array slightly against it by a 48/41 margin.
>
> Americans within pretty much every demographic group continue to oppose gay marriage. Whites are against it 58/34, Hispanics

57/27, and African Americans 52/34. Women oppose it [gay marriage] 55/35, and men oppose it at 59/31. Voters under 30 do at 52/44, ones between 30 and 45 do 51/37, ones between 46 and 65 do 59/29 and those over 65 oppose it at a rate of 61/31.[81]

These findings suggest that social pressures on individuals have made many of them less likely to divulge to human pollsters their genuine views on this subject.[82] What people tell pollsters on this sensitive issue may actually depend on whether a person or a robotic voice poses the question.

In April 2009, the Pew Research Center found that the majority of people surveyed opposed gay marriage, as they had since 1996 when Pew first started asking about public support on the issue. Pew found that most Americans supported civil unions by a margin of 53 percent to 39 percent.[83]

Jeni Loftus, professor of sociology at Indiana University, has studied shifting American attitudes during the years 1973–1998. Loftus noted that in 1990, the public expressed increasingly positive attitudes toward gays and lesbians.[84]

In April 2009, the Pew Research Center found that the majority of people surveyed opposed gay marriage.

Most opposition to same-sex marriages now comes from older people, frequent churchgoers, and religious conservatives. Scriptures that condemn homosexual practices no doubt influence their opposition. Leviticus 18:22 states, "You shall not lie with a male as with a woman; it is an abomination." Leviticus 20:13 prescribes death for violating this command, providing a portion of the scriptural basis for rejection of male homosexuality. In the New Testament, Romans 1:24–27 is frequently cited as condemning same-sex acts: "Therefore God gave them up in the lusts of their hearts to impurity, to the dishonoring of their bodies among themselves. . . . For their women exchanged natural relations for those that are contrary to nature; and the men likewise gave up natural relations with women and were consumed with passion for one another, men committing shameless acts with men and receiving in themselves the due penalty for their error." In addition, many Christians cite God's destruction of Sodom and Gomorrah as their basis for condemning same-sex unions and state their belief that God, who does not change his standards of conduct, will deal harshly with a nation that endorses such behavior (Genesis 19:1–29).

C. S. LEWIS ON BIBLICAL MARRIAGE

C. S. Lewis, the influential Christian writer and professor of Medieval Renaissance English at Cambridge University, offered words of wisdom about marriage and divorce that apply well to the debate over same-sex marriages. When it came to the ease of obtaining a divorce, Lewis forcefully argued that Christians should not seek to impose their lifestyles on nonbelievers. Lewis said:

> Churches should frankly recognize that the majority of . . . people are not Christians and, therefore, cannot be expected to live Christian lives. There ought to be two distinct kinds of marriage: one governed by the State with rules enforced on all citizens, the other governed by the Church with rules enforced by its own members. The distinction ought to be quite sharp, so that a man knows which couples are married in a Christian sense and which are not.[85]

Christians must be about the business of repairing and strengthening their own marriages and relationships so that they can be the salt and light of the world. If Christians must live side by side with gay couples in a culture with a homosexual agenda, their only hope is to strengthen themselves spiritually and to live boldly and teach the truth to their children and loved ones.

FORCES OF CULTURAL CHANGE

A number of factors have caused Americans to change their attitude about homosexuality. Although most religious groups oppose same-sex marriages, notable exceptions exist.[86] Episcopalians, Unitarian Universalists, and members of the United Church of Christ support gay marriages.[87] Episcopalians and some Presbyterians and Baptists allow openly gay priests and pastors. In July 2010, the Evangelical Lutheran Church in America ordained seven gay pastors, causing a split[88] and formation of a new denomination.[89] While conservative Christians believe that the Bible's standards do not change, contemporary attitudes reflect the liberal view that the Bible is a "living document" that changes over time, and is particular to people and cultures. This view is like a liberal method of constitutional interpretation, which argues against textual analysis and original intent and in favor of methods that reflect changes in society.

᛫ The media, of course, exerts its pervasive influence. As early as 2000, soap operas such as *All My Children* introduced gay themes and gay relationships. More recently, inroads were made with movies such as *Brokeback Mountain* and *Precious* and through the efforts of outspoken celebrities who have come out as gay and who represent the gay lifestyle as mainstream.

In addition, some public schools have taught children that homosexual relationships are normal rather than deviant. In 1992, New York City embroiled itself in a controversy over the reading list for the first-grade curriculum. Recommended readings included *Heather Has Two Mommies*, a book about a lesbian couple that conceives a child through artificial insemination, as well as *Daddy's Roommate*, about a child with two male parents. The intent is to teach children that lesbian and gay family structures are as normal as heterosexual two-parent families. Some public schools allow girls and boys to cross-dress rather than risk lawsuits and controversy.[90]

Rather than offering students the freedom to examine biblical teachings on sexuality, secularists have misused the US Constitution to ban the Bible in most public schools, resulting in Bible readings marginalized only as part of literature courses. Books such as Robie Harris's *It's*

Perfectly Normal present homosexuality, bisexuality, and gay and lesbian sexual attraction as normal and condemn opposition to these lifestyles as bigotry.[91]

The Girl Scouts of America has also joined forces with pro-gay ranks. Since 2000, the organization has adopted a political correctness that runs counter to former core principles of the organization, such as belief in God, loyalty to nation, and traditional morality. Unlike the Boy Scouts of America, which has suffered criticism for its conservatism, the Girl Scouts allows gay troop leaders.[92] Writer Kathryn Lopez notes:

> Girl Scout policy forbids sex on Girl Scouts time. But the book *On My Honor: Lesbians Reflect on Their Scouting Experience*,[93] published in 1997, is filled with coming-of-age stories sparked by gay encounters in the Girl Scouts. Along with an essay titled "All I Really Need to Know About Being a Lesbian I Learned at Girl Scout Camp," and various stories of "butch" counselors who "wore men's clothes and had slicked back short hair," is testimony to the prevalence of lesbians in Girl Scouting. One writer remembers: "By the time I was a junior counselor, Mic was assistant camp director and her gruff, deep-voiced directives no longer scared me. I didn't know that most of the counselors were lesbians." Others remember how sleepovers and camping trips were opportunities for same-sex sexual experimentation. Girl Scout staffers writing in the book claim that roughly one in three of the Girl Scouts' paid professional staff is lesbian.[94]

Unfortunately, most parents don't know that the Girl Scouts has undergone radical changes. Its politically correct and feminist agenda can be destructive to the family. The Girl Scouts of today is not the Girl Scouts of former years. Interestingly, Boy Scouts of America, which does not allow gay troop leaders, recently settled more than twelve hundred cases of child sexual abuse the organization has been accused of hiding.[95]

The homosexual agenda seems to be much broader than procuring public acceptance of gay marriages. Appeals for gay marriage and

*Most parents don't know that the Girl Scouts has undergone radical changes.
Its politically correct and feminist agenda can be destructive to the family.*

polygamy seem tame when compared to the demands of the North
American Man/Boy Love Association (NAMBLA), founded in 1978 by
scholars hoping to promote "intergenerational intimacy" between adult
men and underage boys.[96] Under current US law, these illicit relationships are prosecutable as pedophilia, but NAMBLA continues to promote
normalizing this behavior. Many proponents of these emerging forms of
sexual freedom are professors at some of the nation's elite educational
institutions and sit on the boards of professional organizations that make
public pronouncements about the normality of homosexual relations and
the rights of individuals to engage in lifestyles of their choice.

Paula Martinac, a lesbian writer, states:

[Some] gay men still maintain that an adult who has same-sex relations
with someone under the age of legal consent is on some level doing the
kid a favor by helping to bring him or her "out" . . . [A]dult-youth sex
is viewed as an important aspect of gay culture, with a history dating
back to "Greek love" of ancient times. The romanticized vision of adult-
youth sexual relations has been a staple of gay literature and has made
appearances, too, in gay-themed films . . . Last summer, I attended
a reading in which a gay poet read a long piece about being aroused
by a flirtatious young boy in his charge. In response, the man went
into the boy's bedroom and [sexually abused the boy as he] slept . . .
Disturbingly, most of the gay audience gave the poet an appreciative
round of applause.[97]

The author concludes that the lesbian and gay community will never
succeed in fighting the pedophile stereotype "until we stop condoning sex
with young people."[98]

Although self-identified homosexuals constitute a small fraction of the population—an estimated 3 percent[99]—they wield enormous influence in many spheres. In 2010, Kevin Jennings, a well-known homosexual activist with a history of having engaged in a series of questionable actions regarding children's safety, served as the Obama administration's assistant deputy secretary of the Office of Safe and Drug-Free Schools.[100] Scandals involving Jennings include the following:

- "Brewstergate"—the case of a young student, "Brewster," whom Jennings knew was having sex with an older man he'd met in a bus station restroom.
- "Fistgate"—the case in which Massachusetts public school educators sponsored by GLSEN (the Gay, Lesbian and Straight Education Network, founded and run by Jennings) instructed children as young as twelve about explicit homosexual practices, including such dangerous practices as "fisting."
- "NAMBLAgate"—Jennings has repeatedly expressed admiration for the late Harry Hay, a member of the Communist Party and one of the most militant homosexuals of the past century. Hay was an icon and "senior statesman" in NAMBLA . . .
- "QueerSchoolsgate"—Jennings wrote the foreword to *Queering Elementary Education* and has acknowledged that he developed the "anti-bullying" label as a way to present the pro-homosexual agenda as a "safety" issue. Jennings's Gay, Lesbian, and Straight Education Network (GLSEN) brigades have subjected millions of schoolchildren to forced "queering" sessions through various GLSEN-sponsored programs.
- "Act-Upgate"—Jennings is a longtime activist in the militant homosexual group Act Up, which invaded churches and physically assaulted clergymen and Christian worshippers. Jennings is notorious for viciously smearing (sometimes in foul language both in his writings and speeches) Christians who disapprove of homosexual behavior. He also advocates censoring former homosexuals who warn youngsters against the gay lifestyle.

- "Drug-gate"—Jennings, who ran the US Office of Safe and Drug-Free Schools, has written ambiguously about his own drug and alcohol abuse—expressing no regrets and even romanticizing it—leaving open to question whether he is encouraging drug use among the nation's youth.[101]

Despite calls from Republicans for his resignation, Jennings remained in his position as the Safe and Drug-Free Schools deputy secretary.[102]

Much of the mainstream media ignored or omitted relevant facts when it reported on Frank Lombard, a former associate director of the Center for Health Policy at Duke University, who was convicted of molesting and offering his five-year-old adopted son for sex acts.[103] Lombard was caught after a witness told police he had seen him having oral and anal sex with the child. The child Lombard molested was one of two black children that Lombard, who is white, and his partner adopted in their infancy. The Associated Press coverage failed to mention the race of the children, and some people took pains to note that Lombard's sexual preferences were irrelevant.[104] Meanwhile, civil rights activists ignored the incident.

Speaking about the slippery moral slope that confronts the nation, philosopher and University of Texas professor J. Budziszewski notes, "The list of what we are required to approve is growing ever longer. Consider the domain of sexual practice. First we are to approve sex before marriage, then without marriage, now against marriage. First with one, then with a series, now with a crowd. First with the other sex, then with the same. First between adults then between children, then between adults and children. The last item has not been added yet, but will be soon: you can tell from the change in language."[105]

CHANGING DEFINITIONS OF *FAMILY*

Marital relationships are only one aspect of "family." As far back as Aristotle, the Greek philosopher and student of Plato, the family was recognized as the basic unit of society.[106] The US Census Bureau defines a family as "a group of two people or more (one of whom is the householder) related by birth, marriage, or adoption and residing together; all such people . . . are considered as members of one family."[107] Traditionally, the nuclear family consisted at least of a male and female living in the same household. This arrangement gave couples an opportunity to produce biologically related children or adopt them into the family unit. The family provided for the education, training, and socialization of children. This family made it possible for individuals to pool resources, create and disseminate wealth, and care for the needs of extended family members. But times have changed. Many traditional functions of the family—such as education, economic support, child rearing, care of the elderly, and even food preparation—have been shifted over to the state and the market.

In recent years, the concept of family has come under attack by social scientists. They argue that there is no ideal family type, that the concept of traditional family is passé, and that it was never more than a social construct. New York University philosopher Paul Boghossian offers a definition of social construction.[108] To say that an institution is socially constructed means, "This thing could not have existed had we not built it; and we need not have built it at all, at least not in its present form. Had we been a different kind of society, had we had different needs, values, or interests, we might well have built a different kind of thing, or built this one differently. The inevitable contrast is with a naturally existing object, something that exists independently of us and which we did not have a hand in shaping."[109] In other words, the theory of social construction argues that societies and cultures create their own realities.

Feminist scholars and activists have argued that the family is a socially constructed institution that has been used to oppress women. Linda Gordon, a New York University professor of law, has argued that "the nuclear family must be destroyed . . . whatever its ultimate meaning, the break-up of families now is an objectively revolutionary process."[110] Expressing similar sentiments, feminist leader Sheila Cronan of the National Association of Women concluded that "since marriage constitutes slavery for women, it is clear that the women's movement must concentrate on attacking the institution. Freedom for women cannot be won without the abolition of marriage."[111]

The concept of family has come under attack by social scientists. They argue that there is no ideal family type, that the concept of traditional family is passé, and that it was never more than a social construction.

Rebecca Walker, daughter of Pulitzer Prize–winning author Alice Walker, who wrote *The Color Purple*, told a reporter that she "very nearly missed out on becoming a mother—thanks to being brought up by a rabid feminist who thought motherhood was about the worst thing that could happen to a woman . . . My mom taught me that children enslave women . . . I grew up believing that children are millstones around your neck, and the idea that motherhood can make you blissfully happy is a complete fairytale."[112]

Phyllis Schlafly, the conservative activist and constitutional lawyer who led the charge against the ratification of the 1972 Equal Rights Amendment, has dedicated her life to countering what she sees as the destructive feminist message. She views feminism as a movement bent on the destruction of families. Schlafly has argued that "society simply has not invented a better way of raising children than the traditional family . . . [The] division of labor is cost-efficient, the environment is healthy, and the children thrive on the 'object constancy' of the mother."[113] Schlafly believes that "the strength and stability of families determines the vitality and moral life of society; thus, as the family goes, so goes the nation."[114]

Just as in the abortion debate, some professional organizations lend credibility and legitimacy to behaviors and lifestyles once considered deviant. In 1999, the American Psychological Association published "Deconstructing the Essential Father" by Louise Silverstein and Carl Auerbach. The article challenged "neoconservative social scientists who have claimed that fathers are essential to positive child development, and that responsible fathering is most likely to occur within the context of heterosexual marriage."[115] The authors conclude:

> Neither the sex of the adult(s) nor the biological relationship to the child has emerged as a significant variable in predicting positive development. One, none, or both of those adults could be a father (or mother). We have found that the stability of the emotional connection and the predictability of the caretaking relationship are the significant variables that predict positive child adjustment. . . . we do not believe that the data support the conclusion that fathers are essential to child well-being and that heterosexual marriage is the social context in which responsible fathering is most likely to occur.[116]

According to Silverstein and Auerbach, "neither mothers nor fathers are essential to child development, and . . . responsible fathering can occur within a variety of family structures."[117]

Largely as a result of research done by Silverstein and Auerbach, and the support of professional organizations, most states allow gay men and women to adopt children. For years, Florida had the most restrictive legislation, but a federal judge in September 2010 declared prohibitions against adoption by gays unconstitutional.[118]

Studies that document harm to children raised in same-sex homes are dismissed as junk science. Gay rights advocates have enlisted numerous professional organizations to support their cause. The American Academy of Pediatrics, American Psychiatric Association, American Psychological Association, and American Psychoanalytic Association all have declared that children raised by gay and lesbian parents are no different from those raised by heterosexual parents.[119]

The increase in acceptance of nontraditional parenting and adoption is at odds with research by distinguished social scientists who have found that children thrive best when raised in homes with their biological mothers and fathers. Princeton University professor Sara McLanahan and University of Wisconsin professor Gary Sandefur have found that "children who grow up in a household with only one biological parent are worse off, on average, than children who grow up in a household with both of their biological parents, regardless of the parents' race or educational background, regardless of whether the parents are married when the child is born, and regardless of whether the resident parent remarries."[120]

Yet acceptance of this trend is growing. "As of 2003, 43.7 percent of custodial mothers and 56.2 percent of custodial fathers were either separated or divorced. Only 63 percent of American children are being raised in the same household as their biological parents—the lowest figure in the Western world."[121]

Clearly, the traditional family is in trouble, and broken marital covenants are at the root of the problem. We can no longer agree on the definition of a family. Nor can we agree on whether one family structure is superior to another for raising and nurturing children. As an example, for the fall 2010 television season, the show *19 Kids and Counting*, which profiles a conservative Christian family with nineteen children, runs alongside *Sister Wives*, a show featuring a polygamous family with four wives.

The traditional family is in trouble, and broken marital covenants are at the root of the problem.

The Center for Marriage and Families believes that disputes among scholars about the definition of family and marriage, and the influence of traditional family structures on the well-being of children and adults, have serious implications for society.[122] Kyle Pruett, a Yale University psychiatrist, has reported confusion and longing among children conceived by homosexual parents using in vitro fertilization. These children frequently ask questions such as, "Mommy, what did you do with my daddy?" "Can I write him a letter?" "Has he ever seen me?" "Didn't you like him? Didn't he like me?"[123] Research has also shown that girls need fathers and that young women who grow up without them are at greater risk of engaging in premature sex.[124] Mothers also bring special comfort and security to their children.[125]

PARENTAL AUTHORITY, SPANKING, AND THE ROLE OF THE STATE

The topic of corporal punishment—spanking as a means of disciplining children—has been in the news over past decades and poses a dilemma for parents who believe a swat on the behind is an effective form of child discipline. Over the years, Christian parents have cited a number of scriptures to support their belief in corporal punishment,[126] including "Folly is bound up in the heart of a child, but the rod of discipline drives it far from him" (Proverbs 22:15), and "Do not withhold discipline from a child; if you strike him with a rod, he will not die. If you strike him with the rod, you will save his soul from Sheol" (Proverbs 23:13–14).

In 1946, pediatrician Dr. Benjamin Spock's best-selling *The Common Sense Book of Baby and Child Care* sold more than fifty million copies. The book turned parents away from spanking and toward a softer approach to child rearing. Spock advised parents against a stricter disciplinary approach while counseling for more verbal interaction—and what some would consider indulgence. According to Spock, spanking teaches children "that might makes right, that it encourages some children to be bullies, and most fundamentally, that to the degree that it results in good behavior it's because of the fear of pain. I have a strong belief that the best reason for behaving well is that you like people, want to get along with them, want them to like you."[127] Spock believed that a link existed between violent behavior in society and childhood spankings.

Several generations of children were raised using Spock's methods. An article in the *Wall Street Journal* reported, "More than five decades after Dr. Spock sent corporal punishment to the woodshed, spanking is making a comeback. A growing number of parents—many of whom were never spanked themselves—are shunning the experts, defying disapproving friends and neighbors, and giving their kids a slap on the bottom, the hand or the leg."[128] Parents state that other methods of discipline are not as effective as spankings and that spankings are needed for some violations of parental rules.

Quigley Moynihan remembers using corporal punishment three times on his boys but never on his daughter:

> Brenda and I and the child would sit down, and she would tell me about the deed that had been done in sort of a "prosecuting attorney" style. I would listen to her and the defense from the child, and then it would be decision time for me to administer the swats. I might say something like four or maybe eight for one particularly gruesome offense.
>
> Then it would be off to the shop with the child—him and me. In my wood shop the child would take a seat and watch me pick a piece of scrap lumber. Maybe a 2x6 about a foot long. Then with care I would draw the outline of my intended paddle, then cut it out . . . The time would come when I was finished, and it was time to do the deed. Bare skin on the butt, and never with my full force.
>
> Now comes the important part. After it was over, I pronounced it over, and I told my child that I was sure I would never need this paddle again.
>
> My shop has the same wood-burning stove from the farm I grew up on. Together, my child and I would make a fire with the paddle and all the leftover scraps. Then we'd watch it burn to cinders in silence as we let our tears dry, and I let the lump go out of my throat.[129]

Christian parents must individually decide when and how they will discipline their children. The Bible makes it clear that children need loving correction and guidance from wise parents and that correction is a form of love. In fact, we are told that God chastens his sons and daughters when they go astray. Hebrews 12:6 states, "The Lord disciplines the one he loves, and chastises every son whom he receives."

FAMILY COURT

Some Christian parents, alarmed about the direction of the culture, have opted to educate their children at home.[130] However, courts are intervening to limit homeschooling parents.[131]

Phyllis Schlafly is among those who have warned about family courts and their increasing tendency to issue decisions that intrude on the rights of parents to make what they consider to be the best decisions for their children.[132] According to Schlafly, family courts have taken the concept of "the best interest of the child" and turned it upside down. Under the English common law of William Blackstone, parents were presumed to act in their children's best interests as long as the parents were deemed fit. The parental prerogative changed in the 1970s, when family courts acting in divorce situations "assumed the discretion to decide the best interest of children of divorced and unmarried parents." The "best interest rule," Schlafly argues, is always subjective. The expert witnesses who testify in these cases can make subjective decisions seem objective because of their academic credentials. She argues that most court decisions go against men. The attack on men, she claims, includes their imprisonment for unpaid child support, even in cases where DNA tests have proven that they are not the biological father of the child. Family courts have refused to reduce child support payments in cases where men, through no fault of their own, have found themselves laid off or unemployed or facing bankruptcy.

THE SPECIAL CASE OF THE BLACK FAMILY

We will soon discover if a nation can sustain itself without strong families and whether the breakdown of the family will ultimately lead to the breakdown of civilization and our American way of life. But the immediate crisis for America is the special case of the black family and what, if anything, can be done to turn around some persistent dangerous trends. An alarm was sounded forty years ago when Daniel Patrick Moynihan, then Harvard University professor and future U.S. senator from New

York, authored the Moynihan Report titled "The Negro Family: The Case for National Action."[133] (Daniel Patrick Moynihan is not related to Quigley Moynihan.) Moynihan warned that conditions in black communities were worsening and that unhealthy patterns of female-headed households were taking root. He concluded his report with a call for a national effort geared toward strengthening black families.

For his efforts Moynihan was roundly condemned by both white and black social scientists who argued that the black family structure was a unique adaptation to oppression and should not be compared to the two-parent family structures commonly associated with Europeans. According to Elizabeth Wright, editor of *Issues and Views*:

> When news about the contents of the Report hit the fan, an armed assault team of social scientists, black and white, set out to discredit its findings. Politically correct ideology was blatantly substituted for objective investigation. In fact, several of these academics condemned what they called the Report's "cold, scientific" approach to the facts . . . Numbers of black academics determined to conduct their own "research," with some of them boldly stating just what they would be looking for. They, by God, were going to locate the "strengths" of the black family and put to rest this talk about its disintegration.[134]

Today, blacks have the lowest marriage rates of any ethnic group. Decades of social science research and governmental intervention appear only to have exacerbated these problems; furthermore, while our nation has its first black president, the hoped-for rise in self-esteem has not come among black families, and problems in families do not appear to be receding. During the economic crisis of 2008–2010, the unemployment rates of black men were comparable to those reported during the Great Depression.[135] According to the US Census Bureau (2001), 43 percent of black men and 42 percent of black women have never been married (compared with 27 and 21 percent, respectively, for whites).[136] One problem affecting black marriages is a shortage of "economically stable" marriageable black men.[137] When blacks do marry, they are more likely to divorce than any other group. Erma Jean Lawson and Tanya Sharpe report that two-thirds of black marriages end in divorce and two of three black children experience divorce in their homes before they reach age sixteen. The situation for black marriages has worsened significantly since 1970, when 68 percent of black families were intact. The impact of divorce has been especially hard on black men, who suffered greater rates of drug abuse and suicide after divorce than married men who remained married.[138]

The immediate crisis for America is the special case of the black family and what, if anything, can be done to turn around some persistent dangerous trends.

Today black families suffer from every imaginable dysfunction. Black men are overrepresented in prison and jail populations.[139] Blacks are more likely to commit violent crimes, such as rape, robbery, and homicide, and to become victims of deadly crimes.[140] As data already cited shows, black children are more likely than whites or Hispanics to grow up in female-headed households, to be born out of wedlock, and to be poor and disadvantaged. Black babies are more likely to be aborted, regardless of whether their parents are married or single. And only 17 percent of black youth—fewer than one in five—live with both married parents.[141]

BLACK MEN, HIV, AND THE DOWN-LOW LIFESTYLE

Blacks are more likely to suffer from sexually transmitted diseases, and they lead the nation in HIV infections. According to the Centers for Disease Control and Prevention (CDC), blacks represent approximately 12 percent of the US population but account for 46 percent of people living with HIV in the country and 45 percent of new infections each year.[112] Gay, bisexual, and other men who have sodomy or homosexual sex with men accounted for 53 percent of new HIV infections each year. Individuals infected by heterosexual contact constitute 31 percent of the new infections and intravenous drug users 12 percent. Black men were six times more likely to be infected than white men, almost three times as likely as Hispanic men, and more than twice as likely as black women. However, black women were fifteen times more likely to be infected than white men and four times more likely than Hispanic women.[143] Anal sex with infected black men was one of the key modes of transmission into the heterosexual population.

In 2002, the CDC estimated that as many as one-third of black men were HIV positive with about 90 percent not knowing their status. Most of these HIV infections came from men engaging in homosexual contact. The District of Columbia has the highest rate of infections in the country, with an estimated 3 percent of its population and 7 percent of its black men infected.[144] Its rates of HIV infections were higher than parts of West Africa. Men having sex with men was the most common mode of transmission, with heterosexual sex and drug use following. Three percent of black women carried the disease.[145]

Women often contract the disease through heterosexual encounters with men who engage in a lifestyle that has been called Down Low.[146] In 2003, Benoit Denizet-Lewis raised public awareness with the article "Double Lives on the Down Low," published in the *New York Times Magazine*. It sheds light on the subject of black men who identify themselves as heterosexual but engage in clandestine homosexual relationships with other men.[147] According to Denizet-Lewis, a segment of the black male gay population has created a subculture distinct from the white gay culture. These black men have rejected the language and effeminate styles sometimes associated with white gay men and have, what they call, a Down Low lifestyle.[148]

Professors Jessie Heath and Kathy Goggin describe the Down Low lifestyle as one that mostly involves young, urban, black men who identify themselves as heterosexual but have male and female sex partners.[149]

The authors note that "by disassociating themselves from the present-day gay culture of the United States, it has been said that men on the Down Low have created a lifestyle absent from the effeminate qualities that are often associated with gay males. They insist that their sexual behaviors do not directly determine their sexual identity and pride themselves on being masculine, though 'real men' who foremost identify as black."[150]

Researchers using the self-identified characteristics of the men describe them as: "(1) Black, (2) not identifying as gay, (3) having sex with both men and women, (4) not disclosing their sexual behavior with men to female partners, (5) never or inconsistently using condoms with males and females."[151] Bisexual black and Hispanic males are more likely than whites to self-identify as Down Low and are less likely to describe themselves as gay, even though they are engaging in homosexual practices.[152] Keith Boykin, author of *Beyond the Down Low: Sex, Lies, and Denial in Black America*, argues that the behavior has been acknowledged in song and literature since the 1930s and was an aspect of black life during the Harlem Renaissance.[153] This behavior has even found its way into some black churches.[154]

Nevertheless, black Americans remain the most conservative group on the issue of homosexual behavior. A 2009 Pew Forum on Religion and Public Life found that "Blacks are much more likely to think that homosexuality is morally wrong (64%) than whites (48%) or Hispanics (43%). At least half of those ages 30 and older say homosexuality is wrong, compared with fewer than four-in-ten (38%) among those under age 30."[155] Some black leaders are working overtime to shift blacks from their biblically grounded positions on homosexual sex practices to more liberal positions. Under the leadership of Ben Jealous, the NAACP has been seeking to convince blacks that opposition to gay sex is a bigoted form of discrimination akin to what blacks suffered before the passage of the 1964 Civil Rights Act.[156] These same black leaders are silent about the connection between gay sexual practices and the HIV/AIDS epidemic ravaging black communities across the nation.

WHAT ACCOUNTS FOR BLACK AMERICA'S FAILURE TO THRIVE?

The recognized leaders of black America are liberal Democrats who endorse the very behaviors that are leading to the decimation of the population. Abortion, homosexual sex practices, and out-of-wedlock births are behaviors that black leaders either endorse or remain silent about. Black leaders are also not in the forefront of confronting the negative impact that high levels of illegal immigration have on America's most vulnerable population. Despite the presence of many elected and appointive black leaders, there is a serious leader void. It does not bode well for the long-term survival of the black masses.

Harvard sociologist William J. Wilson and others have attributed certain behavioral problems of the black underclass to discrimination and a lack of economic opportunity. Some of the most compelling data come from political scientist Charles Murray, whose highly controversial book *Losing Ground: American Social Policy, 1950–1980* offers a wealth of data to buttress what he argues is a connection between poorly conceived social welfare policies and the decline of the black family.[157] Beginning in approximately 1963, Murray's data shows a steady decline of economic and social well-being and a sharp increase in behaviors that most Americans would consider dysfunctional.

There is a serious leader void. It does not bode well for the long-term survival of the black masses.

Black conservatives have pointed out hard truths about black behavior. Commenting on the high infant mortality rate among blacks, conservative economist Thomas Sowell lamented the fact that people would incorrectly assume that the problem was caused by "poverty, race, racism, lack of 'access' to Medicare care, poor education, and all the rest of the familiar litany of welfare state liberals."[158] Instead, Sowell argues, the problem rests with the people. Despite the availability of numerous health-care services, some people refuse to get prenatal care.

Perhaps Brown University economist Glenn Loury hit the nail on the head when he argued, "Sterile debates over policy fail to engage fundamental questions of personal morality, of character and values. We do not have to give voice to the judgments that it is wrong to abuse drugs, to be sexually promiscuous, to be indolent and without discipline, to be disrespectful of legitimate authority, to be unreliable, untruthful, unfaithful."[159] Loury's observations can apply to other groups in today's permissive culture. One thing is certain: families, marriages, and children face a new and uncertain future in a society where traditional families are devalued.

Brad Wilcox of the University of Virginia and University of Utah sociologist Nicholas Wolfinger found that urban families' frequent church attendance has a positive impact on unmarried women who have children out of wedlock. These women are more likely to marry within a year of giving birth.[160] Since the 1930s, social scientists studying the black ghetto have acknowledged the importance of the church in helping stabilize lower-class urban neighborhoods.[161] Moreover, Dr. Patrick F. Fagan of the Family Research Council has surveyed the research on religious practice and its impact on the family. He has found direct links between religious practice and educational attainment, showing higher grade point averages and higher graduation rates for students from homes where church attendance takes place. The highest gains were found among children from low-income neighborhoods.[162]

In short, people who attend church regularly, who read the Bible, and who meet together with like-minded Christians for prayer are by and large not the sort of people who wind up as the statistics of crime, delinquency, and drug addiction. These people do best at breaking the generational cycle of poverty, hopelessness, and self-destruction.[163]

This makes it even more disturbing when churches prove to be unsafe places. In some churches, an emphasis on the prosperity gospel—

distorting Jesus' teachings on stewardship and sacrifice into a message that claims Jesus desires for everyone to be rich—has replaced sound biblical teachings on morality and personal responsibility.

People who attend church regularly, who read the Bible, and who meet together with like-minded Christians for prayer . . . do best at breaking the generational cycle of poverty, hopelessness, and self-destruction.

WHERE DO WE GO FROM HERE?

In the 1940s, Richard Weaver, University of Chicago professor and father of modern-day conservatism, warned of the disintegration of modern society in his book *Ideas Have Consequences*. For Weaver, the real question is whether we would continue to believe in the existence of a "source of truth higher than, and independent of self" or opt for our own, self-created morality and philosophy.[164] How we as a society answer the question, he felt, would profoundly affect the health and well-being of our nation. Weaver was especially concerned with growing materialism and the decay of Western civilization and values. This decay, he said, manifests itself in the denial of universal truths, which leads men and women to deny accountability to higher forms of authority, such as God. Instead of reverence for our elders and the ideals of statesmen, more and more people come to see themselves as the final arbiters of truth.

Weaver's assessments certainly stand true in America's endorsements of ungodly behaviors and our use of influence to spread our unbiblical standards to poorer nations as conditions for receiving our aid. Rather than leading, we now copy and borrow from the laws and customs of other nations. We no longer desire to stand above other nations. Nor do we embrace our Christian heritage. As a result, we can expect only a further decline in our standard of living and our quality of life.

THE MANHATTAN DECLARATION

We should not despair. A new movement is sweeping America. Men and women are committing themselves to pray and fight for the preservation of constitutional values and principles, traditional marriages, protection of the unborn, religious liberty, and protections for workers who are being asked to participate in activities that offend their consciences (for example, doctors and nurses who are expected to perform abortions). In November 2009, Professor Robert P. George of Princeton University released a document he drafted along with Charles Colson, founder of Prison Fellowship, and Tony Perkins of the Family Research Council. This document, known as the Manhattan Declaration, is a petition that as of December 2010 had garnered almost a half million signatures for protecting and reclaiming families. It reads in part:

> We, as Orthodox, Catholic, and Evangelical Christians, have gathered, beginning in New York on September 28, 2009, to make the following declaration, which we sign as individuals, not on behalf of our organizations, but speaking to and from our communities. We act together in obedience to the one true God, the triune God of holiness and love, who has laid total claim on our lives and by that claim calls us with believers in all ages and all nations to seek and defend the good of all who bear his image. We set forth this declaration in light of the truth that is grounded in Holy Scripture, in natural human reason (which is itself, in our view, the gift of a beneficent God), and in the very nature of the human person. We call upon all people of goodwill, believers and non-believers alike, to consider carefully and reflect critically on the issues we here address . . . In this declaration we affirm: 1) the profound, inherent, and equal dignity of every human being as a creature fashioned in the very image of God, possessing inherent rights of equal dignity and life; 2) marriage as a conjugal union of man and woman, ordained by God from the creation, and historically understood by believers and non-believers alike, to be the most basic institution in

society and; 3) religious liberty, which is grounded in the character of God, the example of Christ, and the inherent freedom and dignity of human beings created in the divine image.[165]

Clearly, the battle lines have formed. We are engaged in a war fought between "cultural enforcers" and conservatives in America. We are engaged in a battle for the soul of our nation. The traditional values and moral foundations of the past are fast disappearing.

Christians in America must prepare for a protracted battle. Although we cannot force the ungodly to abide by biblical principles and values, we can renew our commitment to God and focus on our own standards of conduct as we strive to be "salt and light" in an ever-darkening world. We cannot stand silently and watch as our families crumble with the nation. We must wage war with meaningful involvement in our churches, communities, and homes. By doing so, we can work to reclaim our families in transformative, life-changing ways, based on the unchanging truth of the Word of God.

ACTION POINTS

1. Join the Family Research Council at
   http://www.frc.org/, and sign up for action alerts.

2. See if your church offers a marriage enrichment course
   or a singles' support group. If not, meet with your
   church leadership and ask how you can help make
   these services available for all.

3. Look for opportunities to help a single parent with
   child care for a night out.

4. Read and sign the Manhattan Declaration at
   http://www.manhattandeclaration.org/home.aspx.

5. Read and discuss the *Be the People* questions for chapter 4,
   posted at www.CarolMSwain.com.

CHAPTER 5

IMMIGRATION, THE RULE OF LAW, AND NATIONAL SOVEREIGNTY

We should insist that if the immigrant who comes here in good faith becomes an American and assimilates himself to us, he shall be treated on an exact equality with everyone else, for it is an outrage to discriminate against any such man because of creed, or birthplace, or origin. But this is predicated upon the person's becoming in every facet an American, and nothing but an American . . . There can be no divided allegiance here.

—PRESIDENT THEODORE ROOSEVELT[1]

[God] made from one man every nation of mankind to live on all the face of the earth, having determined allotted periods and the boundaries of their dwelling place.

—ACTS 17:26

THRONGS OF ONLOOKERS, JOURNALISTS, CAMERA OPERATORS, AND STAFFERS lined the halls of the Rayburn House office building, the atmosphere growing more charged as the restless crowd waited. As the moments ticked by, one member of Congress quipped, "We've not seen this much interest in a committee hearing since the impeachment."

I was present that day on Capitol Hill to testify at the invitation of the House Judiciary Committee's Subcommittee on Immigration, Citizenship, Refugees, Border Security and International Law.[2] Comedy Central's Stephen Colbert, as well as Arturo Rodriguez, president of the United Farm Workers (UFW), and Phil Glaize, an apple grower from northern Virginia, had also been invited to testify before the sub-committee. We represented a racially and ethnically diverse panel: two white men, one Mexican-American, and a black woman.

I was outnumbered in the hearing room and had opponents sitting behind me and along the sides of three walls. Directly behind me sat pro-amnesty activists, as well as members of the antiwar group Code Pink. Employees of apple grower Phil Glaize had placed a bushel of apples in the space in front of them. Activists had strategically positioned themselves behind me so cameras would capture their frowns and disapproving headshakes as I testified.

With three Democrats testifying, I sat as the lone witness of the Republican minority. However, I was encouraged by friendly faces and smiles of appreciation from the Republicans in the room: Steve King (R-IA); Lamar Smith (R-TX), ranking Republican of the full committee; Dan Lungren (R-CA); Ted Poe (R-TX); as well as staff members. I spoke first, which is unusual, given that protocol dictates that the minority witness speak last. However, in retrospect, I came to see that God ordained my testimony be given first in order that it might establish foundational arguments and be clearly heard. My role was to represent the views of millions of Americans and legal immigrants who desire the enforcement of existing immigration laws, enforcement our government has not carried out for decades.

When my statements were concluded, Phil Glaize argued that "without workers, some agricultural production could halt, causing growers to lose crops and shut down." He characterized the existing guest worker program for farmer workers (H-2A) as "bureaucratic, inefficient, and downright unreliable." The program, he argued, forced growers to "hire migrant workers who present documents that appear to be 'good' but [that represent workers] who may or may not be in this country legally."

Arturo Rodriguez, president of the UFW, had brought to the hearing several reportedly illegal farm workers who wore matching red shirts. Rodriguez had them stand as he introduced them as professional farm workers, and one by one, he listed their years of experience.

Rodriguez's real goal was to convince the panel that his union's "Take Our Jobs" initiative, which invited unemployed Americans to take jobs from immigrants, was a serious effort to hire American workers. According to Rodriguez, the program could locate only seven people, out of the more than eight thousand who inquired about the program's jobs, who were actually willing to work in the fields. Rodriguez argued that the US government should legalize workers who toil on the farms, performing work that Americans simply will not do. If America refuses to take action, he said, farm production will move to other countries. However, Rodriquez did not address how the existing H-2A visa program that brings agricultural workers to the country on short-term visas fits into his recommendations.

Stephen Colbert, the main attraction for the hearing, spoke last and entertained the crowd with a monologue designed to mimic conservatives and satirize their bigotry against immigrants. "This is America," Colbert railed. "I don't want a tomato picked by a Mexican. I want it picked by an American, then sliced by a Guatemalan and served by a Venezuelan in a spa where a Chilean gives me a Brazilian." Earlier, Colbert had suffered the indignity of having John Conyers (D-MI), chair of the full committee, invite him to leave. "We have your written testimony," Conyers said, "so it's not necessary for you to testify." However, Zoe Lofgren (D-CA), chair of the subcommittee, who had invited Colbert to testify, stepped in and successfully argued for him to stay.

Colbert and Representative Lofgren had each spent a day working in farm fields, and they were reportedly at the hearing to testify to the fact that farm work was really hard, a reality that would seem obvious to most people. Colbert provided comic commentary throughout the hearing until the end, when he responded to a serious question from Rep. Judy Chu (D-CA), who asked him why he was there. Assuming a serious tone, Colbert replied, "I have always been interested in the powerless, and I can't think of anyone in America more powerless than migrant farm workers."

As I listened to Colbert's response, I immediately thought about America's blacks, legal Hispanics, and poor whites—groups that are powerless as well. However, these groups are not represented by a voice in the media—by lobbyists or powerful television personalities like Colbert, who are willing to fight for their cause. To the contrary, CNN's award-winning Lou Dobbs of *Lou Dobbs Tonight* was America's only major media personality who regularly addressed issues affecting voiceless middle- and working-class people. Dobbs was pressured to leave CNN because of his forceful, sustained coverage of the negative impact of illegal immigration on working-class people and the harm that US trade policies were inflicting upon the nation. Dobbs has written a book relevant to these issues.[3] Organized leftist groups, such as the Southern Poverty Law Center (SPLC) and the National Council of La Raza (Latin for "the race"), organized smear campaigns and boycotts against *Lou Dobbs Tonight*. Dobbs eventually took a lucrative buyout from the network he helped Ted Turner found.

As I pondered the implication of Colbert's words, I also considered facts regarding the Take Our Jobs initiative—for instance, that in some parts of the country, native workers have successfully worked alongside immigrant farm workers.

I told the committee about a conversation I had had the previous day with a Nashville businessman who ran a one-year experiment in Helena, Arkansas, involving sweet potato planting and harvesting. Don Kerr of Kerr Industries had invested more than a quarter million dollars of his own money in a plan to help unemployed Americans secure agricultural jobs. The unemployment rate for black workers hovers at around 40 percent in the region of the country surrounding Helena, Arkansas.

Kerr's experiment involved H-2A workers and native-born black workers who were picked up at a central location, transported to a job site, provided with bathroom and lunchroom facilities, and paid a decent wage. Mr. Kerr saw no differences in the quality of the work provided by native-born workers. American workers, he said, will do farm work if they have accessibility to transportation and are provided decent working conditions.

Even though he initiated a program that was providing jobs for unemployed Americans, Kerr could not get state or federal agencies to invest in his initiative. Consequently, he discontinued the effort.

Kerr would like to see an independent farm service company created to hire workers, provide transportation in air-conditioned buses, offer bathroom and lunch facilities, and serve as a buffer between agricultural workers and the growers. No matter how successful Kerr's experience might have been in employing American workers, he would have been hard-pressed to find an advocate in the US Congress or state house to take his ideas seriously.

Conversely, newspaper articles and news clips about Colbert's testimony dominated the news for several days. Journalist Kay B. Day was the first to write an article of length focusing on testimony supporting unemployed American workers. She stated that "pop media has provided little information about . . . the real testimony given by Dr. Carol M. Swain, professor of political science and law at Vanderbilt University." She further raised the provocative question, "Did Democrat representative Zoe Lofgren (Calif.) invite Stephen Colbert to distract from Dr. Swain's reasoned, fact-based testimony?"[4] The answer to Day's question is, no: Colbert's invitation came first. The Democrats were counting on his celebrity status to get them enough media attention to ram a liberal immigration reform bill through Congress. But Democrats had not anticipated that the Republicans would invite a conservative black woman knowledgeable about the issue to testify.[5]

Even though he initiated a program that was providing jobs for unemployed Americans, Kerr could not get state or federal agencies to invest in his initiative.

I pointed out that the UFW's Take Our Jobs initiative has a name that would discourage many would-be applicants. Calling the initiative "Take Our Jobs" implied that the jobs belonged to someone else. I stated, "America cannot continue to bring in low-skilled guest workers to compete with its most disadvantaged citizens: poor whites, blacks, and legal Hispanics." I also noted that "surplus labor that starts in the fields migrates into other industries. Without this surplus labor, employers would have to pay higher wages, and many would have to improve substandard working conditions. Instead of paying eight or nine dollars per hour, employers might have to pay twelve or thirteen dollars." I explained that labor economist Phil Martin calculated that an increase in the wages of farm workers would not substantially increase the average family's grocery bill.[6] Martin estimated that better pay for farm workers would raise the average family's grocery bill by only eight dollars a year. As one Republican congressman pointed out, eight dollars is less than the cost of a movie ticket.

AMERICA'S UNACCEPTABLY HIGH UNEMPLOYMENT RATES

My knowledge of unemployment rates for American workers influenced my testimony. Unemployment rates in the second quarter of 2010 revealed a bleak situation for American workers, with an overall unemployment rate of 9.6 percent. However, the Bureau of Labor Statistics' broader measure of employment, called U-6, revealed a gloomier picture. This measure is an important indicator because it calculates the unemployment rate by including unemployed people who would like to work but have not looked recently, as well as those working part-time but who would prefer full-time jobs.

Using the U-6 assessment, the overall unemployment rate for native workers was a whopping 16.5 percent.[7] Low-skilled native-born workers with less than a high school education reported an overall unemployment rate of 20.8 percent and a U-6 rate of 32.4 percent. Those with only a high school education reported an unemployment rate of 20 percent and a U-6 rate of 36 percent.

Black Americans with less than a high school education reported an unemployment rate of 29 percent and a U-6 measure of 43 percent.

That means almost half of the people who would like to work can't find employers who will hire them. Those with a high school diploma fare only slightly better. They reported an unemployment rate of 27.4 percent and a U-6 rate of 40.7 percent.

The picture improved only slightly for Hispanics. Native-born Hispanics with less than a high school education reported an unemployment rate of 22.9 percent and a U-6 rate of 35 percent. Surprisingly, those with a high school diploma had an almost insignificantly different unemployment rate than high school dropouts. Their unemployment rate was 23.3 percent, with a U-6 rate of 36 percent.

Admittedly, government could do more to help unemployed Americans. For instance, we could begin by enforcing our existing laws and regulations and couple that with tougher penalties for breaking existing laws. A multifaceted approach could provide incentives for compliance. Because the Obama administration has chosen to bypass Congress and take administrative action under the radar, many of their actions fall into the category of stealth immigration reform. In some cases, government officials have made decisions favoring illegal immigrants at the expense of native-born Americans, particularly African Americans, first-generation Hispanics, and working-class whites. For example, the Department of Homeland Security, under the direction of Janet Napolitano, has modified workplace raids and in some cases allowed undocumented workers to keep their jobs by giving them temporary work visas.[8] Mark Krikorian reports of a bizarre incident where "immigration agents stopped several van loads of illegal aliens in Massachusetts on their way to work. After taking some in custody, the agents not only released all the other illegal aliens, they actually drove them to work."[9]

To address the issue of illegal immigration, the Obama administration has increased the number of labor audits of businesses, asking employers to produce I-9 documentation (Social Security cards, birth certificates, and passports) to show that employees are eligible to work in the United States. Employer raids, often conducted at night, are simply not as effective a deterrent as workplace raids, which were effective in motivating about one million illegal aliens to deport themselves by voluntarily returning home. We could increase these numbers even more if our government was simply willing to enforce existing federal regulations.

One of the most effective federal programs for identifying illegal workers is a voluntary program called E-Verify. The E-Verify program is an online program run by the Department of Homeland Security that allows employers to check Social Security numbers against a national database. It has a 96 percent accuracy rate, and it yields results in a matter of seconds.[10] If legislators were serious about addressing the employment of illegal workers, they would pass a law making participation with E-Verify mandatory for new and existing employees.

MY EXPERIENCES WITH IMMIGRANTS

My experience with immigrants has been deeply personal. My mother named me after my Uncle Leon's Korean girlfriend, whose name was Carol. Following the Korean War, Carol made her way to Bedford, Virginia. Although it might not seem obvious, I'm named after an Asian woman.

An African student from Sierra Leone named Abou touched my life and convinced me I was smart enough to go to college. I met Abou in the late 1970s when we were both working the same shift at Liberty House Nursing Home in Roanoke, Virginia. At the time, I was a high school dropout with a GED (high school equivalency diploma). College, I thought, was beyond my reach. Abou convinced me that I was smarter than many of the students who attended college with him. Because of his nudge of encouragement, I applied to Virginia Western Community College and subsequently earned what would become the first of five degrees.

While at Virginia Western, I made friends with Vietnamese refugees who had resettled in the city and were attending college. I also had many Lebanese friends, and I remember their fears for their personal safety when the Iranians took Americans hostage. My friend Steve resorted to wearing a T-shirt that said "Lebanese, not Iranian." Over the years I have dated African men, and, to my disappointment, I have learned that our cultural differences are often far-reaching; many held quite different standards of truth and reality than my own.

More recently I have served as an altar worker at Christ Church in Nashville, praying with immigrants who have sought prayers for their green cards and other immigration-related issues. Madhu Gammon, one of my regular prayer partners, trained in India as a dermatologist; her husband, Keith, as a surgeon. Keith came to the United States on an H-1B visa and brought Madhu and their handicapped son. I have observed the saga for legal immigrations through their eyes and discovered that America's broken bureaucracy seems to work more slowly and inefficiently for legal immigrants.

Several years ago I was vacationing in Gatlinburg, Tennessee, in a remote cabin nestled on a hillside. As I was walking down an isolated road, I met a Mexican woman from Pittsburgh. Later she visited my cabin, and she told me her married boyfriend had brought her and her two daughters to the cabins and abandoned them two weeks before school was to start. We sat on the back porch and swapped stories about our lives, and I prayed with her about her difficult situation.

A few days after our visit, I looked out the window of my cabin and noticed two girls around the ages of ten and twelve outside the cabins. I called out and asked them if their mother was named Sonia, and when they replied yes, I inquired about her health. One of the girls replied that their mother was in bed sick. Then eyeing me curiously, the older sister asked, "Are you the woman our mother met the other day?" I replied yes. A look of disappointment swept across the child's face as she said, "Oh, we thought you were an angel."

Although I was not an angel, I became an angel to that family for a day. By the grace of God, I found a church willing to pay for bus tickets to Pittsburgh. The family hurriedly packed, and I gave them some cash and then drove them to the nearest Greyhound bus terminal in Knoxville. Later that night, I heard the roar of the motor of the boyfriend's truck as he sped into the parking lot of our cluster of cabins. I listened in the darkness as he entered their cabin, discovered them missing, and then roared off down the highway. I confess to being a bit afraid, not knowing if he would guess me to be their accomplice and kick down my door. Fortunately, God was with me, and he kept on driving. I kept in touch with the family for a few months as they gratefully settled back in their hometown.

My dealings in immigration have also taken place in more politicized contexts. In 2005, the Bush State Department offered me the privilege of traveling to Southeast Asia on a speaking tour during Black History Month. My topic was the global impact of the civil rights movement. My first stop on the tour was Burma (Myanmar), followed by Malaysia, Vietnam, and the Philippines. As part of the tour, I spoke at colleges and universities, but I also traveled in the interior of the country and saw the grueling poverty of poor people whose unfortunate circumstances make legal travel to the United States impossible. The conditions I saw made me wish that a prescribed number of legal visas were available for the world's poor. We should make allowances for those who cannot qualify for a legal visa or sneak across a border. I would like to see a system that offered legal visas to the most industrious members of the world's poor. Of course, this cannot happen until we address current enforcement problems.

I share this information to clarify that my involvement in the immigration debate is not born out of hostility toward immigrants. The immigrants I have encountered have blessed my life enormously. I understand their pain, the injustices many of them have suffered, and the fact that we don't get to choose our families, our race, or our nation of birth. As I stated earlier, I am proud to be an American. I would like to see our country remain a beacon for people around the world. At the same time, I cannot condone illegal immigration, nor can I close my eyes to the negative impact of mass immigration on the quality of life and opportunities of native-born American citizens who so desperately want their own taste of the American dream.

UNDERSTANDING THE COMPLEXITY
OF IMMIGRATION REFORM

Throughout this book I use the term *illegal alien* to describe a foreigner who enters the country without authorization. In defining the term in this manner, I am rejecting the politically correct definition of *undocumented person*. Under US law, an alien "means any person not a citizen or national of the United States."[11] In 2010, an estimated eleven million illegal immigrants lived and worked in the United States. Since they are undocumented, experts do not know how many are here. The numbers could range anywhere from twelve million to eighteen million. If our government offered amnesty, we have no idea how many people would show up to claim the benefit.

Although tighter border security is essential, border security will not solve the problem of illegal migration. About 40 percent of illegal aliens overstay tourist, work, or student visas,[12] including four of the 9/11 terrorists who were responsible for the deaths of almost three thousand persons. Right now, our nation has no reliable system of tracking when people enter and exit our country. Moreover, Janet Napolitano, the head of Homeland Security under the Obama administration, expressed her reluctance to take the necessary steps to adopt the technology that would take the guesswork out of the process.[13]

The numbers [of illegal immigrants] could range anywhere from twelve million to eighteen million. If our government offered amnesty, we have no idea how many people would show up to claim the benefit.

Too many illegal aliens are currently in the labor force at a time when millions of American citizens have joined the ranks of the long-term unemployed. In 2007, illegal aliens constituted 5 percent of the workforce. Many of them entered the US with low work skills and low levels of education. This occurred during an era when federal resources for fighting the poverty of native-born Americans were shrinking. In light of the high unemployment in the US, no sensible argument can be made for legalizing millions of undocumented persons currently holding jobs to which they are not entitled.

In 2009, we had an estimated undocumented population of twelve million people, with roughly eight million working in the labor force. According to the Pew Hispanic Center, 76 percent of illegal immigrants are Hispanics, with the majority (59 percent) coming from Mexico, a country that shares a contiguous border with us. The next largest groups of illegal aliens are Salvadorans, Guatemalans, and Hondurans, constituting together 74 percent of the illegal population.[14] Heather McDonald of the Manhattan Institute points out that "a significant portion of second- and third-generation Latinos are assimilating downward into underclass culture. Hispanics have the highest rate of teen pregnancy in the US and the fastest-growing rate of illegitimacy (now fifty-three percent) compared with blacks and whites. The incarceration rate of Mexican immigrants jumps more than eightfold between the first and second generations, resulting in a prison rate 3.5 times that of whites."[15]

In many areas of the country, the volume of new immigrants has created enormous drains on educational institutions, hospitals and clinics, jails and prisons, and the supply of low-income housing. This poses a tremendous dilemma and trade-off for a nation that has a long legacy as a haven for refugees and immigrants from around the world.

In light of the high unemployment in the US, no sensible argument can be made for legalizing millions of undocumented persons currently holding jobs to which they are not entitled.

Within the United States, impetus is growing to legalize the unknown millions of current illegal aliens. Given the needs of native-born Americans, this action would be a serious mistake. It would adversely affect millions of blacks, poor whites, and legal immigrants whose wages and opportunities are already suffering because of the overflow of cheap labor, and it would greatly increase our poverty levels and welfare costs. The overwhelming majority of the illegal aliens compete in the same job sectors as low-skilled Americans; the low pay they earn means that more families would qualify for governmental assistance, increasing costs for all taxpayers.

Congress has repeatedly tried to address the immigration problem, with mixed results. In 1986, it passed the Immigration and Reform Control Act (IRCA), four years later the 1990 Immigration Act, and later the Illegal Immigration Reform and Immigrant Responsibility Act of 1996 (IIRIRA). IRCA included four main provisions designed to address illegal migration. It instituted strong employer sanctions that were later gutted, legalized long-term undocumented residents and agricultural workers, and also sought to protect American citizens and permanent residents against discrimination from employers hiring people under the table. The 1990 Immigration Act raised the immigration ceiling to seven hundred thousand and created new preferences for relatives of US citizens and foreigners with specialized skills. IIRIRA made it easier to deport illegal aliens by restricting the judicial review of administrative removal orders while also limiting appeal processes.

Each congressional act has brought with it negative unintended consequences, causing what were once regionally confined problems to spread across the nation and create major social and economic upheavals. Much of the illegal immigration stems from Mexico. Princeton professor Douglas Massey has argued that US policy implanted in 1986 has been a policy of contradictions. Rather than reducing illegal immigration, US policies have made it less likely that illegal aliens from Mexico will voluntarily return home.[16]

The experiences of the United States and Europe suggest that amnesty provisions like the one offered in 1986 only attracted more illegal aliens into the country. Amnesty could have the unintended effect of increasing the flow of new illegal aliens who sneak into the country and wait for the next legalization. In 1986, we offered amnesty as a onetime solution.

An Alice-in-Wonderland reasoning exists amid the voices of those who argue that no harmful consequences flow from our haphazard efforts to absorb millions of illegal aliens into a country challenged with the needs of millions of poor people already. Illegal aliens who mean us no good and who desire to radicalize the disaffected among our native born live within our borders. Recent among the ranks are people who have rejected American values and principles, as well as disenchanted Americans who have joined hate groups and who are ripe for recruitment. Some of our own citizens would like to see the downfall of our once-great but now tottering nation. These include Mexican, Latino, and black hate groups who receive less media attention and generally less scrutiny from so-called watchdog groups like the Southern Poverty Law Center than Caucasian-dominated groups. Radical groups such as the Mexica Movement,[17] the National Council of La Raza, and MEChA (Movimiento Estudiantil Chicano de Aztlan) hope to "one day reclaim Aztlan, the mythical birthplace of the Aztecs. In Chicano folklore, Aztlan includes California, Arizona, Nevada, New Mexico and parts of Colorado and Texas."[18] Among blacks, the New Black Panther Party and the Nation of Islam preach hatred of white Americans and Jews.

THE SOUTHERN POVERTY LAW CENTER (SPLC)

The Southern Poverty Law Center (SPLC), which now advises the Obama Department of Homeland Security (DHS), is a far leftist organization that harasses conservatives—both groups and individuals, while ignoring others that would seem to fit their definition of hate-mongers.

I came under attack by the SPLC because of an August 10, 2009, Huffington Post blog post I wrote that criticized the organization.[19] A November 4, 2008, video showing members of the New Black Panther Party, in full regalia, patrolling a polling precinct in Philadelphia spurred my post. Video footage showed the Black Panthers wielding nightsticks and intimidating white voters. Although news organizations covered the story, resulting in Bush Department of Justice charges against the

Panthers, the Obama Department of Justice dropped charges against the group. I pointed out that the SPLC, which monitors hate groups, never reported the story. Instead, it spent an incredible amount of time hounding conservative organizations and individuals like Lou Dobbs.[20]

The SPLC's attacks on Dobbs were unrelenting and shameless. I concluded my Huffington Post piece by saying, "There is a name for what has happened. It is called 'mission creep.' Mission creep occurs when an organization strays beyond its original purpose and engages in actions antithetical to its goals. Rather than monitoring hate groups, the Southern Poverty Law Center has become one."[21]

The SPLC claimed credit for Lou Dobbs' decision to end production of *Lou Dobbs Tonight*. Since leaving CNN, Dobbs has worked with Democrats and Republicans to construct an acceptable immigration policy. I know the issue tears at his heart. His wife, Debi Segura, is Mexican-American, and their two daughters have mixed ancestry. Additionally, his mother-in-law, Lee Segura, is an outspoken woman who has observed how immigrants suffer. In 2011, Dobbs was preparing to return to television with a new show on the Fox Business Channel.

FURTHER SPLC REPRISALS

Shortly after my public critiques of the SPLC, Mark Potok instigated a payback with the cooperation of my local newspaper, the *Tennessean*. Quoting Potok, the *Tennessean* ran a front page article under the headline "Carol Swain Is an Apologist for White Supremacists." This negative article made its way to the front pages of several newspapers across the state, and the accusation went viral nationally and became the talk of black radio hosts. Only host Tom Joyner allowed me on his show to explain my position. The attack backfired after James Taranto, online editor for the *Wall Street Journal*'s The Best of the Web column, authored a response entitled "In Defense of Carol Swain."[22]

Since that time a number of articles have exposed the SPLC's witch hunts, and one emeritus professor, Guenter Lewy at the University of

Massachusetts, successfully sued and forced the organization to issue an apology and retraction and settle the case for an undisclosed amount. Lewy sought eight million dollars.[23] Of course, the SPLC's questionable practices have not prevented the Department of Homeland Security from relying on it as a law enforcement tool, even to the point of allowing it to help the government write a report on terrorism that slandered Christians, returning veterans, immigration restrictionists, and pro-life activists.[24] The SPLC now lists pro-family, anti–gay marriage organizations among its growing list of hate groups.

ELVIRA ARELLANO: A SYMBOL OF A BROKEN SYSTEM

Elvira Arellano, a twice-deported Mexican illegal immigrant mother of an American-born son, became a cause célèbre after she defied a deportation order and took refuge in Adalberto United Methodist Church in South Side Chicago, where she lived in open defiance of US immigration laws from August 2006 through August 19, 2007. Arellano's eventual arrest and repatriation to Mexico came after she held a press conference and then left the church for speaking engagements in Los Angeles.[25] Arrested outside Our Lady Queen of Angels Catholic Church, she has consistently portrayed herself as the Hispanic counterpart of civil rights icon Rosa Parks, who refused to give her bus seat to a white man during the 1950s. The inappropriateness of this comparison caused one veteran of the civil rights movement to complain, "The differences in the actions and backgrounds of the two women are glaring. Parks was a US citizen whose rights under the 14th Amendment to the US Constitution were violated and ultimately vindicated by the US Supreme Court."[26]

Since Arellano's deportation, other immigrants have taken refuge in churches. Bishop Harry Jackson, senior pastor of Hope Christian Church, and Tony Perkins, president of the Family Research Council, have pointed out that the sanctuary movement is illegal and does not address "the long-term problems that our nation faces with immigration.

Those who are here illegally, as well as those who benefit from illegal labor, must be held accountable."[27]

In 2002, Arellano founded United Latino Family. Her stated goal is to force the US government to stop its deportation of illegal aliens with families. Her son Saulito was born in the United States two years after her first deportation. Critics of Arellano have accused her of returning to the country and having a child as insurance against deportation.[28] Saulito is an "anchor baby." This uncharitable expression refers to the offspring of women who give birth while living illegally in the United States. Once the child reaches the age of twenty-one, he or she can apply for US visas for his or her parents through the family reunification program. The birth of an anchor baby entitles the family to welfare benefits such as Medicaid and food stamps for the child.

BIRTHRIGHT CITIZENSHIP AND THE FOURTEENTH AMENDMENT

The basis for birthright citizenship for the children of illegal aliens, temporary residents, and tourists comes from the Fourteenth Amendment's citizenship clause, which states, "All persons born or naturalized in the United States, and subject to the jurisdiction thereof, are citizens of the United States and of the State wherein they reside." Adopted in 1868, the amendment was a corrective to an injustice against African slaves and American-born blacks that stripped them of their US citizenship, leaving them in political limbo. This occurred in the infamous *Dred Scott v. Sandford* decision (1857),[29] in which Chief Justice Taney, writing for the majority, ruled that African slaves and their American-born descendants had no constitutional protections, were not US citizens, and could never become citizens. The amendment excluded from automatic citizenship anyone not subject to the jurisdiction of the United States. The "subject to the jurisdiction thereof" clause was understood to mean Indians, foreign diplomats, and soldiers. No need existed to address illegal immigrants because at the time, the country had no immigration restrictions.[30]

Within thirty years of the Fourteenth Amendment's passage, the Supreme Court upheld a principle called *jus soli*, Latin for "the right by soil," which was borrowed from English common law.[31] The policy of *jus soli* is based upon the idea that birth within a specific jurisdiction or nation is sufficient for citizenship and allegiance. On the other hand, *jus sanguinis* is Latin for "the right by blood," which confers citizenship on the basis of the parents' status. The United States uses a combination of *jus soli* and *jus sanguinis* for allocating citizenship by birth.

The Court upheld *jus soli* in the case of *United States v. Wong Kim Ark* (1898), which involved the citizenship claims of Wong Kim Ark.[32] Ark was a child of Chinese guest workers, born during a period when his parents were legally residing in the United States and before Congress passed the 1882 Chinese Exclusion Act.[33] In a 6–2 decision, the Supreme Court upheld Ark's rights to US citizenship and gave a more expansive reading of the "subject to the jurisdiction thereof," than it had several years earlier in the 1884 case of *Elkins v. Wilkins*.[34] In the Elkins case, the Court ruled that Indians were not US citizens regardless of whether they remained in their tribes. It is through these cases that the Court affirmed the in-eligibility of native Indians, foreign diplomats and their children, as well as hostile occupying forces for United States citizenship. The Court has never addressed the legal status of children born to illegal immigrants, but it is assumed that they automatically become citizens through *jus soli*. People concerned about the growth of illegal immigration and the rise in mixed-status families argue that appropriate legislative action could close the loophole.

In 1985, Yale University professor Peter Schuck and University of Pennsylvania professor Rogers Smith argued that "the Fourteenth Amendment's Citizenship Clause makes birthright citizenship for the chil-dren of illegal and temporary visitor aliens a matter of congressional choice rather than constitutional prescription."[35] According to this argument, ille-gal aliens are not subject to the jurisdiction of the United States. Vociferously disagreeing with Schuck and Smith, Harvard Law School professor Gerald Neuman testified before Congress in 1995, arguing that there is nothing in "the language, legislative history, or traditional interpretation of the Citizenship Clause that would exclude children born in the United States to aliens not lawfully present here."[36] Neuman argued that since illegal aliens are deportable and liable for criminal punishment if they commit crimes, they are subject to the jurisdiction of the United States.

> The Court has never addressed the legal status of children born to
> illegal immigrants . . . Appropriate legislative action could close
> the loophole.

More recently Professor Schuck reiterated his position in a *New York Times* op-ed.[37] Schuck pointed out that at the time the Fourteenth Amendment was ratified, Congress viewed citizenship as a "mutual relationship to which both the nation and the individual must consent."[38] Schuck notes that "one day before the citizenship clause was ratified, Congress passed the Expatriation Act, which allowed Americans to 'shed their American or foreign citizenship.'"[39] Thus, a grant of US citizenship required the consent of both parties: the immigrant and the receiving nation. It was not a unilateral decision. Presumably the would-be immigrant's application for a visa and the nation's grant of admission would be proof of a consensual relation. When illegal aliens have babies in the United States, the *mutual* aspect of the relationship is not present. Illegal aliens may consent to live in the United States, but the US government surely does not consent to their residing here illegally. An illegal presence in the United States indicates that only one party—the illegal party—has consented to the arrangement. Therefore, can the person possibly be "subject to the jurisdiction thereof"?

Congress should flex its muscles by passing a law that clarifies the scope of the citizen clause.[40] According to legal analyst Jon Feere, closing the loophole would bring the United States in line with other nations that have modified their citizenship criteria in recent years, including Australia, Ireland, India, New Zealand, the United Kingdom, Malta, and the Dominican Republic.[41] Feere reports that of the world's 194 countries, only 30—that is, 15 percent—grant automatic citizenship to the children of illegal aliens.[42]

The big question now is this: apart from a new constitutional amendment, does Congress have the authority to restrict birthright citizenship? Some of the best legal minds in the country believe that it does.[43] Resolution of this issue will center on interpretation of the subject-to-the-jurisdiction-thereof clause and whether the Supreme Court agrees that Congress has the constitutional authority to modify the rule to address current realities.

When it comes to the question of birthright citizenship, the stakes are high. More than three hundred thousand babies are born in the United States each year to parents who are living in our country illegally.[44] Yet suggesting deportation for those who are residing here illegally incites a backlash of criticism against the government. Governmental officials face accusations of ripping babies from their mothers' breasts.

Automatic citizenship of children born to parents who illegally reside in the country creates mixed-status households. It places the children in awkward situations where they can become angry and alienated from their parents and their homeland. As long as our country awards citizenship to every child born in the United States, we will continue to have mixed-status families, the heartbreaking trauma of deportations, and guest workers who refuse to leave.

BIRTH TOURISM

The growth of "birth tourism" is an excellent reason to close the loophole in the Fourteenth Amendment. This term refers to an increasingly common practice whereby wealthy foreigners travel to the United States for the sole reason of giving birth so that the child will be a US citizen.[45] *Washington Post* reporter Keith Richburg describes an organization that offers packages to foreigners, assisting them with getting US passports—and thus, indirectly, citizenship for babies—for $14,750.[46] The fee covers a three-month stay in a California "baby care" center, a room with a cable television and wireless Internet connection, three meals a day, and a Chinese-speaking doctor and staff. The Marmara Manhattan, located in New York's Upper East Side, offers a one-bedroom suite "for $5,100, plus taxes, for a month, with airport transfer, baby cradle and a gift set for the mother." Medical fees are additional.[47] The Tucson Medical Center in Arizona offers a similar package for wealthy Mexican women. For fees of $2,300 to $4,600, women can arrive up to two weeks before their due date and stay at the medical center. Their fee covers the hospital stay, exams, and massages.[48] Incredibly, birth tourism is legal in the United States, and people come from around the world to take advantage of it. The Marmara Manhattan caters to tourists from Hong Kong, South Korea, and Turkey. It would be ludicrous to argue that the intent of the Fourteenth Amendment was to protect the growth of birth tourism in the United States. Certainly, this industry does not serve US interests.

CLOSING THE LOOPHOLE

As part of a true comprehensive immigration reform, Congress must address birthright citizenship and family reunification. Otherwise, we will continue to have mixed-status families and long waits for foreigners who apply for US visas using the system we currently have in place. Rather than leave millions of children in limbo, Congress should include a provision that would allow the American-born children of illegal aliens who have been in the country for ten years or more to apply for citizenship, regardless of their parents' status.[49]

As part of a true comprehensive immigration reform, Congress must address birthright citizenship and family reunification.

Failing to address the immigration problem means that our nation will continue to attract guest workers, illegal aliens, and tourists desiring to give birth on US soil. Furthermore, refusing to address the problem distorts the role of the US government, painting our government as a villain seeking to destroy families when it seeks to enforce its own laws enacted to protect its own citizens.

STATE AND LOCAL INITIATIVES

The failure of federal legislators to reform immigration has led state and local governments to initiate their own policy prescriptions, some of dubious constitutionality. States have recognized the effect of immigration on the distribution of social services such as public education, health care, and law enforcement, as well as the collection of tax revenue. In perhaps one of the most famous attempts to withhold taxpayer-funded services from illegal immigrants, the voters of California passed Proposition 187 in 1994. Proposition 187, signed into law by Governor Pete Wilson, withheld social services such as public education and nonemergency medical treatment from illegal aliens. A federal judge later ruled the law unconstitutional, but not before it spawned a national debate about what obligations state government owes its residents, including illegal aliens.

In December 2007, the Congressional Budget Office (CBO) published an article that shed light on the actual expenses incurred by states for the services provided to illegal aliens.[50] In an attempt to synthesize twenty-nine independent studies on the impact of immigrants on state and local budgets, the CBO stated that finding an aggregate effect was difficult. The study concluded that because of various federal and state statutes that mandate the provision of certain social services, it is difficult for state and local governments to deny those services. In addition, the actual amounts spent on providing services to the unauthorized population represent a very small percentage, typically less than 5 percent of the whole budget for providing those same services to the rest of the population. In certain states such as California, the percentage is higher, but even then, the amount accounts for less than 10 percent of the state budget. The CBO has determined that, overall, the taxes collected from the unauthorized population do not cover the amount of services they consume, but the net impact on state and local budgets is likely modest.

Arizona has stood as ground zero in the immigration debate. In April 2010, Arizona governor Jan Brewer signed Senate Bill 1070 into law and later amended the original version to address the concerns of opponents.[51] Her effort to appease her opponents was unsuccessful. According to the legislature, the bill's intent was "to assist the federal government in enforcing existing immigration law."[52] Described as the toughest law in the nation, it was supposed to become effective July 29, 2010. However, a successful lawsuit by the Obama Department of Justice (DOJ) has delayed its implementation.[53] Arizona appealed the decision. As of October 2010, a final decision from the United States Court of Appeals for the Ninth Circuit was pending. Eleven foreign nations filed briefs (statements) against the law, stating that implementation would hurt international relations. Adding insult to injury, in August, the Obama administration submitted the Arizona law to the Human Rights Council of the United Nations for review.[54]

SANCTUARY CITIES

No fewer than thirty states have adopted sanctuary policies. These policies usually forbid city employees and local law enforcement agencies from identifying and reporting known or suspected illegal immigrants to the Department of Homeland Security's Immigration and Customs Enforcement (ICE), where they could face deportation. Although adopted with good intentions to encourage illegal immigrants to report criminal victimization, the laws can have the unintended effect of sheltering drug dealers, human traffickers, and other criminals who can blend into immigrant communities. Federal and state partnerships like Section 287(g) of the Immigration and Nationality Act (INA)—which authorizes state and local enforcement to run background checks for suspected illegal immigrants, then detain and arrest them if they are, in fact, found to be in the country illegally—are under attack by those who wish to see amnesty granted to the nation's illegal immigrants. This situation poses a challenge for the rule of law and for the sovereignty of nations. Unfortunately, the Obama administration has indicated that it has no plans to enforce immigration law in sanctuary cities.[55] By making this decision, the administration is trampling the Constitution and the rule of law.[56]

Immigration enforcement in the United States has historically been lax, but respect for our nation's immigration laws has hit a new low. Not only has the Department of Homeland Security (DHS) filed a lawsuit against a sovereign state struggling to handle massive illegal migration and gang violence, but it is now working toward gutting the 287(g) program. A month after DHS reviewed Houston's immigration court docket, the *Houston Chronicle* reported that immigration judges had tossed more than two hundred cases and these represented a 700 percent increase from the previous month. Almost half (45%) of the over three hundred cases heard in September 2010 resulted in dismissals.[57]

Immigration enforcement in the United States has historically been lax, but respect for our nation's immigration laws has hit a new low.

However, the administration has been aggressive about identifying and deporting criminal aliens, while leaving others to remain in the US. Meanwhile, Mexican drug cartels have spread their businesses in at least 230 US cities.[58] DHS has also signaled its opposition to implementing a system for tracking the entry and exit of visa holders. A reliable tracking system is essential for getting control of illegal immigration. Both the Republican and the Democratic policy positions on immigration reform are reflections of party interests, and neither party has been able to forge a consensus amenable to their constituency groups. Democrats would like to legalize all illegal aliens because the party sees them as millions of potential new voters. The desire to satisfy corporate and business demands for cheap labor seems to have hampered Republican actions on the issue. For decades, the majority of Americans have wanted strict enforcement of immigration laws, but the elitist leaders of both parties have been unwilling to comply.[59]

BIBLICAL, ETHICAL, AND MORAL CONSIDERATIONS

The Judeo-Christian Bible presents numerous scriptures about how the Israelites were to treat "strangers" in the land. One example is Leviticus 19:33–34: "When a stranger sojourns with you in your land, you shall not do him wrong. You shall treat the stranger who sojourns with you as the native among you, and you shall love him as yourself, for you were strangers in the land of Egypt: I am the LORD your God." Another example is Exodus 22:21: "You shall not wrong a sojourner or oppress him, for you were sojourners in the land of Egypt."

For years amnesty and open-borders advocates have quoted these scriptures to question the faith of Jews or Christians who favor immigration enforcement or a more restrictive approach to rampant illegal immigration. The issue for Christians centers on just who the "stranger" is that the Bible repeatedly references. Brad Hirschfield, a rabbi and president of the National Jewish Center for Learning and Leadership, has addressed the issue of illegal immigration and the proper interpretation of the Hebrew Scriptures. Hirschfield says that the "stranger of the Hebrew Bible is better understood as a resident alien, a non-citizen who agrees to abide by the laws of the community into which he or she has come. To that extent then, many if not most, illegal aliens in this country, would not qualify."[60] The biblical "strangers" had to observe the laws and customs of the Israelites, including its worship practices.

For Christians, the New Testament makes clear the obligations for citizens and noncitizens. Romans 13:1–4 states:

> Let every person be subject to the governing authorities. For there is no authority except from God, and those that exist have been instituted by God. Therefore whoever resists the authorities resists what God has

appointed, and those who resist will incur judgment. For rulers are not a terror to good conduct, but to bad. Would you have no fear of the one who is in authority? Then do what is good, and you will receive his approval, for he is God's servant for your good. But if you do wrong, be afraid, for he does not bear the sword in vain. For he is the servant of God, an avenger who carries out God's wrath on the wrongdoer.

Christians, as well as illegal aliens, are responsible to obey the civil authorities. Churches can minister to their material needs and should encourage their congregants to obey the laws of the land.

Repeatedly, the Bible refers to Israel's borders or other nations' borders and boundaries. These passages include "You have fixed all the boundaries of the earth" (Psalm 74:17) and "He made from one man every nation of mankind to live on all the face of the earth, having determined allotted periods and the boundaries of their dwelling place" (Acts 17:26). Boundaries provide protection and demarcate the places where particular social mores and rules of law prevail. A nation cannot stand without boundaries and a strong security system.

One hundred and twenty-five times the Bible directs the Israelites regarding how to treat foreigners, aliens, and sojourners in their land. And while the United States is not ancient Israel, the biblical principles set forth regarding treatment of aliens are simple, just, and applicable. The foreigner is to be granted the same rights as citizens of the land, to be released from work on the Sabbath, and to be paid just wages in a timely manner. However, in no instance except when the nation of Israel is under God's judgment were foreigners free to influence the nation by worshipping other gods or living by the practices of the countries they had fled.

A nation cannot stand without boundaries and a strong security system.

Concerns about church growth can affect positions on immigration enforcement. Outspoken amnesty voices include Cardinal Roger Mahony, the archbishop of Los Angeles. Mahoney has called immigration laws a sin and has expressed his support for civil disobedience.[61] Self-interest could lie at the heart of his position. A 2008 Pew Study of Religion showed that the Catholic Church had lost more than one-third of its members. The newly arrived Latino immigrants were helping Catholic churches offset some of their losses.[62]

COMPREHENSIVE IMMIGRATION REFORM[63]

The immigration debate is replete with buzzwords. Proponents of "comprehensive immigration reform" would bring immigrants "out of the shadows" and offer them an "earned path to legalization." I suspect that such slogans have emerged from focus-group testing to see which phrases resonate with the American public. But do these buzzwords tell the truth? The word *comprehensive* implies "everything." Hence one should not speak of comprehensive immigration reform without addressing a host of issues, including birthright, citizenship, and family reunification. Likewise, one should not discuss an "earned path to legalization" without asking what signal this would send to legal immigrants who have respected and followed the country's rules.

The failure to enforce our laws heretofore should not stop us from taking corrective measures in the present to restore the rule of law. Until immigration is comprehensively reformed, the federal government—with state and local assistance—should increase enforcement of existing immigration laws and procedures. If Congress is unable to do so, the president should establish a commission of scholars and religious leaders that is bipartisan, ideologically balanced, and autonomous—not beholden to existing ethnocentric interest groups such as the National Council of La Raza[64]—to craft a reform package on which members of Congress can vote up or down. The model already exists for such a commission. In 1990, Congress created the US Commission on Immigration Reform, which it dissolved in 1997. Its members included Rep. Barbara Jordan (D-TX), Brandeis University professor Lawrence Fuchs, and *Dallas*

Morning News editor Richard Estrada. Unfortunately, Congress never acted on the Commission's recommendations.

Before any steps are taken toward legalizing currently illegal aliens, Congress must commission studies of how legalization would affect vulnerable populations in the US workforce, such as low-skilled blacks, poor whites, and native-born Hispanics. Policy makers also need to assess the impact legalization would have on social welfare services and the tax burden of state and local governments. Some reports indicate that the legalization of illegal aliens would greatly increase poverty, stimulate population growth to astronomical proportions, and possibly add considerably to state and local governments' unfunded mandates.[65]

Until immigration is comprehensively reformed, the federal government—with state and local assistance—should increase enforcement of existing immigration laws and procedures.

Here are my suggestions for a truly comprehensive immigration policy:

1. Prioritize border security and the completion of a fence on the United States' southern border.
2. Pass new legislation that requires all illegal aliens to register in the country within six months. Anyone failing to do so should be subject to immediate deportation.
3. Since 40 percent of illegal aliens entered on a valid visa,[66] impose stiff penalties for anyone overstaying his or her visa as a student, tourist, or worker.
4. When admitting professional and highly skilled guest workers, ensure that their backgrounds have been thoroughly examined. This might help avoid embarrassing episodes such as Operation Paperclip, where inadequate screening resulted in the US employment of Nazi scientists.[67]
5. Limit all guest worker visas as short-term and nonrenewable.

6. Mandate and enforce employer participation in E-Verify, a
    federal program that allows employers to check Social Security
    cards online against a national database with 96 percent
    accuracy.[68] Stolen identifications reduce the accuracy rate.

7. Reinstate the Social Security no-match regulation.

8. Punish employers of illegal aliens with stiff fines and jail
    sentences for repeat offenders.

9. Return the family reunification definitions to the pre-1965
    categories of spouse, children, and parents.

10. Clarify when birthright citizenship should apply.[69] The
    "subject to the jurisdiction thereof" clause of the Fourteenth
    Amendment is a potential avenue for closing the "birth tourism"
    loophole.

11. Make it a felony triggering automatic deportation to present fake
    identification and Social Security cards.

12. Offer financial subsidies for any illegal aliens who want to leave
    voluntarily. Mass deportation and mass legalization are not the
    only choices we have.

13. Provide assistance for any illegal alien who would like to relocate
    to a willing third-party country.

14. Modify the proposed Development, Relief, and Education for
    Alien Minors Act (DREAM Act), which would allow foreign-
    born graduates of an American high school to gain permanent
    residency if they attend college or serve in the military for
    two years. The present choice is elitist. Attending college is
    not comparable to serving in the military. Instead, include all
    foreign-born youth (twenty-four and under) without criminal
    records who have lived in the country for more than ten years,
    regardless of their willingness to serve in the military or their
    ability to gain college admission. This would also end potential
    discrimination against young people with limited skills and
    against conscientious objectors.

15. Give border states the latitude to develop laws and procedures

that enable them to protect their citizens by helping the federal government enforce immigration laws.

THE RULE OF LAW

Any Christian approach to immigration reform must respect the rule of law. The idea that nations need predictable and enforceable rules and regulations that apply equally to all individuals is fundamental to the rule of law. It is the rule of law that separates civilized countries from uncivilized ones. In *The Leviathan*, seventeenth-century philosopher Thomas Hobbes warns that life without law is necessarily "solitary, poor, nasty, brutish, and short."[70]

The rule of law separates trustworthy governments from abusive and terroristic regimes. This idea is ancient, dating back to Plato and the Old Testament. The Ten Commandments and the Levitical laws distinguished the Israelites from the pagan nations surrounding them. The Levitical laws included prohibitions against bestiality, homosexuality, and incest.

Any Christian approach to immigration reform must respect the rule of law.

Leviticus 18:1–23 outlines the laws, and verses 24–29 explain why God required that aliens be driven from the promised land:

> Do not make yourselves unclean by any of these things, for by all these the nations I am driving out before you have become unclean, and the land became unclean, so that I punished its iniquity, and the land vomited out its inhabitants. But you shall keep my statutes and my rules and do none of these abominations, either the native or the stranger who sojourns among you (for the people of the land, who were before you, did all of these abominations, so that the land became unclean),

lest the land vomit you out when you make it unclean, as it vomited
out the nation that was before you. For everyone who does any of these
abominations, the persons who do them shall be cut off from among
their people.

When the Israelites repeatedly broke their own covenant laws, terrible
but predictable consequences ensued. Judges 21:25 speaks of rampant
lawlessness after the deaths of Moses and Joshua. "In those days there
was no king in Israel. Everyone did what was right in his own eyes," with
consequent national decline.

In the United States, the Constitution forms the foundation for the
rule of law. Our Founding Fathers established a government in which
all governing officials—including the president, members of Congress,
Supreme Court justices, military officials, and political appointees—are
subject to the law, which they affirm by taking a standard oath before
they can assume office. No one is above the law. America's sovereignty
and its standing in the world suffer damage when its leaders fail to abide
by constitutional principles and values that have guided previous generations and that they have bound themselves to follow. Failure to enforce
our laws and statutes undermines their authority and the constitutional
protections that we expect to frame our interactions with fellow citizens
and others throughout the world. And illegal aliens who have entered
our country without our consent have broken our laws and diminished
respect for the rule of law.

Jurisprudence scholar and political theorist Brian Tamanaha has
observed that the rule of law has suffered a "marked deterioration" in
the West even as it takes root in other parts of the world. Activist judges,
lawyers, and other liberal elites have been catalysts of this deterioration.[71]
In particular, disregard for the rule of law, often associated with states
committed to the expansion of the welfare state, has resulted in situations
where judicial activism has allowed judges, lawyers, and other elites to
impose their own will upon the people.[72] This approach drives the thinking behind the contemporary lack of immigration enforcement.

Tamanaha describes circumstances much like those we have witnessed in the United States: judicial activism resulted in legalized abortion, as well as halting prayer and Bible reading in public schools, and now seeks to institute gay marriages. The American people are increasingly at the mercy of nonelected officials who have the power to impose their ideological agendas on the people under the guise of operating under the rule of law. However, the rule of law is often perverted. Other nations—for example, Mexico—have not cooperated with our efforts to enforce laws against illegal migration. In fact, Mexico's government encourages its citizens to break our laws. In 2005, many Americans grew angry when the Mexican government issued a manual on how to cross the desert and enter the United States safely.[73]

THE UNITED STATES MILITARY: THE ABANDONMENT OF COMMON SENSE

Our military leaders no longer exercise common sense when it comes to military recruitment. Leo Shane, a reporter for Military.com, cites Department of Defense statistics of seventy thousand foreign-born troops in the US military. This number includes legal permanent residents, as well as illegal immigrants who hope to receive expedited citizenship.[74] The US military, in its desperation to fill quotas in its all-volunteer ranks, has enlisted tens of thousands of foreign-born troops, some of whom are illegal immigrants promised an expedited citizenship for their service. Deborah Davis, a reporter for *In These Times*, alleges that recruiters have falsely told Latino recruits that the military service would grant legal status for their entire family, which is a blatant lie.[75] In 2006, an estimated 69,300 were foreign-born immigrants from different nations.[76] While their willingness to die for our country is admirable, their desperation to achieve citizenship makes exploitation a possibility worth considering.

When the US abandoned a national draft, it made the recruitment of foreign-born soldiers a necessity. Offering expedited citizenship to illegal aliens who serve in the military places them in the unique situation of having to risk their lives for a nation other than their own. This arrangement strikes me as morally wrong and fraught with risks.

In December 2009, five Muslim soldiers were arrested at Fort Jackson for their part in a plot to use food to poison troops at the base.[77] The soldiers were part of the Arabic translation-training program.[78] In light of America's war on terrorism, many US citizens find it stunning that the military enlists anyone who is not a permanent resident of the United States. But because we have abandoned the draft that ensures Americans from all socioeconomic backgrounds serve our country, we are now a nation desperate for recruits to serve to defend us.

RADICAL ISLAM AND AMERICA

In 2007, the Pew Research Center released a report that showed nearly half (47 percent) of American Muslims self-identified as Muslims rather than Americans. Youths were found to have "pockets of sympathy for Islamic extremism" and "a much-higher-than-average expression of support for suicide bombing." Fifteen percent of the Muslims under thirty years of age said that suicide bombing could be justified "often" or "sometimes," as compared to "less than five percent among Muslims over thirty years of age."[79] The FBI has estimated that at least 10 percent of the more than two thousand mosques in America have links to radical terrorist groups.[80]

We do not know how many Americans have been radicalized by radical imams and al Qaeda operatives in the United States.[81] Several, including Nidal Hasan and Abdulhakim Muhammad, enlisted in the US military and then attacked, murdered, and maimed fellow soldiers. Hasan, an army psychiatrist, killed thirteen people in a shooting spree at Fort Hood military base in Texas.[82] Abdulhakim Muhammad, who shot two soldiers and killed one at the Arkansas Recruiting Center in 2009, was an African-American Muslim convert who changed his name from Carlos Bledsoe. He was reportedly upset about the wars in Iraq and Afghanistan and the killings of Muslims.[83] In 2003, Hasan Akbar, a black sergeant who converted to Islam, used a grenade to kill two fellow officers in Iraq.[84]

It is foolish for the US military to place Muslim recruits in situations where they must engage in actions condemned by their religion. In August 2010, Pfc. Naser Abdo, recognizing the inherent conflict of his faith and military expectations, filed for conscientious objector status rather than be deployed to Afghanistan.[85] The exchange is listed below, and the reply is now disabled. I cut and pasted the exchange in December 2009.

Abdo posted, "Are Muslims allowed to join an un-Islamic military such as that of the United States, where they may be put in a position to kill a fellow Muslim brother or sister? Also what is Allah's punishment for this if such thing happens? Because I hear some Muslim leaders say it is okay to join the US Military?"

Sheikh Faysal Mawlawi, vice chairman of the European Council for Fatwa and Research, replied, "No doubt that the American Muslim soldier is between the devil and the deep blue sea and he is facing a difficult situation . . . As a basic rule in Islam, a Muslim is not allowed to fight against his fellow Muslim brother. This is also a stated fact in the Shari`ah."[86]

Clearly the dictates of religion place enormous burdens on soldiers. Abdulhakim Muhammad told an Associated Press reporter that his attack on fellow soldiers at the Arkansas Recruiting Center was "an act, for the sake of God, for the sake of Allah, the Lord of the World, and also a retaliation against the US Military . . . US soldiers are killing innocent Muslim men and women. We believe in eye for eye. We don't believe in turning the other cheek."[87]

It is foolish for the US military to place Muslim recruits in situations where they must engage in actions condemned by their religion.

Information that has surfaced about Nidal Hasan, the Fort Hood psychiatrist who killed thirteen of his fellow soldiers and wounded others, indicates that he was motivated by Islamic extremism. Evidence about Hasan includes statements he allegedly made in justification of suicide bombings and in support of Muhammad's shooting at the recruitment center. Hasan reportedly yelled, "Allahu Akbar" (Arabic for "God is Great") before he began his rampage.[88]

In an October 2010 interview on ABC's *This Week*, British radical Muslim activist Anjem Choudary said, "We do believe, as Muslims, the East and the West will one day be governed by the Shariah . . . Indeed, we believe that one day, the flag of Islam will fly over the White House."[89] According to Princeton University's WordNet, *sharia* is "the code of law derived from the Koran and from the teachings and example of Mohammed; sharia is only applicable to Muslims; under Islamic law there is no separation of church and state."[90]

Prudence would suggest that the US military must carefully consider when and where it deploys Muslim soldiers and the subsequent level of risk for fellow soldiers. This type of reasoning, of course, involves a trade-off between the religious freedom rights of the soldiers and the needs of the military. Concerns regarding political correctness and fear of discrimination charges should not impede old-fashioned common sense when it comes to recruiting and deploying Muslim soldiers when we are at war with Muslim-dominated nations. Our nation must acknowledge the tenets of the Islamic religion that view us as infidels or else relinquish the upper hand to our proven enemies.

IMMORAL BEHAVIOR

The United States was founded as a nation based on godly principles and values, proud to stand above other nations of the world. Had it continued to pursue its vision and kept its covenant, America would have retained its elite status among nations—strong and independent, a model for the world to follow. But we have bowed to the United Nations, the International World Court, and more recently the International World Police; we have blurred the unique distinctions between nations and brought into our nation practices and behaviors detrimental not only to ourselves but also to the rest of the world. Instead of exporting positive values, we have exported permissiveness, materialism, and perversion. We demand that needy nations abandon their moral standards as conditions for receiving our financial support as foreign aid. In the end, America has lost its moral, ethical, and economic authority in the world—and with it, our status of blessing and advantage.

In recent years our nation has been shocked and embarrassed by the actions of US troops who have committed atrocities and tortured, murdered, and raped other human beings. The Old Testament makes clear the brutalities and horrors that are part of war. We might ask how soldiers from our predominantly Christian nation could commit the horrific acts that occurred at Abu Ghraib prison in Baghdad and Guantánamo Bay. The answer, I believe, lies in the ungodly model of leadership that has been patterned in our nation—for instance, the burning of Christian Bibles at the order of military officials,[91] the acceptance and accommodation of Wiccans in our military ranks,[92] and the passing of resolutions that ban American soldiers from witnessing to others about their Christian faith.[93] Under current military rules, American soldiers home on leave or stationed within the United States are prohibited from sharing their Christian testimony while wearing their military uniform. Clearly, we have strayed from the religious foundations of our nation and our belief in the providence of a God who watches over us. So-called secular progress in recent years is actually our nation's decline from grace, common sense, and wisdom.

America has lost our moral, ethical, and economic authority in the world—and with it, our status of blessing and advantage.

While Islamic extremists advocate violence as a solution to moral and political problems, Christian principles suggest a different approach, one that does not involve the subjection and destruction of other nations. The

Bible teaches that man's atrocities against man occur because of humanity's fallen condition. Jeremiah 17:9 reminds us, "The heart is deceitful above all things, and desperately sick; who can understand it?" Some translations refer to the heart as "desperately wicked." God's Word makes it clear that, when left to his own devices, man does not prove to be trustworthy or kind. First Corinthians 1:19–20 states, "It is written, 'I will destroy the wisdom of the wise, and the discernment of the discerning I will thwart.' Where is the one who is wise? Where is the scribe? Where is the debater of this age? Has not God made foolish the wisdom of the world?"

Today we are seeing foolishness from men and women who think themselves wise—leaders in American government, including the Congress, White House, and Supreme Court—as America becomes a shell of its former self. We are walking in the footsteps of the ancient Israelites, who rejected God and demanded kings like those of surrounding nations. God gave them their wish, and with the granting of their wish came great suffering.

NATIONAL SOVEREIGNTY AND BORDERS

What does it mean to be a "sovereign nation"? Matthew Spalding writes that to "claim a separate and equal status among nations is to make a claim of 'sovereignty' in the context of international law. A nation is sovereign if it is independent of rule by other nations."[94] It does not mean that the nations have to be of equal size, rank, or wealth. Nations must be separate and equal with borders intact before they are truly a sovereign nation.[95] Ambassador John R. Bolton has argued that President Barack Obama's worldview threatens and endangers the national sovereignty of the United States because of his willingness to subjugate American interests.[96] Globalists reject the fact that every nation is formed by unique geographic boundaries within which particular cultural and religious traditions exist, and from which the resulting rules of law prevail.

Immigrants who make demands on Americans to make accommodations for the cultural practices of nations left behind are failing to respect our culture, and by doing so they disregard our laws and customs. Israeli public transportation does not run on the Sabbath, regardless of the requests of nonnatives. Most Muslim nations request, if not require, that women dress modestly. In America, however, immigrants and refugees who have been given a new life apart from the world's most horrible living conditions file lawsuits against the nation that harbors them and demand that America accommodate their customs.

E PLURIBUS UNUM: "OUT OF MANY, ONE"

At the birth of our nation in 1776, *E pluribus unum*, Latin for "out of many, one," became America's official motto. Today it remains a part of the official seal of the United States. *E pluribus unum* embodies the view of America as a melting pot, a nation where people of diverse nationalities shed their old identities and loyalties to forge a new nation, irrespective of bloodlines. The melting pot has stood as a metaphor for American immigration, symbolizing individuals from different parts of the world blending to become a new nation of Americans. But *E pluribus unum* has never become a reality. America has never come close to achieving a melting pot. Arthur Schlesinger Jr., former Harvard University professor and adviser to President John Kennedy, lamented the fact that we abandoned a "brilliant strategy for [addressing] the inherent fragility of multiethnic society."[97] We, instead, embraced political correctness and multiculturalism.

Multiculturalism gave birth to political correctness. Multiculturalism is an educational movement that attempts to facilitate an appreciation for diverse cultures and lifestyles. It teaches that "all cultures should be empowered to preserve, unchanged, their unique cultural reality. Any effort to change or reform a cultural group is actually repression, domination, and colonizing of one group by another."[98] Multiculturalism teaches that superior cultures do not exist. The concept was borrowed from the

Canadians, and American colleges and universities have embraced it with a religious fervor. Political correctness allows "cultural enforcers" to push for conformity in the manner in which we evaluate culture, prescribing what we can and cannot say and think about history, truth, values, and society. Political correctness has blurred distinctions between illegal aliens and legal immigrants, as cultural elites insist that the former be addressed as "unauthorized migrant" or "undocumented person," because to do otherwise is to dehumanize the immigrant.

WHERE DOES THIS LEAVE US?

E pluribus unum is dead. The concept died because America abandoned the noble quest of instilling in our young people a respect for the rule of law, civic principles, and love of flag and country. We no longer know or honor our country's unique heritage. America is a nation peopled with competing clusters of peoples with different values, cultures, and languages. Our citizens are no longer encouraged to become American. Instead, our nation exists as a polyglot of different peoples with different interests and competing stories of victimization as groups struggle against one another for rights and privileges. In the process, we have lost the idea of the one America. It behooves us to return to the commonsense wisdom of Theodore Roosevelt quoted in the opening of this chapter: "We should insist that if the immigrant who comes here in good faith becomes an American and assimilates himself to us . . . There can be no divided allegiance here."[99]

ACTION POINTS

1. Report businesses and contractors suspected of
    hiring illegal aliens to ICE, which is a division of
    the Department of Homeland Security. The new
    toll-free number to call to report employers who are
    knowingly hiring illegal aliens is: 1-866-DHS-2-ICE
    (866-347-2423).

2. Encourage state and local businesses to participate
    in DHS's E-Verify Program, a free service that allows
    employers to check the employment eligibility of
    workers. Employers can call 888-464-4218,
    877-875-6028 (TTY), or e-mail for more information:
    E-Verify@dhs.gov.

3. Write letters to the newspapers and phone state and
    federal legislators to tell them you believe they should
    honor the rule of law by enforcing state and federal
    immigration laws.

4. Read and discuss the *Be the People* questions for chapter 5,
    posted at www.CarolMSwain.com.

CHAPTER 6

MOVING BEYOND RACE AND RACISM

The point is not that we have racial problems in America, but how much progress
we have made in the last 50 years. I remember segregation. My children went to
segregated schools, but we have made remarkable progress. Sure there are problems
and always will be, but that is the genius of this country. We slowly work them out.

—JOHN R. TURBYFILL, FORMER NORFOLK SOUTHERN CORPORATION
VICE CHAIRMAN[1]

I attended the Glenn Beck Rally in DC, traveling with a friend from East Tennessee,
Ron Harwell, who happens to be black. . . . As I traveled with Mr. Harwell to
Washington, I watched proudly as others stopped him and wanted to interview him
on video, asking him why he was there. I felt like I was with a celebrity, and I was
proud to say I was with him. He's a war veteran, a brother-in-Christ, and a believer
in our founders' principles. We share the same values. I didn't mind one bit blending
into the background.

—MATT MOYNIHAN, COFOUNDER OF THE
SUMNER COUNTY, TENNESSEE, TEA PARTY[2]

AMERICA HAS MADE TREMENDOUS STRIDES IN RACE RELATIONS OVER THE
past decades. John Turbyfill expresses the pride all Americans should
feel in the enormous progress we have made in race relations since
the passage of the 1964 Civil Rights Act and the end of government-
sanctioned segregation in public schools. Blacks and Hispanics now
share power with whites in both the public and private sector. We have
had a black president, Barack Obama; two black secretaries of state,

Colin Powell and Condoleezza Rice; and a black attorney general, Eric Holder. We have also witnessed the election of numerous black politicians from majority white constituencies. Since 1977, blacks have served in seventeen cabinet-level positions. The United States has more black millionaires than ever before, and Oprah Winfrey and Black Entertainment Television founder Bob Johnson have both cracked the ranks of billionaires. Another indicator of positive change is a tripling in the most resistant form of interracial marriage; marriages between blacks and whites have tripled since 2000.[3]

Nevertheless, racial problems remain that we would be foolish to ignore. Unfortunately, we have a tendency to mischaracterize some forms of human behavior as racist, even when more factors lie behind the behaviors we observe. Nowhere is this more apparent than in the media's efforts to characterize the 2009 Tea Party movement as being racist in its origins.

MATTHEW MOYNIHAN AND THE INTEGRATED SUMNER COUNTY, TENNESSEE, TEA PARTY

In chapter 4 I introduced Quigley Moynihan, a faithful husband and father of three whom I met in December 2009. Matt Moynihan is the more conservative of Quigley and Brenda's firstborn twins. He is a Vanderbilt University graduate who double-majored in communications and psychology and now works as a communications manager for a technology company, as well as being a small business owner. He is also the cofounder of the largest Tea Party in Tennessee, and he writes a conservative column for a local newspaper.

Matt and a friend started the Sumner County Tea Party on February 19, 2009, eight days after CNBC financial reporter Rick Santelli went on his now-famous tirade about our nation's founding, relating how America was birthed as a tax revolt against the 1765 Stamp Act. Santelli reminded viewers that with great intentionality and regard for the weaknesses of the human heart, the framers of the Constitution created a governmental structure with limited and enumerated powers, a system of checks and balances, with power divided between levels of government. This governmental structure would prevent tyranny in a system where the propertyless majority might be tempted or persuaded to redistribute wealth by unfairly taxing wealthier citizens. Eight days after Santelli's tirade, Matt Moynihan, who had never been involved in politics, took his place on the steps of the legislative plaza in Nashville alongside three hundred other American citizens who were protesting Barack Obama's attempts to reshape their country. Concerns about the Constitution, family values, and fiscal responsibility motivated their actions. Matt embraces the Tea Party themes of God, country, and family.

Matt Moynihan bristles at the charge of racism that the NAACP and other organizations have hurled at the Tea Party movement. He points to his longstanding brotherly friendship with black veteran Ron Harwell and their shared Christian values, the invitation he extended for me to headline his tax-day rally, as well as what his eyes have seen within the Tea Party movement.

Matt explains, "I've been a founding member of the Tea Party movement and have not seen one incident of racism. In fact, it's often you see people of color take the stage at Tea Party events, clearly even more diverse than the crowds they speak in front of . . . Tea Partiers, indeed, look for shared values, not racial quotas. If someone shares our values and can articulate our beliefs in the role government should play in our lives, then color is completely irrelevant." He continues, "Unfortunately, over the past forty years, despite filibustering [a legislative tactic to kill a bill] civil rights legislation in the 60s, the Democratic Party has co-opted a demographic by promising to care for the African-American community. The African Americans I know never asked for a handout, but unfortunately, too many have grown dependent on government subsidy, which seems to have perpetuated a generational expectation of taxpayer provision. This results in a lack of self-reliance, and worse, self-confidence in their ability to provide for themselves."

When asked what he wanted for the nation, Matt responded, "Restore the country back to family values, moral principles, and self-respect for all individuals. Government shouldn't dictate our way of life. We should live by God's will; that's what made America benevolent. We shouldn't have to give the fruits of our labor over to the government. I can make my own decisions about causes like helping underprivileged children. Everybody has their passion to serve and to give as God calls them."[4]

In November 2010, largely as the result of national Tea Party support, Republicans elected a record number of racial and ethnic minorities across the nation. Officials voted in include Nikki Haley, South Carolina's first female governor and first Indian-American governor; Susanna Martinez of New Mexico, who became the nation's first female Hispanic governor; and Brian Sandoval, Nevada's first Hispanic governor. Other victories included black congressmen Allen West of Florida and Tim Scott of South Carolina, the first blacks in their states to serve since Reconstruction, and Marco Rubio, the son of Cuban exiles.[5]

Propelled to victory on the strength of Tea Party votes, Rubio on election night echoed Moynihan's concerns about the direction of the country. Rubio said that our nation is following the wrong path and he accused politicians of both parties of ignoring the voters who sent them to Washington as their representatives. Americans, he argued, have been struggling to make a better future for their children and grandchildren. For Rubio, changing the Washington culture was about making America a better place for generations of Americans. Therefore, he was quick to point out that the election was about more than his place in history.[6]

Although accusations of racism are regularly hurled against politicians and activists, the evidence of the 2008 election of President Barack Obama and the rise of black Republicans across the country offer the possibility that our nation is finally transcending the constraints of historical racism. However, in spite of recent gains, racially rooted problems persist.

THERE IS ONLY ONE RACE: THE HUMAN RACE

Racism encompasses the belief that some groups of humans are genetically inferior to others. Man devised this belief system, and it is deeply rooted in the heart of humanity. Racism emerged in the nineteenth century with eugenicists helping to advance the idea. Among the eugenicists of the era were Planned Parenthood founder Margaret Sanger, who wrote *The Pivot of Civilization*;[7] Madison Grant, a lawyer, historian, and anthropologist, who wrote *The Passing of the Great Race: Or, the Racial Basis of European History*;[8] and Lothrop Stoddard, who wrote *The Rising Tide of Color Against White World*.[9] The authors introduced the world to the idea of compulsory sterilization and other ideologies that have brought decades of racial devastation to ethnic and politically powerless groups, like the mentally retarded. Stoddard's work played a role in the shaping and passage of the Immigration Act of 1924,[10] which established the nation-of-origin quotas limiting the number of immigrants who could enter the United States from certain countries.

Hard-core racists argue for the existence of at least three races: Asians, blacks, and Caucasians, as well as a hierarchy of intelligence within the races; however, scientific evidence supports the existence of one human race. Scientists studying genetics and mitochondrial DNA have proven that all human beings descend from a common human ancestor who lived in Africa. That ancestor's offspring are responsible for the world's diversity.[11] Evidence from the Human Genome Project supports the one-race, common-ancestor theory. Scientific mappings have demonstrated that all human beings share 99.9 percent of the same DNA.[12] All races of human men and women can mate with each other and invent nonverbal ways of communicating, even when language barriers exist.

Viktor Frankl, the concentration camp survivor who wrote *Man's Search for Meaning*, survived his ordeal and from his experience shared his observations about the nature of mankind and about race: "There are two races of men in the world, but only these two—the 'race' of the decent man and the 'race' of the indecent man. Both are found everywhere; they penetrate into all groups of society. No group consists entirely of decent and indecent people. In this sense, no group is a 'pure race.'"[13]

What significance do Frankl's words hold for us? Racism came from man, not God. It attests to the sinful heart of man. When we look at the vast variety of the human species, we find that our Creator God designed unique men and women with different shapes, colors, talents, and ability groupings. In spite of God's vast diversity in creation, however, people congregate based upon their similarities. This natural inclination produces problems in society when one group possesses superior resources to other groups and uses those resources as a means of suppression. Throughout history, humanity has used skin color to create rankings of racial superiority, with lighter-skinned people typically designated as superior to those with darker skin. Discrimination based on skin color has been a hallmark of history.

Scientific mappings have demonstrated that all human beings share 99.9 percent of the same DNA.

Matt Moynihan's affection for his friend Ron Harwell reflects a glorious truth about the body of Christ. The love of Christ transcends skin color and runs counter to our human tendency to show preference for members of our own ethnic groups—people who typically reflect similar self-interests and reinforce a sense of security.

Both the Old and New Testaments promote the idea of a common Creator and a brotherhood of man that is inconsistent with notions of racial superiority, competition, suppression, prejudice, and hatred. Genesis 1:27, for instance, provides an account of creation in which all humans are depicted as descending from a single human ancestor, Adam (Hebrew for "man"), who is created "in the image of God." Similarly, in Acts 17:26 (NKJV), the apostle Paul declared the peoples of all nations to be of "one blood."

The Exodus story of the Israelites' four-hundred-year bondage and redemption offered powerful hope to enslaved blacks in America and fueled their agitation for freedom from their ungodly masters. Exodus 21:16 offers further evidence for the rightness of the slaves' moral position. The passage states, "He that stealeth a man, and selleth him, or if he be found in his hand, he shall surely be put to death" (KJV).

The love of Christ transcends skin color and runs counter to our human tendency to show preference for members of our own ethnic groups.

Slaves also rejected the interpretation of Ham and of Joshua's curse of the Gibeonites that some white slave owners used as a supposedly scriptural basis for black enslavement. Bible-believing Christians who contend that African Americans are the cursed descendants of Ham must confront what the Bible has to say about the cleansing power of the blood of Jesus and the new covenant redemption. African Americans have repeatedly cited Galatians 3:28: "There is neither Jew nor Greek, there is neither slave nor free, there is no male and female, for you are all one in Christ Jesus" and similar passages in the letters of the apostle Paul that stress the universal redemptive power of Christ's mission and message.

Although segregated churches and segregated worship are still the norm in much of America, non–racially linked reasons exist for segregated churches. These reasons include differing tastes in music, styles of response during services, and expectations about lengths of services. Just as whites and blacks sometimes behave differently in movie theaters—with blacks sometimes engaging in a dialogue with the action on the screen—similar cultural differences often carry over into worship styles. While Christian principles about a universal humanity and the brotherhood of man have inspired reform movements of great benefit to mankind, Christians have historically responded to these principles more in their breach than in their observance. Unfortunately, Christianity's checkered history concerning racial issues gives atheists and secular humanists much fodder for ridiculing America's majority religion.

NEGLECTING AND PERVERTING
THE BIBLICAL MESSAGE

Scientific data and biblical data stand in agreement that humanity descended from one race. However, during the period of American slavery, scriptures detailing curses against the sons of Ham and the Gibeonites provided inspiration for racist groups who sought religious justification for their position. According to Genesis 9:22–27, Noah's son Ham was cursed because of an implied sexual transgression committed against his father while Noah was in a drunken state. Genesis 9:24–25 states, "Noah awoke from his wine, and knew what his younger son had done to him. Then he said: 'Cursed be Canaan [Ham's son]; a servant of servants he shall be to his brethren'" (NKJV). In a similar passage, Joshua cursed the Gibeonites as their punishment for tricking the Israelites into sparing their lives. Joshua 9:22–23 states, "Then Joshua called for them, and he spoke to them, saying, 'Why have you deceived us, saying, "We are very far from you," when you dwell near us? Now therefore, you are cursed, and none of you shall be freed from being slaves—woodcutters and water carriers for the house of my God'" (NKJV).

In the ultimate representation of perversion, the Ku Klux Klan appropriated the salvation symbol of the cross for its own racist purposes. Crosses have been lit in ceremonies where Klan members sing beloved Christian hymns like "Amazing Grace," "The Old Rugged Cross," and "Onward Christian Soldiers." Yet another racist movement called Christian Identity distorts Scripture by teaching that Caucasians are God's "chosen people" and that Anglo-Saxons are "true Israelites." Of course, Scripture taken out of context can be used to support almost any theology.[14]

As part of their defense of slavery and the subordination of blacks, Christian racists have cited Colossians 4:1: "Masters, give unto your servants that which is just and equal; knowing that ye also have a Master in heaven" (KJV). They also reference Ephesians 6:5, a passage that urges servants to "be obedient to them that are your masters according to the flesh" (KJV). Racists never explain that slavery as practiced in the ancient world was not based on race (slaves could be of any race) and that the New Testament proclaimed a religion that transcended racial categories.

To this date in history a world that transcends racial and ethnic categories has not emerged, and until the return of Christ, we will never see the eradication of racial barriers and tensions. To the contrary, nationalism and racism are rearing their ugly heads at unprecedented levels worldwide, and we know from the histories of other multiracial, multiethnic societies the horrors that can occur when men are given free rein to sow the seeds of racism in the hearts of mankind. In *The Disuniting of America*, Arthur Schlesinger Jr. writes, "Within nation-states, nationalism takes the form of ethnicity or tribalism. In country after country across the third world—India, Burma, Sri Lanka, Indonesia, Iraq, Ethiopia, Nigeria, Angola, Trinidad, Guyana—ethnic groups struggle for power and, in desperate cases, for survival. The ethnic upsurge in America, far from being unique, partakes of the global fever." He argues, "The cult of ethnicity exaggerates differences, intensifies resentments and antagonisms, and drives awful wedges between races and nationalities."[15]

We cannot and should not assume that racial and ethnic harmony in America is a goal easily within our grasp. A move toward secularism holds great risk for our goals of racial and ethnic harmony. As our nation systematically removes God from our national conscience, we will reap the consequences as humanity works out their worst impulses against other human beings. Racism's insidious root lies in the denial of the sanctity of human life; as we dehumanize one another, we become capable of depriving those we deem less than ourselves not only of liberty, but of life itself.

RACE AND THE FEAR FACTOR[16]

The nationalistic impulses of blacks, whites, and Hispanics threaten race relations by causing leaders to pursue racial-group interests rather than strategies that focus on the well-being of the nation as a whole. Among whites, well-developed literature feeds hatred and animosity toward minorities. *The Communist Manifesto*,[17] *Mein Kampf*,[18] and *The Sayings of Chairman Mao*[19] are well-known examples of movement-inspiring literature. Among the more radical white nationalist, white supremacist, and neo-Nazi groups in America, certain books have played a parallel role, the most important of these being William Pierce's futuristic racial apocalypse, *The Turner Diaries*.[20] The FBI has called this book the "Bible of the racist right."[21] Many Americans first knew of *The Turner Diaries* when it was revealed that Timothy McVeigh, the Oklahoma City bomber, may have been partially inspired to carry out his murderous deed after reading this work.[22]

Pierce, a former university physics professor and founder of the influential white supremacist group the National Alliance, published *The Turner Diaries* under the pseudonym Andrew Macdonald in the late 1970s. (Pierce is now deceased.) The novel describes in graphic detail a race war in which white patriots in California (collectively known as the Organization) launch a successful attack against the Zionist Occupied Government (ZOG) in Washington for its crimes against white Americans. Members of the Organization assassinate federal officials, law enforcement personnel, and politicians. They slaughter Jews, non-white minorities, and race traitors and then launch a nuclear attack upon the state of Israel with the nuclear arsenal assembled by ZOG. The book's conclusion offers Pierce's view of the necessity of violence. "There is no way to win the struggle in which we [whites] are engaged without shedding torrents—veritable rivers—of blood."[23]

Despite the brutal violence, an unknown number of whites who have read *The Turner Diaries* seem to be attracted to its vision of an all-white America purged of racial minorities and Jews. Journalist Susan Eastman interviewed one such reader, a white woman, captivated by the book's vision of a homogeneous white community. This woman said, "I remembered reading in the *Turner Diaries* at the end where the white people were finally separate. I imagined that this celebration was for that. It seemed so fitting, it looked like the America we long for. I hope one day we can live like that, friendly white people, no one afraid of anything, it was an atmosphere hard for me to describe."[24]

As I noted in *New White Nationalism in America*, "Eastman was amazed—and appalled—that a seemingly ordinary woman could be so attracted to a novel that condones mass violence to achieve its vision of an ethnically purified America."[25] Eastman writes:

> The "regular white woman" glosses over the descriptions in the book . . . of the blood revolution where Jews are dispatched on death marches at the rate of a million a day, [and] African Americans and Jews are marched out of captured white enclaves. To get to the all-white world that "a regular woman" finds so appealing, white separatists bomb buildings, disrupt power to cities, and wind up hanging 55,000 to 60,000 white people from lampposts, power poles, and trees all over Los Angeles on a day called the "Day of the Rope."[26]

Minister Louis Farrakhan's Nation of Islam and the New Black Panther Party have produced Black Nationalist speakers who preach racial hatred of white people. In 1993, Khalid Abdul Muhammad gave an infamous Kean University speech in which he lambasted Jews and spoke of killing white South Africans who refused to leave the country: "We kill the women. We kill the babies. We kill the blind. We kill the cripples. We kill them all . . . When you get through killing them all, go to the graveyard and kill them again because they didn't die hard enough."[27]

The Nation of Islam suspended Muhammad for his speech. However, Malik Zulu Shabazz, a member of the New Black Panther Party, echoed Khalid Muhammad's theme of killing white people in 2010. Glenn Beck played the video of Shabazz spewing racist expletives and venom: "I hate white people, all of them. Every last iota of a [white man], I hate him. . . . You want freedom? You are going to have to kill some [whites]. You are going to have to kill some of their babies."[28]

Political scientists Darren Davis and Ronald E. Brown report that black nationalism "stresses the importance of a connection to African origins and identity, pride in being black, a desire for blacks to control their own communities, and sometimes a desire to establish a black nation in Africa or some part of the United States.[29] On the other hand, the Nation of Islam, under Minister Louis Farrakhan, has set itself apart as an "intolerant, racial separatist, patriarchal [organization], promoting black self-sufficiency and anti-Semitics."[30]

Latinos jumped onto the racist bandwagon as well and formed their own hate organizations. The most prominent of these is MEChA, which stands for Movimiento Estudiantil Chicano de Aztlan. The preamble to MEChA's constitution states that "Chicano and Chicana students of Aztlan must take upon themselves the responsibilities to promote Chicanismo within the community, politicizing our Raza with an emphasis on indigenous consciousness to continue the struggle for the self-determination of the Chicano people for the purpose of liberating Aztlan."

In May 2007, authorities in California arrested members of Latino gangs and charged them with engaging in a "violent campaign to drive blacks out of the unincorporated Florence-Firestone neighborhood that allegedly resulted in 20 homicides over several years."[31] Rutgers University professor Tanya Hernandez has written that "murder was a manifestation of an increasing common trend: instances of Latino aggression toward African Americans in multiracial neighborhoods."[32] Hernandez points out that "racism and anti-Black racism in particular is a pervasive and historically entrenched reality of life in Latin America and the Caribbean . . . The legacy of the slave period in Latin America and the Caribbean is similar to that of the United States. Lighter skin and European features increases one's chances of socioeconomic opportunity, while darker skin and African features severely limit mobility."[33]

Nicolas Vaca, author of *The Presumed Alliance: The Unspoken Conflict Between Latinos and Blacks and What It Means for America*, has observed that in "the 1960s, relations between Blacks and Latinos were viewed through rose-colored glasses. It was the 'brothers under the skin,' 'a house divided will fall,' Latinos and Blacks united against the 'white oppressor' that swept differences under the rug."[34] Blacks and Latinos now fight over affirmative action, housing, jobs, and political power. According to Vaca, the emotions behind the shared discrimination in the early days blinded minority leaders to "the frictions that existed or could exist in the future between coalesced minorities."[35]

No racial group can claim a monopoly on decency. Fear is the catalyst that pushes ordinary citizens to embrace extremist causes where they believe they can reshape society.[36] As I explain in my 2002 book, *The New White Nationalism in America: Its Challenge to Integration*, "A combination of factors can drive seemingly ordinary and reasonable people toward extremism. One such factor is fear for personal safety and security. If people believe their life or property is genuinely threatened, they may seek to eliminate that threat as expeditiously as possible. White racial leaders prey upon this fear in whites by focusing on crime statistics that paint African Americans as criminals."[37]

No racial group can claim a monopoly on decency.

But fear, however, does not necessarily motivate people toward extremism; fear can also motivate people toward acts of courage. These acts can include the courage to debate unpopular issues, the courage to tell the truth and stand up to extremist views, and the courage to search for responsible answers to complex issues all Americans face. Far too many political leaders and policymakers lack the courage to confront the legitimate issues racial demagogues exploit because of the context of silence among mainstream politicians.

WHY AFFIRMATIVE ACTION IS DUE
FOR A MAKEOVER

Many people express grievances over affirmative action programs. Affirmative action refers to public and private initiatives that offer preferential treatment to members of officially designated racial or ethnic minority groups (or to other groups thought to be disadvantaged), usually to compensate them for the effects of past and present discrimination or in some cases to enhance institutional and corporate diversity.[38] Covered groups include Asians, blacks, Hispanics, Native Americans, women, the disabled, and in some cases gays and lesbians. Covered areas include hiring, promotions, admissions to colleges and universities, disbursement of scholarships and grants, government contracting, and electoral redistricting. Some forms of affirmative action are acceptable to the American public—for example, policies designed to create opportunities for disadvantaged Americans on a race neutral basis. Other forms such as racial "plus-factoring," race-norming, and numerical quotas are opposed.

Legally minded critics of the policy often point to what they see as the incompatibility of racial preferences with both the letter and spirit of the 1964 Civil Rights Act, as well as with the equal protection clause of the Fourteenth Amendment to the United States Constitution. The clear wording of these documents would seem to support their claim. "No state," the Fourteenth Amendment declares, "shall make or enforce any law which shall abridge the privileges or immunities of citizens of the United States; nor shall any State deprive any person of life, liberty, or property, without due process of law; nor deny any person within its jurisdiction the equal protection of the laws."[39]

The 1964 Civil Rights Act is even more explicit:

No Person in the United States shall, on the ground of race, color, national origin, be excluded from participation in, be denied the benefits of, or be subjected to discrimination under any program receiving Federal financial assistance.[40] . . .

    (a)   It shall be an unlawful employment practice for an employer

          (1)   to fail or refuse to hire or to discharge any individual, or otherwise to discriminate against any individual with respect to his compensation, terms,

conditions, or privileges of employment because of
such individual's race, color, religion, sex, or national
origin; or

(2) to limit, segregate, or classify his employees in any
way which would deprive any individual of employment opportunities or otherwise adversely affect his
status as an employee, because of such individual's
race, color, religion, sex, or national origin.[41]

The language of both the constitutional amendment and the statutory provisions of the Civil Rights Act seem at odds with a policy of
preference for any group, since the rights discussed are framed as the
protected rights of all *individuals*. Over the years, a series of Supreme
Court decisions and ballot initiatives have chipped away at the policy of racial preferences, but affirmative action remains a major force
in American society, and it enjoys widespread support among many
of America's social, economic, and political elites, including college
and university presidents, business leaders, television and print media
moguls, and leading politicians.[42]

Ordinary Americans not well versed enough to understand perceived
contradictions between public policy directives and the language of civil
rights laws react from a gut feeling that it is wrong to advantage or disadvantage anyone because of an immutable characteristic such as race
or sex.

Michael Kinsley, a liberal journalist, has written that the actual harm
done to nonminorities by affirmative action is small, yet the policy causes
great anxiety among whites who fear that they may become its victims.
The policy of affirmative action, Kinsley says, "has become a scapegoat
for the anxieties of the white middle class. Some of those anxieties are justified; some are self-indulgent fantasies. But the actual role of affirmative
action in denying opportunities to white people is small compared with
its role in the public imagination and public debate."[43]

Race-based affirmative action at educational institutions is here to stay for the immediate future. Writing for the Supreme Court's majority in the 2003 *Grutter v. Bollinger* case,[44] Justice Sandra Day O'Connor stated that the Constitution does not prevent the "narrowly tailored" use of race in university admissions decisions if the goal of the institution is to obtain a "critical mass" of minority students. A law fails the narrowly tailored test, if the government could have found another means of reaching the goal that would not impinge on a constitutional right.[45] Justice O'Connor concluded that in perhaps twenty-five years, affirmative action would no longer be necessary to guarantee racial and ethnic diversity.

Addressing affirmative action in order to reduce racial tensions is a pressing concern. If current demographic shifts continue at present rates, non-Hispanic whites will be a minority of the population by 2045. As the country becomes more and more racially diverse, and the white majority faces minority status, it becomes harder to justify a policy of racial prefer- ence. As I wrote in 2002, "Whatever benefits affirmative action may have conferred in the past—and it can be argued that they are sizeable—it now seems undeniable that on balance, current policies of racial prefer- ence are a negative force in American society, and that they threaten to undermine public support for those principles of racial integration and racial justice that so inspired the nation during the Civil Rights Era of the 1950s and 1960s."[46]

OVERCOMING THE LIES WE TELL OURSELVES

American blacks look to a handful of nationally prominent black leaders to advance their cause; yet their trusted leaders often deceive and manipulate them regarding their best interests. Elitist black leaders encourage black Americans to view themselves as victims at the mercy of the political sys- tem rather than as resilient people who have overcome enormous odds and have made tremendous individual and collective strides. By misdirecting the focus to white people as the source of racial problems, as well as by failed remedies (welfare, race-based affirmative action, and government programs), many blacks miss the tremendous power they have to chart their own courses by starting businesses and creating jobs for themselves and their children. Entrepreneurship empowers minorities and helps lead the way to greater wealth. Not all business investments require millions of dollars, but instead, the investment of ideas and the willingness to work hard to carry out one's vision. True empowerment often comes from individual effort that can help place someone at the right place at the right time.

Unfortunately, too many black leaders have perfected the art of complaining—issuing demands and whining about white racism while they themselves openly express virulent racism against members of other groups. As journalist David Shipler writes:

African Americans do not hear themselves parroting age-old slanders against Jews and others. They do not hear themselves echoing the pernicious logic, under which they themselves have suffered, that projects one individual's faults onto an entire group. Negative imagery travels in many directions across America's ethnic lines; no group has a monopoly on malice. Unkind caricatures of African Americans flourish among Latinos, Asians, and Jews just as they do among the majority Christian white population. And in return, such visible blacks as Louis Farrakhan, Al Sharpton, and Leonard Jeffries find license to express their prejudices acerbically, souring the atmosphere of debate and making black America appear more bigoted than it is.[47]

Likewise, as Seymour Martin Lipset has pointed out, the failure of black leaders to acknowledge the progress that African Americans have made has led some whites to conclude that there must be something "inherent in the black situation which prevents them from getting ahead."[48] This plays into the hands of racists who believe in the inferiority of blacks and their incapacity for improvement.

White Americans tell themselves lies about race too. Some white Americans falsely believe that they bear no responsibility for the problems of blacks; at the other extreme, some whites believe they bear total responsibility for the failure of blacks to thrive. The latter position leaves individuals anguishing in a white guilt that can lead them to support programs and initiatives that serve as Band-Aids for significant problems. The truth lies between the two extremes. White racism has resulted in limited opportunities for blacks. However, the actions of whites alone do not explain the inability of blacks to thrive. Attitudes about personal responsibility and group cultural traits also play a role in whether the race prospers.

Whites can become involved in helping minorities. I have benefited greatly from the mentorship of whites, and my children benefited from cross-racial friendships and opportunities to participate in activities with white families who exposed them to another culture as they were growing up. White people can help by acknowledging that racial profiling does exist, that racism is real, and that racial tensions will not disappear until we all begin treating each other with respect. Sometimes white people are in the best positions to challenge the racism that takes place behind closed doors. Standing up for others can sometimes involve risk, but Christians should be willing to speak up against injustice and bigotry.

Some illegal aliens have deceived themselves into believing that the United States owes them amnesty, health care, access to a free or reduced-cost education, affirmative action programs, and in the extreme case, land in the Southwest region of our nation. Of course, this type of entitlement thinking is counterproductive. Legal and illegal immigrants should learn the history of our country and the tremendous struggles that blacks and others have endured in order to enjoy the rights and privileges many of them take for granted.

Our national interests are best supported when people understand that our nation as a whole thrives when all its people thrive. Historically, many of the programs and policies established to help poor minorities have failed to alleviate their problems. America's approach to race relations has fostered unhealthy competition, jealousy, and rivalries over increasingly scarce resources. In short, human ingenuity has ended in a string of failed solutions; the efforts of multiculturalism and cultural relativism have resulted in a grand deception that all cultures are equal and that right and wrong are moral relatives and, in essence, do not exist.

Our national interests are best supported when people understand that our
nation as a whole thrives when all its people thrive.

America's culture of entitlement has eroded our work ethics, and our lost sense of identity has set us adrift among the nations of the world as our nation's leaders call out for a new vision—a vision without values and without virtue, and unanchored to the roots of our national heritage. Until we gain a clear grasp of the principles of work, purpose, and identity, we will continue to grapple with the attitude of racism that lies rooted in our flawed human hearts.

ACTION POINTS

1. Get to know people from other races who live or work near you. Identify common values and principles. Learn their life stories. Invite them to dinner or to your church and attend theirs for one or more Sundays.

2. Watch some movies that deal with racial and ethnic themes. I found these movies quite enlightening for the questions they raised about human behavior and its complexity: *Crash* (2004), *Falling Down* (1993), and *Gran Torino* (2008).

3. Read and discuss the *Be the People* discussion questions for chapter 6, posted at www.CarolMSwain.com.

CHAPTER 7

RACIAL POLITICS: PRESIDENT OBAMA AND ME

Now even as we speak, there are those who are preparing to divide us—the spin masters, the negative ad peddlers who embrace the politics of "anything goes." Well, I say to them tonight, there is not a liberal America and a conservative America—there is the United States of America. There is not a Black America and a White America and Latino America and Asian America—there's the United States of America.

—SENATE CANDIDATE BARACK OBAMA ADDRESSING
THE DEMOCRATIC NATIONAL CONVENTION, JULY 27, 2004[1]

A wise leader cannot and should not keep his word when keeping it is not to his advantage or when the reasons that made him give it are no longer valid. If men were good, this would not be a good precept, but since they are wicked and will not keep faith with you, you are not bound to keep faith with them.

—NICCOLÒ MACHIAVELLI, *The Prince*[2]

RACE HAS BEEN AN INTEGRAL PART OF AMERICAN POLITICS FOR DECADES. AS blacks who have risen to national prominence, both President Obama and I grew up to become persons of influence in our respective spheres. Despite squabbles in our nation about affirmative action and black disadvantages, I can attest that I never viewed myself as disadvantaged because of my race, sex, or social class. For the early years of my academic experience, I walked through life as if I were wearing giant blinders that would not allow me to see the full reality of race in America. I benefited from an "I'll show them" attitude that proved the naysayers wrong.

Thankfully, God has endowed me with a gift of transparency and a willingness to take risks for others.

Although I did not vote for Barack Obama to become president, I did write an *Ebony* article in December 2006 that may have helped influence the timing of his decision to run for the highest office in the land. The article, published alongside one written by Reverend Al Sharpton, responded to the question: "Is America ready to elect a black President?" Sharpton and I agreed the nation was ready but disagreed on the attributes of the ideal candidate. In my article, I said:

> I believe America is ready to elect a Black president who has the attributes and the credentials to make our nation feel good about its trajectory and how far it has come. But the first successful Black president will not be a Jesse Jackson or an Al Sharpton or any veteran activist of the Civil Rights Movement.
>
> Such a candidate laden with heavy baggage would evoke too much White guilt, and he (or she) would be seen more as a "Black" candidate than one who happened to be Black.
>
> *The first successful Black candidate will be a person like Barack Obama or Gen. Colin Powell, both of whom embody the hope of the American Dream.* It will be a person who ascribes to the mainstream political and social values that places heavy emphasis on hard work and individual responsibility.
>
> These examples are lighter-skinned offspring of foreign-born immigrants, but one could easily imagine that a Black-American descendant of slaves with the right set of credentials could garner the heart and mind of a majority of the American public. The hard-core racist element that would oppose a black man because he is a black man is not sufficiently large enough to deny the nomination or election of the right person.[3]

Some months later, I heard the future president state that an article he had read while on vacation influenced his decision. I wonder if it was the *Ebony* article. At the time, I viewed Barack Obama as a good presidential candidate for a future bid. When I wrote the article, he came across as someone who espoused mainstream values and principles. And while my observations held merit, they proved to hold a limited view of what would ultimately become Barack Obama's vision for our nation.

PEGGY JOSEPH AND THE POLITICS OF WISHFUL THINKING

Shortly before the November 2008 presidential elections, Peggy Joseph, an attractive black woman from Sarasota, Florida, took her daughter home from school early so they could attend an Obama rally. Bubbling with excitement after having heard Barack Obama's speech, Ms. Joseph offered a startling retelling of the campaign speech. "I never thought this day would happen," she said. "I won't have to work on putting gas in my car. I won't have to work at paying my mortgage. You know. If I help him, he's gonna help me."[4]

Where did Ms. Joseph get her fanciful idea? Perhaps it came from a portion of the candidate's speech where he identified with the plight of struggling families by saying, "It's gotten harder and harder to make the mortgage, or fill up your gas tank, or even keep the electricity on at the end of the month."[5] Ms. Joseph also heard candidate Obama say, "If you will stand with me and fight by my side, and cast your ballot for me, then I promise you this—we will not just win Florida, we will not just win this election, but together, we will change this country and we will change the world."

Ms. Joseph's world changed that evening, but probably not as she expected. She achieved instant notoriety after someone posted her interview on YouTube. As of February 2010, her video had received almost two million hits. Conservative blogger Michelle Malkin dubbed her Peggy the Moocher. "'E Pluribus Unum' is no longer our national motto," Malkin wrote. "These three words are: 'Do For Me.' As in: What will the government do for me?"[6]

DECEIVED BY THE CULT OF CELEBRITY

Obama did not run as an African American candidate but as a candidate who happened to be African American. Throughout most of the campaign, he downplayed his ethnic background, while at the same time using his race and relative youthfulness to reach out to entire new subsets of voting blocs.[7]

Peggy Joseph was not alone in her enthusiasm for candidate Obama or her belief that a single election could change her life. Millions of Americans voted to send to the White House a man who offered hope and who promised them change and transparency. The fact that Barack Obama was a black man seemed to matter in a positive manner for millions of white people who cast votes for him because they thought electing a black president with his attributes would be good for America. For a brief moment in time, we believed we had entered a postracial era in American politics. We were wrong.

For many people, a vote for Barack Obama meant a chance to change a world that was in crisis. Most people persuaded by his message were minorities and young people between the ages of eighteen and twenty-nine, who recorded their second-highest turnout since 1972, when eighteen- to twenty-year-olds were first given the right to vote in a presidential election.[8]

Unlike Ms. Joseph, who voted with an expectation and vision, many young people interviewed on radio and television could not cite a specific reason for supporting President Obama. YouTube clips featured interviewees who responded to questions about the candidate's appeal by repeating an Obama campaign slogan; others spoke in vague terms about hope. Many African Americans responded to the opportunity to elect a candidate who shared their race and political party. Many whites, I believe, saw an opportunity to prove that they had transcended race by casting a vote for a black man. Others wanted to send a message to George W. Bush and the Republican Party, whom they blamed for the economic collapse the nation was facing.

Historic numbers of racially diverse voters elected Barack Obama as America's first black president in the 2008 election. Blacks made up 12.1

percent of the voting electorate, with a turnout rate that jumped from 60.3 percent in 2004 to 65.3 percent in 2008. However, black women showed the strongest turnout, at 68.8 percent, while white Americans recorded their lowest turnout on record at 66 percent, in comparison to a 2004 turn-out of 67.2 percent. Even with the lowered turnout in 2008, white turnout was higher than the white percentage of the US population (65.8 percent).[9] Hispanic-Americans, who represent 7.4 percent of the electorate, increased their participation from 47.2 percent in 2004 to 49.9 percent in 2008. Asians, representing 2.5 percent of the electorate, increased from 44.6 per-cent in 2004 to 47 percent. The Democratic Party also made significant gains among younger, less religiously observant white evangelicals.

For a brief moment in time we believed we had entered a postracial era in American politics. We were wrong.

But candidate Obama failed to sway the most religiously observant white Christians.[10] Weekly churchgoers were resistant to his message of hope and change.[11] Many from the faith community were wary of his lib-eral positions on abortion, gay rights, and the role of government. Elected with veto-proof Democratic majorities in both houses of Congress, the candidate who inspired so much hope in Peggy Joseph and millions of other Americans was voted in as president of the United States.

President Obama is not a descendant of slaves, but his election remains a momentous achievement for a nation that experienced slavery, as well as the Jim Crow era that followed. His election also stands as a grand achievement for the offspring of a white woman and an African immigrant. Post-election polls placed President Obama's approval rating at 70 percent, while the incumbent George W. Bush's popularity stood at 27 percent one week after the election.[12] Unfortunately, the election of Barack Obama as the nation's first black president was not the healing balm that many people anticipated, nor did it provide the hope and promise many blacks expected.

Questions about candidate Obama's background and lack of solid leadership experience escaped the notice of many Americans who were fed up with President George W. Bush and the financial crisis confronting the nation. Some conservatives have argued that the mainstream media, enamored with Obama's oratory skills and persona, abandoned their traditional journalistic standards and neutrality in their coverage of his campaign. "Sure, mainstream journalists always root for the Democrat," argued CBS News, Emmy Award–winning correspondent Bernard Goldberg. "But this time it was different. This time journalists were not satisfied merely being partisan witnesses to history. This time they wanted to be real players and help determine the outcome. This time they were on a mission. Everyone wanted to help make history. It became more important for the narrative to help elect the nation's first black president than to make history by electing the first woman."[13]

Unfortunately, the election of Barack Obama as the nation's first black president was not the healing balm that many people anticipated, nor did it provide the hope and promise many blacks expected.

In many ways, candidate Obama achieved rock-star status: women fainted at his events, he was the subject of tributes, and performances were staged on sets that made him seem larger than life. No doubt, these factors played a role in the election outcome. Chris Hedges, author of *Empire of Illusion: The End of Literacy and the Triumph of Spectacle*, has argued that "a public that can no longer distinguish between truth and fiction is left to interpret reality through illusion."[14] Hedges goes on to state, "Those captivated by the cult of celebrity do not examine voting records or compare verbal claims with written and published facts and reports. The reality of their world is whatever the latest cable news show, political leader, advertiser, or loan officer says is reality. The illiterate, the semiliterate, and those who live as though they are illiterate are effectively cut off from the past. They live in an eternal present."[15]

In 2009, the president's popularity stood at 53 percent,[16] but by early 2010, black leaders including Tavis Smiley, Cornel West, and the Congressional Black Caucus had begun to criticize President Obama for not having done enough for African Americans.[17] In grading Obama's performance on black issues, West said, "I think on a symbolic level I would give him an A in terms of uplifting the spirits and providing a sense of hope and possibility going into the inauguration and sustaining it up to a certain point." But, West continued, "On a substantial level I would give him a C- when it comes to policy, when it comes to priority, when it comes to focusing on poor people and working people—which has to do with the vast majority of black people—that he has really not come through in any substantial and significant way."[18]

THE PRESIDENT'S SLIPPING POPULARITY

Admittedly, President Obama took office at a difficult time in American history. In January 2009, the Center for American Progress released economic data that revealed a nation in deep distress.[19] The Center reported that the gross domestic product was showing negative numbers, job losses were accelerating, unemployment was increasing, and families were burdened with debt, foreclosures, and losses in personal wealth. Deficits were deepening, business investment had declined, trade deficits loomed, and the national debt was steadily growing. Unfortunately, the president's American Recovery and Reinvestment Act (stimulus legislation) failed to have the expected results of jump-starting the economy.[20] The act, along with unpopular policy initiatives and the naming of questionable presidential appointees, took a huge toll on the president's popularity.

Conservative columnist Michelle Malkin's best-selling book *Culture of Corruption: Obama and His Team of Tax Cheats, Crooks, and Cronies* examined the backgrounds and connections of President Obama and his wife, Michelle, and revealed some troubling patterns.[21] Fox commentator Sean Hannity and the authors of *Catastrophe*, Dick Morris and Eileen McCann, were among the high-profile conservatives who published books geared toward defeating what they saw as President Obama's radical agenda.[22] Hannity warned:

Obama and his party stand for America's economic bankruptcy, virtual surrender in the war on terror, and a culture of death, from abortion to embryonic stem cell research to health-care rationing tantamount to death panels. He stands for a comprehensive radicalization of our culture, from turning schools over to homosexual activities, to undermining the sanctity of heterosexual marriage, to expanding dependency of classes. He stands for polarization and alienation between racial and ethnic groups, and between those of different economic circumstances.[23]

Questions about his religion, as well as his birthplace, have dogged President Obama. An August 2010 national survey by the Pew Research Center found that nearly one in five Americans (18 percent) believe Obama is a Muslim. This figure is up from 11 percent in March 2009. Only about one-third of adults (34 percent) said Obama was Christian, a number that has dropped from 48 percent in 2009. Forty-three percent of those surveyed said they did not know the president's religion. The Pew survey was completed before the president indicated his support for the construction of a mosque near the site of the former World Trade Center[24] at a White House dinner celebrating Ramadan. President Obama told his dinner guests, "As a citizen, and as president, I believe Muslims have the same right to practice their religion as anyone else in this country. That includes the right to build a place of worship and a community centre on private property in lower Manhattan, in accordance with local laws and ordinances. This is America, and our commitment to religious freedom must be unshakable."[25] The president made these comments at a time when public opinion polls showed 68 percent of Americans opposed to the building of a mosque near Ground Zero.[26]

THE RISE OF THE BIRTHERS

People uneasy with President Obama's background have questioned his eligibility to serve in the Office of the Presidency. Several factors have created an air of suspicion around the man who campaigned for office promising transparency. These include a foreign adoption and persistent allegations about his birth, with some claiming that he was actually born in Kenya and his parents later registered his birth in Hawaii, a procedure that Hawaii law allowed at the time. People seeking to prove Obama's ineligibility for the presidency have requested his "kindergarten records, Punahou school records, Occidental College records, Columbia University records, Columbia thesis, Harvard Law School records, Harvard Law Review articles, scholarly articles from the University of Chicago, passport, medical records, files from his years as an Illinois state senator, Illinois State Bar Association records, any baptism records, and his adoption records."[27]

The most recent effort to keep the issue alive is a November 8, 2010, WorldNetDaily article that includes a link to an April 9, 2009, internal Congressional Research Service Memo written to help members of Congress respond to inquiries from their constituents. The memo states, "It should be noted that there is no federal law, regulation, rule, guideline, or requirement that a candidate for federal office produce his or her original birth certificate, or a certified copy of the record of live birth, to any official of the United States government; nor is there a requirement for federal candidates to publicly release such personal record or documentation."[28]

People uneasy with President Obama's background have questioned his eligibility to serve in the Office of the Presidency.

The label "birther" is an epithet applied to those who question whether President Obama is a natural-born citizen who meets the constitutional requirements to serve as president. Those who question the president's background draw distinctions between the status of natural-born US citizens and that of naturalized citizens, the foreign born who go through the naturalization process but are barred from ever becoming president because of a stipulation in the Constitution that the president must be a natural-born citizen. Article II of the Constitution outlines the criteria for eligibility for president. It reads: "No person except a natural born Citizen, or a Citizen of the United States, at the time of the Adoption of this Constitution, shall be eligible to the Office of the President; neither shall any Person be eligible to that Office who shall not have attained to the Age of thirty-five Years and been fourteen Years a Resident within the United States." Some people have argued that the purpose of this stipulation was to ensure that the president of the United States would never have divided loyalties. Those who make this argument base their contentions on legal philosopher Emer de Vattel, who wrote an important book called *The Law of Nations*. Vattel describes "natural-born citizens" as "those born in the country, of parents who are citizens."[29] These questions have spawned legal challenges from some who question President Obama's status as commander-in-chief.[30]

Questions about President Obama's birthplace arose after Sarah Obama, his stepgrandmother, told interviewers through an interpreter that she was present at his birth in Kenya. Israel National News and other news outlets reported on the grandmother's statement.[31] Numerous attempts by the president's supporters to debunk rumors have failed to satisfy part of the population. In 2011, Neil Abercrombie, Hawaii's newly elected Democratic governor announced he was going to release the birth certificate to shut the mouths of the birthers.[32] After a period of silence, Abercrombie told reporters that the document was misplaced, but he had found some notation about the birth in the archives, thereby raising eyebrows.[33] Within days of Abercrombie's interview, the Hawaii attorney general said that Abercrombie did not have the authority to release the document because of privacy concerns.[34] An August 2010 CNN Public Opinion Poll found "more than a quarter of the public have doubts about Obama's citizenship, with 11 percent saying Obama was definitely not born in the United States and another 16 percent saying the president was probably not born in the country." The results varied by political party. "Eighty-five percent of Democrats say that Obama was definitely or probably born in the US, compared to 68 percent of independents and

57 percent of Republicans. Twenty-seven percent of Republicans say he was probably not born here, and another 14 percent of Republicans say he was definitely not born in the US."[35]

The cumulative weight of the above factors and more—economy, race, unpopular policies like the health-care initiative dubbed "Obamacare," and persistent rumors about the president's birthplace and religion—have taken an enormous toll on the president's popularity. By February 2010, President Obama's popularity had dropped to 49 percent.[36] As of October 26, 2010, his approval rating was at 43 percent, with 48 percent disapproving.[37] Sources of dissatisfaction included a litany of complaints, and for some Americans, "buyers' remorse" had set in. For many Americans, the euphoria of 2008 had dissipated. A September 2010 Gallup Poll found 91 percent of black America continuing to support the president, 55 percent of Hispanics, and 36 percent of whites.[38] The 2010 midterm elections proved to be a blowout for the Republican Party, which was able to reclaim the House of Representatives, seven governorships, twenty-nine state legislative districts, and six Senate seats. However, by January 2011, a string of legislative victories in the lame-duck session and a move to the political center raised the president's popularity above the 50 percent approval mark.

A MORE RACIALLY POLARIZED NATION

Despite the hype and a flurry of media attention, President Obama's election has not caused America to transcend the complexities of race. If anything, his election has heightened racial tensions, causing many blacks to view all criticism of the president as racially motivated, shrouding larger issues, such as a socioeconomic agenda that many Americans regard as socialist. Moreover, instead of making decisions that build confidence for a broad spectrum of Americans, the president has nominated individuals such as Sonia Sotomayor to the Supreme Court. During the confirmation hearings, she became known for having said on more than one occasion that she "would hope that a 'wise Latina woman' with the richness of her experiences would more often than not reach a better conclusion than a white male who hasn't lived that life." Given the rapid growth of the nation's Hispanic population, few people would question the raw politics behind nominating this controversial appointee to become our country's first Hispanic female Supreme Court justice.

Unfortunately, the Obama administration has missed multiple opportunities to take a leadership position on race. In fact, the Obama administration unwisely sided with the city of New Haven against white firefighters in the Supreme Court case of *Ricci v. DeStefano*, a case where federal Judge Sotomayor was overturned.[39] The case involved seventeen white and two Hispanic firefighters who passed a test qualifying them for promotion to management positions, only to have the city of New Haven invalidate the results because none of the black firefighters had passed the test. In a 5–4 decision, the Court ruled against the city of New Haven, determining that their decision to throw out the results was a violation of Title VII of the Civil Rights Act of 1964. President Obama, a constitutional law expert, could have urged his administration to take a different stance on the issue.

President Obama's election has not caused America to transcend the complexities of race. If anything, his election has heightened racial tensions.

President Obama also waded into a controversy involving Henry Lewis Gates, a Harvard University professor arrested at his home for failing to show identification to police who were responding to a report of a possible burglary at the residence. Before getting the facts, Obama sided with Gates and accused the police of acting stupidly. Embarrassingly for the president, Sgt. James Crowley, the officer who made the arrest, was an expert on racial profiling who had taught classes on the subject for the previous five years and had an impeccable record on issues related to minorities.[40]

A lack of strong leadership was revealed when a Department of Justice

(DOJ) employee was accused by insiders of not protecting white voters from voter intimidation tactics at a polling booth in north Philadelphia that was patrolled by members of the New Black Panther Party. Obama appointee Eric Holder and his staff at the DOJ dropped the charges against the New Black Panther Party, whose members were Obama supporters. Because President Obama appointed Holder, the action or inaction of the DOJ reflects poorly on both men.

Similarly, the Department of Homeland Security under Obama appointee Janet Napolitano cut back its enforcement of federal immigration laws, as evidenced by its increasing reluctance to deport noncriminal illegal aliens. These actions have caused some white people to charge racism.

We are not moving in the direction of a postracial society. By the summer of 2009, a YouTube video titled "Whites Are People Too" was popularized on the Internet.[41] Fox News commentator Glenn Beck was calling President Obama a racist who hates white people. The evidence Beck cited included Obama's long-term membership in Reverend Jeremiah Wright's ethnocentric church, the fact that the Obama administration dropped charges against members of the New Black Panther Party, his nomination of Sonia Sotomayor to the US Supreme Court, as well as his quick decision to side with Professor Gates before examining the evidence.

The frustration of whites was manifesting itself in various forms. I received an e-mail from a Jewish woman I'll call Hadassah who described herself as being frustrated by racial preferences and racial double standards. Hadassah wrote to inquire whether I would be willing to serve as an interpreter between the races:

I myself never harbored any racialist or racist attitudes until the advent of the playing of the race card, affirmative action, reverse racism against White people, and the myriad attempts by liberals in government to make life unbearable for those of the White Race, such as forced integration, forced busing, and the ruination of White neighborhoods. I have met many Asian people who share these exact concerns as well.

Because of the many efforts by professional race mongers such as the SPLC, the NAACP, and the like, hatred against your people has heightened to a level I have never before seen in my half-century of life on this earth. It terrifies me, and I wonder if perhaps fair-minded persons like yourself could help ameliorate this in some way? It seems you have indeed been trying; I try to do the same within the Jewish community, to make Jewish liberals understand that many of their actions only harm the Jewish people in the eyes of the Gentile community.

Hadassah's willingness to e-mail me suggests she is willing to engage in constructive dialogue. She is not the only Jewish person who identifies herself as a white nationalist. In *The New White Nationalism in America*, I quote two Jewish professors who expressed sentiments quite similar to Hadassah's. Their interview transcripts are in my book *Contemporary Voices of White Nationalism*.[42]

Campaigning for Democratic candidates during the fall 2010 midterm elections, a desperate President Obama told a Hispanic audience: "If Latinos sit out the election instead of saying, 'We're gonna punish our enemies and we're gonna reward our friends who stand with us on issues that are important to us,' if they don't see that kind of upsurge in voting in this election, then I think it's gonna be harder."[43] To a predominantly black audience, he said, "They think, 'Oh, well, Obama's name is not on the ballot, maybe they're not going to turn out.'" Referring to African American voters, he said, "You've got to prove them wrong." Delivering the same message at historically black Bowie State University in Maryland a few days earlier, the president said, "Don't make me look bad, now."[44] To some people, Obama's comments seemed remarkable for a president whom many people thought would work to move the nation beyond persistent racial and partisan barriers.

On the eve of the November 2010 elections, a Rasmussen report found that 65 percent of Americans believed the country was headed in the wrong direction.[45] Sixty-one percent of blacks disagreed by stating that the country is on the right track. These statistics reveal racial polarization and capture black reluctance to criticize the nation's first black president. It should be kept in mind that the president's party normally loses seats in the midterm election. Most likely, the election was a referendum on the president's performance. At the time of the election, the national unemployment rate stood at 9.6 percent, and that figure did not include the millions of Americans, many of them black, who had given up on finding a job.

THE PRESIDENT'S NONTRADITIONAL BACKGROUND

Nontraditional details in Obama's background could hold clues to his attitudes on issues such as gay rights and how he approaches the job of president. During President Obama's November 2010 visit to Indonesia, the *New York Times* published an article on his childhood that included a revelation about his childhood influences. According to reporter Norimitsu Onishi, "His nanny was an openly gay man who, in keeping with Indonesia's relaxed attitudes toward homosexuality, carried on an affair with a local butcher, longtime residents said. The nanny later joined a group of transvestites called Fantastic Dolls, who, like the many transvestites who remain fixtures of Jakarta's streetscape, entertained people by dancing and playing volleyball."[46]

Barack Obama's first school in Indonesia was a Catholic school called St. Francis of Assisi that he entered at age six with his religion listed on the application form as Muslim and his name as Barry Soetoro. Barry Soetoro lived in Indonesia from the age of six through ten with his mother, Stanley Ann Dunham, and stepfather, Lolo Soetoro, who had adopted him. Israella Pareira, one of his grade-school teachers at St. Francis of Assisi, remembers a paper that Barry wrote "that foreshadowed his future."[47] She said, "Since the very beginning, because we have seen his character, especially with the story he wrote on 'I Want to

Become a President,' we're sure he would have come to this accomplishment."[48] He later spent two years at State Elementary School Menteng 01, also called the Besuki school, a public school in Jakarta where he studied the Qur'an as part of the school's educational curriculum. On page 142 of the first printing of his autobiography, *Dreams from My Father*, he states,

> In Indonesia, I'd spent 2 years at a Muslim school, 2 years at a Catholic school. In the Muslim school, the teacher wrote to tell mother I made faces during Koranic studies. In the Catholic school, when it came time to pray, I'd pretend to close my eyes, then peek around the room. Nothing happened. No angels descended. Just a parched old nun and 30 brown children, muttering words. Sometimes the nun would catch me, and her stern look would force my lids back shut. But that didn't change how I felt inside.[49]

In his 2006 book, *The Audacity of Hope*, written after his election to the Senate, he explains the choice of schools. "Without the money to go to the international school that most expatriate children attended, I went to local Indonesian schools and ran the streets with the children of farmers, servants, tailors, and clerks."[50]

Daniel Pipes, director of the Middle Eastern Forum and a distinguished fellow at the Hoover Institute, has investigated the claims of whether the president was raised as a Muslim or Christian.[51] Pipes concludes that the weight of the evidence suggests Obama was raised a Muslim, at least during the four years in Indonesia, a Muslim country; took classes in the Qur'an; and attended events at the local mosque. Anticipating a bid for the presidency, Obama denied having practiced Islam as a child. He told an NBC news reporter:

> My father was from Kenya and a lot of people in his village were Muslim. He didn't practice Islam. Truth is he wasn't very religious. He met my mother. My mother was a Christian from Kansas, and

they married and then divorced. I was raised by my mother. So, I've always been a Christian. The only connection I've had to Islam is that my grandfather on my father's side came from that country. But I've never practiced Islam. . . . For a while, I lived in Indonesia because my mother was teaching there. And that's a Muslim country. And I went to school. But I didn't practice.[52]

Because America is a country where an overwhelming majority of the population describe themselves as Christian and because of fears of radical Muslims spawned by the 2001 bombing of the World Trade Center and the Pentagon, it is only logical that someone with presidential ambitions distance himself from Islam, as did candidate Barack Obama.

Obama's spiritual journey speaks of receiving Jesus Christ and becoming a Christian at Trinity United Church in Chicago, a Black Nationalist church where pastor Jeremiah Wright gained much publicity because of his sermons wishing damnation upon America. The church does not require the traditional confession of faith and water baptism for Muslim converts—tenets that many Christians feel lie at the heart of their faith.[53] In "Barack Obama's Search for Faith," reporter Jodi Kantor cites 1988 as the year of his conversion and the date he joined Trinity.[54]

Traditional Christianity requires a renunciation of sins and a public confession of faith, and many denominations require a water baptism. Christianity explicitly rejects the idea of one god, many faiths. In John 14:6, Jesus clearly stated, "I am the way, and the truth, and the life. No one comes to the Father except through me." This statement rejects Muhammad and the Buddha as avenues to salvation. Obama's positions on gay, lesbian, and transvestite rights; his vigorous fight against the Born-Alive Infants Protection Act; his position in favor of late-term abortions; and his quest to allow openly gay men and women to serve in the United States military (breaking a two-hundred-year military tradition) seem at odds with what many Christians believe the Bible requires of followers of Christ.

LINGERING QUESTIONS

The Office of the Presidency is the highest position in the land, and implicit in that office is the authority to bind the United States to other nations and to actions of international consequence through treaties and executive orders. The individual who holds the position of president holds the reins to the security of our nation and determines the integrity of the office. Therefore, as the nation's first black president, it is especially troubling that his background includes sealed records. Those who press the issue are summarily dismissed as racists or "birthers," a pejorative term suggesting mental instability. This is unfortunate. The well-being of our nation rests on both the ability of the people to determine the integrity and veracity of leadership and the existence of an appropriate process for gaining access to relevant and substantiating information.

Barack Obama's July 27, 2004, speech at the Democratic National Convention propelled him to the national spotlight. At the convention, he stole the limelight with rhetoric that resonated with many people who love their country. Candidate Obama said:

> The pundits, the pundits like to slice-and-dice our country into Red States and Blue States; Red States for Republicans, Blue States for Democrats. But I've got news for them, too. We worship an "awesome God" in the Blue States, and we don't like federal agents poking around in our libraries in the Red States. We coach Little League in the Blue States and yes, we've got some gay friends in the Red States. There are patriots who opposed the war in Iraq and there are patriots who supported the war in Iraq. We are one people, all of us pledging allegiance to the stars and stripes, all of us defending the United States of America.[55]

However, since his election, the president has operated as a pure partisan politician, even engaging in actions that have contributed to racial tensions in the country.

President Obama and his advisers have done the nation a disservice by failing to release records that would help scholars and researchers document his life beyond the information he has given us in his two autobiographical books.[56] It is critical for scholars and biographers to have access to documents to study all aspects of the lives of our presidents. Failure to release documents does not reflect openness for a president who promised healing and transparency, and it has created an unnecessary distraction for a quarter of the nation's population. Although some people may argue that President Obama's sealed records are none of the public's business, I disagree. Once an individual becomes the president of the United States, he or she belongs fully to the people; therefore, certain aspects of privacy rights should no longer apply.

Since his election, the president has operated as a pure partisan politician, even engaging in actions that have contributed to racial tensions in the country.

Political appointees are typically required to submit to in-depth background checks and open disclosure of scrutinous details regarding every aspect of their lives. To my knowledge, the president of the United States and members of Congress are not required to undergo any background checks before gaining access to high-level security information affecting the health and well-being of our nation. It therefore becomes more important than ever that an independent media seriously scrutinize and vet all candidates for high office and not allow considerations of race to hamper the process. Because the Constitution of the United States outlines the qualifications for serving in federal office, a constitutional amendment would be required to change the existing system that requires more information about the backgrounds of political appointees than about the president who makes the nominations and the senators who advise and approve them. The Constitution sets the qualifications for office and the terms of office. Consequently, any effort to require background checks, release of documents, or mandatory term limits would require a constitutional amendment because the citizens of various states cannot arbitrarily add to existing constitutional qualifications.

Federal courts have dismissed challenges to the president's eligibility brought under the "natural born" citizen clause because of the plaintiff's lack of standing to bring a charge. *Standing* is a legal standard derived from Article III of the Constitution that must be met before a person can sue for relief in federal court. One legal dictionary explains the concept of *standing* this way:

> Standing, sometimes referred to as standing to sue, is the name of the federal law doctrine that focuses on whether a prospective plaintiff can show that some personal legal interest has been invaded by the defendant. It is not enough that a person is merely interested as a member of the general public in the resolution of the dispute. The person must have a personal stake in the outcome of the controversy . . .
>
> Once a federal court determines that a real case or controversy exists, it must then ascertain whether the parties to the litigation have standing. . . . Basically, a plaintiff must have suffered some direct or substantial injury or be likely to suffer such an injury if a particular wrong is not redressed. A defendant must be the party responsible for perpetrating the alleged legal wrong.[57]

Daniel P. Tokaji, associate professor of law at Ohio State's Moritz College of Law and an expert in election law, has concluded that the standards for federal courts have made it impossible for anyone seeking to challenge the eligibility of a presidential candidate to prevail because of their inability to document legal standing. Tokaji advised plaintiffs that the most fruitful avenue is to file complaints in state courts challenging ballot eligibility of the candidate before the election takes place.[58]

WHAT CAN PRESIDENTS DO?

Presidents can take positive actions to improve race relations. For example, the president can remind Americans of the importance of forging a national identity that transcends racial and ethnic membership. Certain problems adversely affecting blacks and other minorities relate to factors other than race and ethnicity. In the case of President Obama, he can use his shared racial membership with blacks to discuss issues in the community that have not proven amenable to governmental solutions: for example, crime, high illegitimacy rates, low achievement levels among the classes, and drug abuse. This conversation can include cultural differences that work against people of lower socioeconomic status.

Lastly, a pressing need exists for a national conversation about the continued job discrimination that many black men and women experience despite the existence of civil rights laws and statutes. Some of this discrimination occurs in low-wage, low-skill jobs where blacks find themselves at a disadvantage when competing with whites and immigrants. Until we acknowledge the problems associated with current policies and practices, we can never develop new strategies for helping disadvantaged Americans.

Despite the current racial challenges facing America, one thing is certain: racial preference policies are no longer a viable solution for addressing disparities in a nation as ethnically diverse as ours has become. Surely, a leadership opportunity now exists for President Obama to bridge the divide and bring about real change for racial and social justice.

A NOTE OF CAUTION

Many of us are prone to criticize leaders with whom we disagree—especially those who are in high political office. The Bible gives Christians reason for pause, even when they disagree with a leader's stance based on biblical reasoning and principles. If we believe God is sovereign, we must also believe he allows the rise and fall of leaders for his own purposes. When Daniel prayed about an ungodly king, he said, "Blessed be the name of God for ever and ever: for wisdom and might are his: And he changeth the times and the seasons: he removeth kings, and setteth up kings: he giveth wisdom unto the wise, and knowledge to them that know understanding" (Daniel 2:20–21 KJV). Similarly, in Romans 13:1 we read, "Let every person be subject to the governing authorities. For there is no authority except from God, and those that exist have been instituted by God."

First Timothy 2:1–4 admonishes us to pray for our leaders, even those we don't support politically. "Therefore I exhort first of all that supplications, prayers, intercessions, and giving of thanks be made for all men, for kings and all who are in authority, that we may lead a quiet and peaceable life in all godliness and reverence. For this is good and acceptable in the sight of God our Savior, who desires all men to be saved and to come to the knowledge of the truth" (NKJV).

Showing respect for leaders does not mean we do not hold individuals accountable for their actions, nor does it relieve us from applying the Word of God to the decisions and programs that We the People are asked to support with our taxes.

A GLIMPSE INTO THE AUTHOR'S FORMATIVE YEARS

Because this chapter and the previous one have been about race, it seems fitting to give you a closer glimpse into my experience growing up in the rural South during the 1960s. I was born and raised in a rural hamlet of Bedford, Virginia, called Chamblissburg. My household consisted of my mother, stepfather, and seven brothers and four sisters. Each of us dropped out of school shortly after completing the eighth grade. Four siblings earned GEDs. My brother Calvin, the most recent of my siblings to earn his GED, earned his diploma about three years ago while he was in prison. He promptly and proudly mailed me a copy of the certificate for safekeeping.

In the birth order, I am number two of my siblings. To date, I am the only child in my family to have attended college. Yet I was not the smartest of the brood. My older sister, Maxine, carried that distinction. My father had a third-grade education, and my mother reached the tenth grade. At different points in my life, I have been racked with guilt and questions about why I was given the opportunities to achieve and why I have been blessed with what I have been given. I can only say, "Thank God."

For the first thirteen years or so of my life, home was a shack situated on the property of the white family for whom my stepfather worked. The white family's name was Padgett, and they owned a tomato-canning factory. One of my childhood dreams was to be old enough to get a summer job at the tomato factory, where I envisioned earning enough money to purchase school clothes.

We did not own an automobile. Getting to the bus stop for school meant a half-mile or so trek down a long, curving red clay road flanked on one side by a church cemetery and on the other side by a slight incline and a thick border of trees. Open fields of pasture surrounded our house. We owned a horse and a cow. Our property boasted a pond, where we fished.

Every day I walked past Beaver Dam Baptist Church, which had a nuclear fallout shelter. I spent quite a bit of my time worrying about whether Nikita Sergeyevich Khrushchev, a Soviet politician who didn't like America, really meant it when he said, "We will bury you!"[59] I was never quite sure if those nice white folks at Beaver Dam Baptist Church would open the door for my family if the Soviets attacked us. Fortunately, we never had to deal with those questions. While I was growing up, I naively thought that all black people could be trusted, but I feared white people because I knew many of them hated blacks.

I have left behind the grueling poverty of Bedford, Virginia, and the four-room shack covered with artificial brick siding that burned so easily. The house I grew up in had no indoor plumbing, which meant no bathroom. Not even an outhouse. We relieved ourselves in the woods by day and in a plastic bucket at night. For toilet paper we used leaves in the spring and summer and old newspapers in the winter. Of course, we couldn't afford luxuries such as deodorant and sanitary napkins. I remember making my own deodorant concoction by pasting detergent under my arms each morning. By the end of the day, my underarms would be raw with soapsuds oozing from my armpits. We were poorer than the other blacks in our community.

The white families that lived near us had nice brick homes with modern conveniences. Our ill-fitting clothes and shoes came from these families. Often we would find treasures in the dumps behind their homes. We also found Ku Klux Klan literature that we would take home and read. The literature didn't frighten me, but I wondered why the cartoons depicted black people with bones through their noses and contorted facial features. Even the nicest of white families had Klan literature delivered into their homes.

I often escaped into my own fantasy world. In my world, I was not black, I was not poor, and I was not female. While it may not be politically correct to share this aspect of my life, my fantasy family was white. I cast myself into the role of a rich white male named David, who was able to do what he wanted. Race was not an issue, because it never came up in my fantasy world. David was too busy traveling the world and dealing with his servants, who for some strange reason were not black. I once shared this aspect of my life with Nobel Prize–winning author Toni Morrison, who was a colleague during my Princeton years. Without the slightest tinge of judgment in her voice, Toni said, "That's so amazing. Even as a child you knew enough to want to be the best thing that one can be in America [a white male]."

Sometimes even when we think we know someone intimately, that person suddenly surprises us with racism that we didn't know was lurking within. I remember a kind white girl named Angie who was smart and compassionate and showed no racism. However, after Martin Luther King Jr. was killed by an assassin's bullet, I was shocked to overhear her telling our classmates that she was glad they killed him because he stirred up the black people.

My sixth-grade teacher, Mrs. Gallagher, was fond of telling the class that George Wallace was going to run for president and he was going to set things right. Bedford County had only recently integrated the schools, and whites and blacks were trying to figure each other out. In those days, I was into my blackness. I adorned my notebooks, and I used a black magic marker to decorate my white fake leather jacket with a black power fist. I frequently told my startled classmates, "I'm black and proud." This elicited comments and whispers that I was going to get into trouble for being so militant.

The best thing that happened to me from school integration was that I learned that I was as smart as the smartest white people, even though I missed a lot of school. The knowledge that I was as smart as kids at the "white" school gave me enormous self-confidence, after having heard for years that whites were smarter than blacks. Whatever my black teachers ingrained into me at Body Camp Elementary School helped me be competitive in all areas except math. Math has always been my struggle.

I cannot think of a time when I was not proud to be an American citizen. As a child, I studied civics and Virginia history and was proud of the fact that Virginia is known as the mother of presidents; George Washington, Thomas Jefferson, James Madison, James Monroe, William Henry Harrison, John Tyler, Zachary Taylor, and Woodrow Wilson were all born in Virginia, and the state gave our country four of its first five presidents. Consequently, I am disturbed when I hear anyone disparage our nation, especially black Americans. Despite our country's racial problems, blacks in America enjoy a higher standard of living than anywhere else in the world. People across the globe are still willing to risk their lives to live on American soil. The vast numbers of foreign citizens wishing to enter the United States, whether legally or illegally, tell us we are an exceptional nation. And although I was born into challenging circumstances, I experienced firsthand the fruits of this exceptional country.

I was a shy kid—always self-conscious about how I looked and whether my mouth would form the words I wanted to speak. Often as a child of nine or ten, I would want a glass of water or a slice of bread, but it was as if the cat had my tongue. I simply couldn't remember how to formulate words. My shyness did not fully leave until after my conversion to Christianity in 1999. Teaching was a nightmare for me up until then. I would try to write out everything I was planning to say about the subject and then read it to the students. There were times I would get so nervous in a public setting that I would forget my name.

With my conversion experience came empowerment, and my desire to communicate what I considered an important message to the world overrode my self-consciousness. Suddenly I no longer needed to clutch the lectern. I was free to speak extemporaneously. While on the Princeton faculty, my shyness had caused me to decline an opportunity to be on *Good Morning America* to discuss my first book, *Black Faces, Black Interests: The Representation of African Americans in Congress*. However, by 2002, I was a new person. When *The New White Nationalism in America: Its Challenge to Integration* was published, I took media training, and I began appearing in a range of media settings all across the country. Since then, I have done hundreds of interviews, and I especially enjoy talk radio. I have become a public intellectual who speaks to the current issues on national television networks like Fox News and CNN.

Over the years I have been a divorced welfare mother of two sons, both of whom, I am proud to report, managed to avoid most of the serious problems that plague black males in America. I have worked as an assistant in a nursing home for the aged, as an unskilled worker in a garment factory, as a door-to-door salesperson, and as a library worker at a community college before becoming a successful university professor. My varied experiences at different occupations and class levels have enabled me, I believe, to relate better to Americans from many different racial, economic, and educational backgrounds.[60]

My experiences with people of different races and social classes have brought me many wonderful relationships that truly transcend race, where we can talk about any topic without fear that the other will take offense. I have learned that racial differences are not nearly as great as the divisions that come with religion and politics for people of similar socioeconomic standing. America's race problems persist for several reasons. First and foremost, humanity is broken and imperfect; we blame other people when our lives don't turn out the way we hoped. Second, we have not learned how to talk across racial lines about behaviors that make us feel uncomfortable when we see them manifested in other racial groups. Unfortunately, we have allowed political correctness to stifle conversations that are needed to promote understanding across racial and ethnic lines, and we have allowed multiculturalism and cultural relativism to preach the often unchallenged lies that all cultures are equally good for promoting success and well-being.

America's future increasingly depends upon our ability to speak truth to one another across the racial, ethnic, and cultural lines that divide us. Moreover, we must be able to forge bonds across conservative and liberal ideological lines at a time in history when America needs leadership with a fixed vision in a changing world.

ACTION POINTS

1. Read the 1996 version of Barack Obama's *Dreams from My Father: A Story of Race and Inheritance* (New York: Times Books, 1995). What aspects of the president's life strike you as most relevant for understanding his values and principles?

2. Think about your own life. Can you identify people and experiences that helped shape your character? Consider contacting those people to thank them for their influence in your life.

3. What role, if any, did faith in God play in making you the person you ultimately became? Pray and thank him for his sovereign role in your life. If you have questions about your faith or want to become a Christian, talk to a pastor or believing friend, or visit http://www.sbc.net/knowjesus/theplan.asp.

4. Read and discuss the *Be the People* questions for chapter 7, posted at www.CarolMSwain.com.

CHAPTER 8

Reclaiming America's Faith and Promise

Politics and religion are different enterprises, and it is understandable that many people would like to keep them as separate as possible. But they are constantly coupling and getting mixed up with one another. There is nothing new about this. . . . What is relatively new is the naked public square. The naked public square is the result of political doctrine and practice that would exclude religion and religiously grounded values from the conduct of public business. The doctrine is that America is a secular society . . . [that] doctrine is demonstrably false and exceedingly dangerous.

—Richard John Neuhaus[1]

The progressive thinkers of the early twentieth century, having rejected the very idea of self-evident truths and enduring principles, created a theory of a "living," evolving Constitution, allowing government to expand and implement "progress" through more and more control over everyday life.

—William J. Bennett, former secretary of education[2]

In recent decades, American society has increasingly chosen to define itself as secular, during a period of time when progressive thinkers have come to construe the Constitution as a living document with meaning that changes with the mores of the American culture. These elements have also influenced how many Americans view the truth of Scripture; increasing numbers of contemporary religious scholars regard the Bible as a document with truth that changes with the pulse of contemporary customs and culture. Consequently, these leaders no longer preach about hellfire or the authority and relevance of biblical scriptures in discussions

219

on divorce, same-sex marriages, fornication (sex between unmarried people), and living together before marriage. And those who do broach these issues often water down the Bible's clear message about sin and its consequences. Professor Luke Timothy Johnson, a New Testament scholar at Emory University, writes, "I think it is important to state clearly that we do, in fact, reject the straightforward commands of Scripture, and appeal instead to another authority when we declare that same-sex unions can be holy and good. *We appeal explicitly to the weight of our experience.*"[3]

Secular humanists, atheists, agnostics, and non-Christians who control America's most elite educational institutions and other bastions of power feel it is imperative to persuade Christians to accept the world's view of human ingenuity as offering a path to human fulfillment and happiness. However, the historical demise of other nations who followed this path tells us that this is a tragic pursuit.

Most Americans tell pollsters they are conservative; however, our national leaders have demonstrated their commitment to a course that runs contrary to the principles and values of most of America's conservatives, and certainly those who worship the God of the Bible. It is my conviction that large segments of the American public are being shrewdly misled by politicians, newspaper and television journalists, religious leaders, and educators who believe they know what is best for the general population and desire to transform American culture into one that is more permissive, more liberal, more embracing of all truth, no matter how contrary to the Bible that truth might be. Unfortunately, these individuals control the flow and content of information vital to the American people. As cultural elites in positions of control, they are free to use deceit and half-truths to serve their own agendas; as a result, ordinary citizens must make heroic efforts to obtain balanced information on the critical issues affecting our nation. Today's cultural elites, like many failed social experimenters who have gone before them, are motivated by a dangerous desire. They seek to manipulate language, revise history, and create social controls in order to produce a utopian society in which human reasoning replaces what they consider to be the superstitious nonsense of religious reasoning. Unless they are stopped, America will quietly but relentlessly move forward in its progressive mind-set as it comes to resemble the worst of atheistic Europe in its laws and ways of life.

Many cultural elites in our country are unwilling to engage in discussion of one central philosophical question: does the God of the broken American covenant still judge nations? The most powerful and elite educational institutions in our nation have for decades chipped away at America's godly heritage as our educational institutions have become bastions of secular indoctrination. Their influence has become powerfully restrictive: individuals who believe in the Judeo-Christian God are forced to act against their consciences by supporting the killing of unborn babies through the use of their tax dollars; believers are asked to watch silently as secular humanists promote sexual activity among our nation's children, at the same time that government-funded Planned Parenthood encourages abortions among distressed women and minors. Christians are expected to bite their tongues and risk their jobs, their professional standing, and the consequences of legal action if they take a stand for biblical behaviors.

Unless [today's cultural elites] are stopped, America will quietly but relentlessly move forward in its progressive mind-set as it comes to resemble the worst of atheistic Europe in its laws and ways of life.

In his book entitled *Unfashionable*, Billy Graham's grandson Tullian Tchividjian has written an indictment of the church that can help us understand how we reached this point.[4] Tchividjian points out that too many of us have become "seduced by cool":

> According to Jesus, Christianity is not cool . . . if what's fashionable in our society interests you, then true Christianity won't. It's that simple.
> Think about it. Jesus said some pretty unfashionable stuff. *If you want to live, you must die. If you want to find your life, you must lose it.*

He talked about self-sacrifice and bearing crosses and suffering and death and the dangers of riches. He talked about the need to lay down our lives for those who hate us and hurt us. He talked about serving instead of being served, about seeking last place instead of first. He talked about gouging out our eyes and cutting off our hands if they cause us to sin.[5]

Tchividjian explains what Jesus meant: "Daily Christian living means daily Christian dying—dying to our fascination with the sizzle of this world and living for something bigger, something thicker, something eternal."[6]

Cal Thomas, a Christian syndicated columnist, has written, "Thirty years of trying to use government to stop abortion, preserve opposite-sex marriage, improve television and movie content and transform culture into the conservative Evangelical image has failed."[7] The moral decline continues because we haven't quite reached the hearts and minds of the majority of Americans who consider themselves Christians yet know very little about biblical teaching, the history of our nation, and its founding documents. Theologian Vern Poythress believes that Bible-believing Christians have not achieved much in politics because they have not devoted themselves to the larger arena of cultural conflict: "Politics mostly follows culture rather than leading it . . . A temporary victory in the voting booth does not reverse a downward moral trend driven by cultural gatekeepers in news media, entertainment, art, and education. Politics is not a cure-all."[8]

Likewise, Roanoke College theologian Robert Benne has noted that whenever nations lose their Christian heritage by a failure to maintain thriving communities, moral conditions erode: "It seems to be a melancholy fact of human history that when humans find themselves in conditions of great affluence in a context of widespread freedom, their values degenerate. They become more devoted to hedonistic pleasures—food, comfort, high living standards, sex, clothes—and bridle anything that constrains the pursuit of pleasure. They become self-oriented, unwilling to endure sacrifices that come with marriage and family, service to others, aspiring to challenging projects, and taking on wider responsibilities beyond their own private lives."[9]

The moral decline continues because we haven't quite reached the hearts and minds of the majority of Americans who consider themselves Christians yet know very little about biblical teaching, the history of our nation, and its founding documents.

However, we should not be disheartened by the sad state of affairs in our nation. We can find inspiration in the life of Caleb, one of the twelve Old Testament spies who were sent ahead of the people of Israel to bring back a report about the people inhabiting the promised land. Unlike ten of the other eleven spies, Caleb returned with a positive report despite the daunting circumstances that lay ahead of the Israelites in claiming the land God had promised to give his chosen people and their future generations (Numbers 14:6–8). Numbers 13:30 tells us, "Caleb quieted the people before Moses and said, 'Let us go up at once and occupy [the land], for we are well able to overcome it.'" Like Caleb, we, too, can pray to see the promise and riches of our land and to share a vision for what *can* be and what *should* be, rather than be discouraged by seeming obstacles in our pathway.

Like Caleb, I have a vision for our land. With a concerted effort and a plan of action, we can help restore America to its former glory. We must begin with the foundational recognition that we have sinned and participated in great evils. Consequently, our nation risks God's wrath; we stand guilty because of our individual personal actions, but also because of the allocation of our tax dollars, as well as the actions of leaders who have repeatedly engaged in and condoned sinful behaviors—the same kinds of sinful behaviors that resulted in the destruction of Old Testament nations. However, unlike the Old Testament nations who have gone before us, America bears a greater burden of responsibility. God has given us the testament of history and his clear commands to guide us in his Word.

We possess the biblical record of God's dealing with the ancient world; the record of God's dealings through history; and the spiritual, moral, and ethical awareness of standards of conduct drawn from Scripture and tested over the course of history.

Christians are supposed to be different from the world—to live in ways that make us distinctive. First Peter 2:9–10 tells us, "You are a chosen people, a royal priesthood, a holy nation, a people belonging to God, that you may declare the praises of him who called you out of darkness into his wonderful light. Once you were not a people, but now you are the people of God; once you had not received mercy, but now you have received mercy" (NIV).

With a concerted effort and a plan of action, we can help restore America to its former glory.

Likewise, we have been given instructions for reclaiming the land. God has always sent his prophets to warn his people through his Word. Second Chronicles 7:14 states, "If my people who are called by my name humble themselves, and pray and seek my face and turn from their wicked ways, then I will hear from heaven and will forgive their sin and heal their land."

PASTOR JOE WRIGHT'S OPENING PRAYER TO THE KANSAS HOUSE

Pastor Joe Wright of Central Christian Church in Wichita used his opportunity as a guest chaplain at the Kansas State House on January 23, 1996, to call for national repentance. Thousands of copies of Pastor Wright's prayer circulated the world in the weeks after he uttered the prayer. His words still reverberate across the nation. Wright's prayer is one that we should all consider praying, with sincerity and conviction, individually, congregationally, and in small groups:

Heavenly Father, we come before you today to ask Your forgiveness and to seek your direction and guidance. We know Your Word says, "Woe on those who call evil good," but that's exactly what we have done. We have lost our spiritual equilibrium and reversed our values.

We confess that:

We have ridiculed the absolute truth of Your Word and called it pluralism.

We have worshiped other gods and called it multiculturalism.

We have endorsed perversion and called it an alternative lifestyle.

We have exploited the poor and called it the lottery.

We have neglected the needy and called it self-preservation.

We have rewarded laziness and called it welfare.

We have killed our unborn children and called it choice.

We have shot abortionists and called it justifiable.

We have neglected to discipline our children and called it building self-esteem.

We have abused power and called it political savvy.

We have coveted our neighbor's possessions and called it ambition.

We have polluted the air with profanity and pornography and called it freedom of expression.

We have ridiculed the time-honored values of our forefathers and called it enlightenment.

Search us, O God, and know our hearts today; cleanse us from every sin and set us free. Guide and bless these men and women who have been sent to direct us to the center of Your will. I ask it in the name of Your Son, the living Savior, Jesus Christ.[10]

MAY GOD HAVE MERCY

Second Timothy 3:1–5 aptly sums up the godlessness we are seeing in the world today: "In the last days there will come times of difficulty. For people will be lovers of self, lovers of money, proud, arrogant, abusive, disobedient to their parents, ungrateful, unholy, heartless, unappeasable, slanderous, without self-control, brutal, not loving good, treacherous, reckless, swollen with conceit, lovers of pleasure rather than lovers of God, having the appearance of godliness, but denying its power."

Despite the godlessness of our world, Scripture assures us that God stands ready to extend mercy to those who accept the offer of faith through Jesus Christ. Romans 8:1–2 states, "There is therefore now no condemnation for those who are in Christ Jesus. For the law of the Spirit of life has set you free in Christ Jesus from the law of sin and death."

May God have mercy on our nation.

STEPS TOWARD RECLAIMING AMERICA

The Ten Commandments, the Declaration of Independence, and the Constitution of the United States of America and its Bill of Rights reveal the power to take back our country. For that reason, I have added these documents as appendices in the back of this book.

Here are several steps we can take toward reclaiming America's faith and values:

1. Make a concerted effort to know the biblical principles that motivated so many of our forebears. Every Christian should know the Ten Commandments (Appendix A), and every family should own a Bible and apply biblical principles to daily life. It is impossible for a Christian to evaluate the media, culture, education, politics, or any message without having firsthand knowledge of Scripture. Many bookstores sell versions of the Bible formatted for reading in one year. In as little as fifteen minutes a day, readers can cover the entire Bible in one year, reaping many benefits. These Bibles are especially helpful for Christians who have never read Scripture outside of church. I favor the New King James Study Bible for general reading.[11] Many people like the New Living Translation.[12] Browse a

Christian bookstore and choose the Bible that meets your needs for size, readability, study notes, and so on.

2. Read the Declaration of Independence and see why our Founding Fathers were willing to die for freedom, the right of self-governance, and national sovereignty (Appendix B).

3. Read the Bill of Rights, which is the first ten amendments to the U.S. Constitution (Appendix C). The First Amendment reads, "Congress shall make no law respecting an establishment of religion, or prohibiting the free exercise thereof; or abridging the freedom of speech, or of the press; or the right of the people peaceably to assemble, and to petition the Government for a redress of grievances." Separation of church and state and restrictions on religion in the public square were twentieth-century developments.

4. Read the Constitution and become familiar with its amendment process. The Constitution forms the basis for the rule of law in the United States (Appendix D). Like the Declaration of Independence, our Constitution is an easily readable document that establishes the functions and duties of the three major branches of government. Each branch of government possesses independent and overlapping powers. Every elected official and political appointee at the federal level swears an oath to uphold the Constitution. We cannot hold them accountable if we are unfamiliar with its contents. It should be as accessible as your Bible.

5. Get your news from more than one source. Although millions of conservatives turn to Fox News for information, it is a good idea to check out more than one news network. I subscribe to the online versions of major newspapers, and I visit other media sources. These include the *Washington Times*, *Wall Street Journal*, *Washington Post*, *New York Times*, BBC, Drudge Report, Politico, and *The Hill*. Each news outlet carries its own ideological slant.

I also follow a range of people and news organizations on Twitter, and I include liberal thinkers and media sources.

6.   Always double-check information you receive in e-mails before forwarding it to your personal list. Many people fall victim to frauds and hoaxes regarding actions in Washington and on Capitol Hill. If you accidentally send out false or erroneous information, try to set things straight as soon as possible with a correction.

7.   Register to vote. Monitor what elected officials do, and hold them accountable, regardless of their political affiliation. Conservative organizations like the Family Research Council (www.frc.org), the Heritage Foundation (www.heritage.org), and Gary Bauer of American Values (www.ouramericanvalues.org) can help keep you informed about issues and legislative actions.

8.   Keep the numbers for the House Office Switchboard (202-224-3121) and the Senate Switchboard (202-224-3121) handy so that you can call and register your opinion on key issues.[13]

9.   Prepare to be ridiculed, persecuted, or even martyred. Understand that your Christian walk as an activist could cost you your life and livelihood. John 16:2 warns, "They will put you out of the synagogues. Indeed, the hour is coming when whoever kills you will think he is offering service to God." In today's society, Christians are often labeled as the bad guys.

10.   Accept the fact that no matter what Christians and other believers do, it may be too late to save the United States of America. Once God determined judgment against the nation of Israel, he told the prophet Jeremiah to cease his prayers on behalf of the nation. Jeremiah 7:16 reads: "As for you, do not pray for this people, or lift up a cry or prayer for them, and do not intercede with me, for I will not hear you." Likewise, Jeremiah 14:11 states, "The LORD said to me: 'Do not pray for the welfare of this people.'" As it stands, we do not know if judgment has been determined for our nation.

CONCLUDING OBSERVATIONS

Christians should not despair about the changing times in which we live or the possibility of God's harsh judgment upon our nation. Our task is to fulfill our calling as believers. Our first and highest priority is to focus on our personal relationship with God. Second, our role is to strengthen our families and churches. Lastly, we should help inform, educate, and enlighten the minds of fellow believers who have strayed into unbiblical thinking because of inadequate knowledge.

Second Timothy 2:15 says: "Be diligent to present yourself approved to God, a worker who does not need to be ashamed, rightly dividing the word of truth" (NKJV). The Bible is the Christian's authoritative guidebook. We need to know what it teaches about the responsibilities we are to assume in our world, and the power of Christ to work in and through us. We are to walk wisely in our world and integrate the truth of the gospel in all spheres of thought and life. As good citizens of both an earthly realm and God's kingdom, Christians need to be well versed in the founding documents of our nation, to be politically astute, and to be committed to excellence in biblical scholarship and the skills and elements of public discourse.

We as believers cannot allow the missteps or shortcomings of past Christian leaders or the finger-pointing of secularists to deter us from speaking out for truth. Fortunately, Christ does not call us to lives of perfection. He died on the cross for our past, present, and future sins. A pastor told me once, if you sin—and we all do—just follow these simple steps: "Admit it, quit it, and forget it." Likewise, Romans 8:1–2 reminds us, "There is therefore now no condemnation for those who are in Christ Jesus. For the law of the Spirit of life has set you free in Christ Jesus from the law of sin and death." Therefore, we can stand boldly and confidently and proclaim truth that does not change.

Christians need to be well versed in the founding documents of our nation, to be politically astute, and to be committed to excellence in biblical scholarship and the skills and elements of public discourse.

Evangelist Billy Graham has reminded America for seven decades of the central message of the Christian gospel found in John 3:16: "For God so loved the world, that he gave his only Son, that whoever believes in him should not perish but have eternal life." Likewise, Jesus said, "I came that they may have life and have it abundantly" (John 10:10). If we claim these foundational scriptural truths and devote ourselves to teaching them to our children and grandchildren, I believe we can produce the critical mass that can turn the tide against the evil gripping our land. Our love for God, our families, future generations—for all who will be required to give an account to God—demands that we take seriously our obligation to warn society of God's impending judgment on those who continue to pursue an ungodly course.

Let us choose wisely the course we will follow.

APPENDIX A

THE TEN COMMANDMENTS

THEN GOD spoke all these words:

I am the Lord your God, Who has brought you out of the land of Egypt, out of the house of bondage.

You shall have no other gods before or besides Me.

You shall not make yourself any graven image [to worship it] or any likeness of anything that is in the heavens above, or that is in the earth beneath, or that is in the water under the earth;

You shall not bow down yourself to them or serve them; for I the Lord your God am a jealous God, visiting the iniquity of the fathers upon the children to the third and fourth generation of those who hate Me,

But showing mercy and steadfast love to a thousand generations of those who love Me and keep My commandments.

You shall not use or repeat the name of the Lord your God in vain [that is, lightly or frivolously, in false affirmations or profanely]; for the Lord will not hold him guiltless who takes His name in vain.

[Earnestly] remember the Sabbath day, to keep it holy (withdrawn from common employment and dedicated to God).

Six days you shall labor and do all your work,

But the seventh day is a Sabbath to the Lord your God; in it you shall not do any work, you, or your son, your daughter, your manservant, your maidservant, your domestic animals, or the sojourner within your gates.

For in six days the Lord made the heavens and the earth, the sea, and all that is in them, and rested the seventh day. That is why the Lord blessed the Sabbath day and hallowed it [set it apart for His purposes].

Regard (treat with honor, due obedience, and courtesy) your father and mother, that your days may be long in the land the Lord your God gives you.

You shall not commit murder.

You shall not commit adultery.

You shall not steal.

You shall not witness falsely against your neighbor.

You shall not covet your neighbor's house, your neighbor's wife, or his manservant, or his maidservant, or his ox, or his donkey, or anything that is your neighbor's. (Exodus 20:1–17 AMP)

APPENDIX B

THE DECLARATION OF INDEPENDENCE[1]

IN Congress, July 4, 1776

The unanimous Declaration of the thirteen united States of America

WHEN IN THE COURSE OF HUMAN EVENTS IT BECOMES NECESSARY FOR ONE people to dissolve the political bands which have connected them with another and to assume among the powers of the earth, the separate and equal station to which the Laws of Nature and of Nature's God entitle them, a decent respect to the opinions of mankind requires that they should declare the causes which impel them to the separation.

We hold these truths to be self-evident, that all men are created equal, that they are endowed by their Creator with certain unalienable Rights, that among these are Life, Liberty and the pursuit of Happiness.—That to secure these rights, Governments are instituted among Men, deriving their just powers from the consent of the governed,—That whenever any Form of Government becomes destructive of these ends, it is the Right of the People to alter or to abolish it, and to institute new Government, laying its foundation on such principles and organizing its powers in such form, as to them shall seem most likely to effect their Safety and Happiness. Prudence, indeed, will dictate that Governments long established should not be changed for light and transient causes; and accordingly all experience hath shewn that mankind are more disposed to suffer, while evils are sufferable than to right themselves by abolishing the forms to which they are accustomed. But when a long train of abuses and usurpations, pursuing invariably the same Object evinces a design to reduce them under absolute Despotism, it is their right, it is their duty, to throw off such Government, and to provide new Guards for their future security.—Such has been the patient sufferance of these Colonies; and such is now the necessity which constrains them to alter their former Systems of Government. The history of the present King of Great Britain is a history of repeated injuries and usurpations, all having in direct object the establishment of an absolute Tyranny over these States. To prove this, let Facts be submitted to a candid world.

He has refused his Assent to Laws, the most wholesome and necessary for the public good.

He has forbidden his Governors to pass Laws of immediate and pressing importance, unless suspended in their operation till his Assent should be obtained; and when so suspended, he has utterly neglected to attend to them.

He has refused to pass other Laws for the accommodation of large districts of people, unless those people would relinquish the right of Representation in the Legislature, a right inestimable to them and formidable to tyrants only.

He has called together legislative bodies at places unusual, uncomfortable, and distant from the depository of their Public Records, for the sole purpose of fatiguing them into compliance with his measures.

He has dissolved Representative Houses repeatedly, for opposing with manly firmness his invasions on the rights of the people.

He has refused for a long time, after such dissolutions, to cause others to be elected, whereby the Legislative Powers, incapable of Annihilation, have returned to the People at large for their exercise; the State remaining in the mean time exposed to all the dangers of invasion from without, and convulsions within.

He has endeavoured to prevent the population of these States; for that purpose obstructing the Laws for Naturalization of Foreigners; refusing to pass others to encourage their migrations hither, and raising the conditions of new Appropriations of Lands.

He has obstructed the Administration of Justice by refusing his Assent to Laws for establishing Judiciary Powers.

He has made Judges dependent on his Will alone for the tenure of their offices, and the amount and payment of their salaries.

He has erected a multitude of New Offices, and sent hither swarms of Officers to harass our people and eat out their substance.

He has kept among us, in times of peace, Standing Armies without the Consent of our legislatures.

He has affected to render the Military independent of and superior to the Civil Power.

He has combined with others to subject us to a jurisdiction foreign to our constitution, and unacknowledged by our laws; giving his Assent to their Acts of pretended Legislation:

For quartering large bodies of armed troops among us:

For protecting them, by a mock Trial from punishment for any Murders which they should commit on the Inhabitants of these States:

For cutting off our Trade with all parts of the world:

For imposing Taxes on us without our Consent:

For depriving us in many cases, of the benefit of Trial by Jury:

For transporting us beyond Seas to be tried for pretended offences:

For abolishing the free System of English Laws in a neighbouring Province, establishing therein an Arbitrary government, and enlarging its Boundaries so as to render it at once an example and fit instrument for introducing the same absolute rule into these Colonies

For taking away our Charters, abolishing our most valuable Laws and altering fundamentally the Forms of our Governments:

For suspending our own Legislatures, and declaring themselves invested with power to legislate for us in all cases whatsoever.

He has abdicated Government here, by declaring us out of his Protection and waging War against us.

He has plundered our seas, ravaged our coasts, burnt our towns, and destroyed the lives of our people.

He is at this time transporting large Armies of foreign Mercenaries to compleat the works of death, desolation, and tyranny, already begun with circumstances of Cruelty & Perfidy scarcely paralleled in the most barbarous ages, and totally unworthy the Head of a civilized nation.

He has constrained our fellow Citizens taken Captive on the high Seas to bear Arms against their Country, to become the executioners of their friends and Brethren, or to fall themselves by their Hands.

He has excited domestic insurrections amongst us, and has endeavoured to bring on the inhabitants of our frontiers, the merciless Indian Savages whose known rule of warfare, is an undistinguished destruction of all ages, sexes and conditions.

In every stage of these Oppressions We have Petitioned for Redress in the most humble terms: Our repeated Petitions have been answered only by repeated injury. A Prince, whose character is thus marked by every act which may define a Tyrant, is unfit to be the ruler of a free people.

Nor have We been wanting in attentions to our British brethren. We have warned them from time to time of attempts by their legislature to extend an unwarrantable jurisdiction over us. We have reminded them of the circumstances of our emigration and settlement here. We have appealed to their native justice and magnanimity, and we have conjured them by the ties of our common kindred to disavow these usurpations, which would inevitably interrupt our connections and correspondence. They too have been deaf to the voice of justice and of consanguinity. We must, therefore, acquiesce in the necessity, which denounces our Separation, and hold them, as we hold the rest of mankind, Enemies in War, in Peace Friends.

We, therefore, the Representatives of the united States of America, in General Congress, Assembled, appealing to the Supreme Judge of the world for the rectitude of our intentions, do, in the Name, and by Authority of the good People of these Colonies, solemnly publish and declare, That these united Colonies are, and of Right ought to be Free and Independent States, that they are Absolved from all Allegiance to the British Crown, and that all political connection between them and the State of Great Britain, is and ought to be totally dissolved; and that as Free and Independent States, they have full Power to levy War, conclude Peace, contract Alliances, establish Commerce, and to do all other Acts and Things which Independent States may of right do.—And for the support of this Declaration, with a firm reliance on the protection of Divine Providence, we mutually pledge to each other our Lives, our Fortunes, and our sacred Honor.

—John Hancock

New Hampshire:

Josiah Bartlett, William Whipple, Matthew Thornton

Massachusetts:

John Hancock, Samuel Adams, John Adams, Robert Treat Paine, Elbridge Gerry

Rhode Island:

Stephen Hopkins, William Ellery

Connecticut:

Roger Sherman, Samuel Huntington, William Williams, Oliver Wolcott

New York:

William Floyd, Philip Livingston, Francis Lewis, Lewis Morris

New Jersey:

Richard Stockton, John Witherspoon, Francis Hopkinson, John Hart, Abraham Clark

Pennsylvania:

Robert Morris, Benjamin Rush, Benjamin Franklin, John Morton, George Clymer, James Smith, George Taylor, James Wilson, George Ross

Delaware:

Caesar Rodney, George Read, Thomas McKean

Maryland:

Samuel Chase, William Paca, Thomas Stone, Charles Carroll of Carrollton

Virginia:

George Wythe, Richard Henry Lee, Thomas Jefferson, Benjamin Harrison, Thomas Nelson, Jr., Francis Lightfoot Lee, Carter Braxton

North Carolina:

William Hooper, Joseph Hewes, John Penn

South Carolina:

Edward Rutledge, Thomas Heyward, Jr., Thomas Lynch, Jr., Arthur Middleton

Georgia:

Button Gwinnett, Lyman Hall, George Walton

APPENDIX C

THE BILL OF RIGHTS[1]

AMENDMENT 1–FREEDOM OF RELIGION, PRESS, EXPRESSION.

Congress shall make no law respecting an establishment of religion, or prohibiting the free exercise thereof; or abridging the freedom of speech, or of the press; or the right of the people peaceably to assemble, and to petition the Government for a redress of grievances.

AMENDMENT 2–RIGHT TO BEAR ARMS.

A well regulated Militia, being necessary to the security of a free State, the right of the people to keep and bear Arms, shall not be infringed.

AMENDMENT 3–QUARTERING OF SOLDIERS.

No Soldier shall, in time of peace be quartered in any house, without the consent of the Owner, nor in time of war, but in a manner to be prescribed by law.

AMENDMENT 4–SEARCH AND SEIZURE.

The right of the people to be secure in their persons, houses, papers, and effects, against unreasonable searches and seizures, shall not be violated, and no Warrants shall issue, but upon probable cause, supported by Oath or affirmation, and particularly describing the place to be searched, and the persons or things to be seized.

AMENDMENT 5–TRIAL AND PUNISHMENT, COMPENSATION FOR TAKINGS.

No person shall be held to answer for a capital, or otherwise infamous crime, unless on a presentment or indictment of a Grand Jury, except in cases arising in the land or naval forces, or in the Militia, when in actual service in time of War or public danger; nor shall any person be subject for the same offense to be twice put in jeopardy of life or limb; nor shall be compelled in any criminal case to be a witness against himself, nor be deprived of life, liberty, or property, without due process of law; nor shall private property be taken for public use, without just compensation.

AMENDMENT 6–RIGHT TO SPEEDY TRIAL, CONFRONTATION OF WITNESSES.

In all criminal prosecutions, the accused shall enjoy the right to a speedy and public trial, by an impartial jury of the State and district wherein the crime shall have been committed, which district shall have been previously ascertained by law, and to be informed of the nature and cause of the accusation; to be confronted with the witnesses against him; to have compulsory process for obtaining witnesses in his favor, and to have the Assistance of Counsel for his defence.

AMENDMENT 7–TRIAL BY JURY IN CIVIL CASES.

In Suits at common law, where the value in controversy shall exceed twenty dollars, the right of trial by jury shall be preserved, and no fact tried by a jury, shall be otherwise re-examined in any Court of the United States, than according to the rules of the common law.

AMENDMENT 8–CRUEL AND UNUSUAL PUNISHMENT.

Excessive bail shall not be required, nor excessive fines imposed, nor cruel and unusual punishments inflicted.

AMENDMENT 9–CONSTRUCTION OF CONSTITUTION.

The enumeration in the Constitution, of certain rights, shall not be construed to deny or disparage others retained by the people.

AMENDMENT 10–POWERS OF THE STATES AND PEOPLE.

The powers not delegated to the United States by the Constitution, nor prohibited by it to the States, are reserved to the States respectively, or to the people.

THE CONSTITUTION OF THE UNITED STATES OF AMERICA (1787)[1]

WE THE PEOPLE OF THE UNITED STATES, IN ORDER TO FORM A MORE PER-fect Union, establish Justice, insure domestic Tranquility, provide for the common defence, promote the general Welfare, and secure the Blessings of Liberty to ourselves and our Posterity, do ordain and establish this Constitution for the United States of America.

ARTICLE. I.

Section. 1. All legislative Powers herein granted shall be vested in a Congress of the United States, which shall consist of a Senate and House of Representatives.

Section. 2. The House of Representatives shall be composed of Members chosen every second Year by the People of the several States, and the Electors in each State shall have the Qualifications requisite for Electors of the most numerous Branch of the State Legislature.

No Person shall be a Representative who shall not have attained to the Age of twenty five Years, and been seven Years a Citizen of the United States, and who shall not, when elected, be an Inhabitant of that State in which he shall be chosen.

Representatives and direct Taxes shall be apportioned among the several States which may be included within this Union, according to their respective Numbers, which shall be determined by adding to the whole Number of free Persons, including those bound to Service for a Term of Years, and excluding Indians not taxed, three fifths of all other Persons [Modified by Amendment XIV]. The actual Enumeration shall be made within three Years after the first Meeting of the Congress of the United States, and within every subsequent Term of ten Years, in such Manner as they shall by Law direct. The Number of Representatives shall not exceed one for every thirty Thousand, but each State shall have at Least one Representative; and until such enumeration shall be made, the State of New Hampshire shall be entitled to chuse three, Massachusetts eight, Rhode-Island and Providence Plantations one, Connecticut five, New-York six, New Jersey four, Pennsylvania eight, Delaware one, Maryland six, Virginia ten, North Carolina five, South Carolina five, and Georgia three.

When vacancies happen in the Representation from any State, the Executive Authority thereof shall issue Writs of Election to fill such Vacancies.

The House of Representatives shall chuse their Speaker and other Officers; and shall have the sole Power of Impeachment.

Section. 3. The Senate of the United States shall be composed of two Senators from each State, *chosen by the Legislature thereof* [Modified by Amendment XVII], for six Years; and each Senator shall have one Vote.

Immediately after they shall be assembled in Consequence of the first Election, they shall be divided as equally as may be into three Classes. The Seats of the Senators of the first Class shall be vacated at the Expiration of the second Year, of the second Class at the Expiration of the fourth Year, and of the third Class at the Expiration of the sixth Year, so that one third may be chosen every second Year; *and if Vacancies happen by Resignation, or otherwise, during the Recess of the Legislature of any State, the Executive thereof may make temporary Appointments until the next Meeting of the Legislature, which shall then fill such Vacancies* [Modified by Amendment XVII].

No Person shall be a Senator who shall not have attained to the Age of thirty Years, and been nine Years a Citizen of the United States, and who shall not, when elected, be an Inhabitant of that State for which he shall be chosen.

The Vice President of the United States shall be President of the Senate, but shall have no Vote, unless they be equally divided.

The Senate shall chuse their other Officers, and also a President pro tempore, in the Absence of the Vice President, or when he shall exercise the Office of President of the United States.

The Senate shall have the sole Power to try all Impeachments. When sitting for that Purpose, they shall be on Oath or Affirmation. When the President of the United States is tried, the Chief Justice shall preside: And no Person shall be convicted without the Concurrence of two thirds of the Members present.

Judgment in Cases of Impeachment shall not extend further than to removal from Office, and disqualification to hold and enjoy any Office of honor, Trust or Profit under the United States: but the Party convicted shall nevertheless be liable and subject to Indictment, Trial, Judgment and Punishment, according to Law.

Section. 4. The Times, Places and Manner of holding Elections for Senators and Representatives, shall be prescribed in each State by the Legislature thereof; but the Congress may at any time by Law make or alter such Regulations, except as to the Places of chusing Senators.

The Congress shall assemble at least once in every Year, *and such Meeting shall be on the first Monday in December* [Modified by Amendment XX], unless they shall by Law appoint a different Day.

Section. 5. Each House shall be the Judge of the Elections, Returns and Qualifications of its own Members, and a Majority of each shall constitute a Quorum to do Business; but a smaller Number may adjourn from day to day, and may be authorized to compel the Attendance of absent Members, in such Manner, and under such Penalties as each House may provide.

Each House may determine the Rules of its Proceedings, punish its Members for disorderly Behaviour, and, with the Concurrence of two thirds, expel a Member.

Each House shall keep a Journal of its Proceedings, and from time to time publish the same, excepting such Parts as may in their Judgment require Secrecy; and the Yeas and Nays of the Members of either House on any question shall, at the Desire of one fifth of those Present, be entered on the Journal.

Neither House, during the Session of Congress, shall, without the Consent of the other, adjourn for more than three days, nor to any other Place than that in which the two Houses shall be sitting.

Section. 6. The Senators and Representatives shall receive a Compensation for their Services, to be ascertained by Law, and paid out of the Treasury of the United States. They shall in all Cases, except Treason, Felony and Breach of the Peace, be privileged from Arrest during their Attendance at the Session of their respective Houses, and in going to and returning from the same; and for any Speech or Debate in either House, they shall not be questioned in any other Place.

No Senator or Representative shall, during the Time for which he was elected, be appointed to any civil Office under the Authority of the United States, which shall have been created, or the Emoluments whereof shall have been encreased during such time; and no Person holding any Office under the United States, shall be a Member of either House during his Continuance in Office.

Section. 7. All Bills for raising Revenue shall originate in the House of Representatives; but the Senate may propose or concur with Amendments as on other Bills.

Every Bill which shall have passed the House of Representatives and the Senate, shall, before it become a Law, be presented to the President of the United States; *[2]* If he approve he shall sign it, but if not he shall return it, with his Objections to that House in which it shall have originated, who shall enter the Objections at large on their Journal, and proceed to reconsider it. If after such Reconsideration two thirds of that House shall agree to pass the Bill, it shall be sent, together with the Objections, to the other House, by which it shall likewise be reconsidered, and if approved by two thirds of that House, it shall become a Law. But in all such Cases the Votes of both Houses shall be determined by yeas and Nays, and the Names of the Persons voting for and against the Bill shall be entered on the Journal of each House respectively. If any Bill shall not be returned by the President within ten Days (Sundays excepted) after it shall have been presented to him, the Same shall be a Law, in like Manner as if he had signed it, unless the Congress by their Adjournment prevent its Return, in which Case it shall not be a Law.

Every Order, Resolution, or Vote to which the Concurrence of the Senate and House of Representatives may be necessary (except on a question of Adjournment) shall be presented to the President of the United States; and before the Same shall take Effect, shall be approved by him, or being disapproved by him, shall be repassed by two thirds of the Senate and House of Representatives, according to the Rules and Limitations prescribed in the Case of a Bill.

Section. 8. The Congress shall have Power To lay and collect Taxes, Duties, Imposts and Excises, to pay the Debts and provide for the common Defence and general Welfare of the United States; but all Duties, Imposts and Excises shall be uniform throughout the United States;

To borrow Money on the credit of the United States;

To regulate Commerce with foreign Nations, and among the several States, and with the Indian Tribes;

To establish an uniform Rule of Naturalization, and uniform Laws on the subject of Bankruptcies throughout the United States;

To coin Money, regulate the Value thereof, and of foreign Coin, and fix the Standard of Weights and Measures;

To provide for the Punishment of counterfeiting the Securities and current Coin of the United States;

To establish Post Offices and post Roads;

To promote the Progress of Science and useful Arts, by securing for limited Times to Authors and Inventors the exclusive Right to their respective Writings and Discoveries;

To constitute Tribunals inferior to the supreme Court;

To define and punish Piracies and Felonies committed on the high Seas, and Offences against the Law of Nations;

To declare War, grant Letters of Marque and Reprisal, and make Rules concerning Captures on Land and Water;

To raise and support Armies, but no Appropriation of Money to that Use shall be for a longer Term than two Years;

To provide and maintain a Navy;

To make Rules for the Government and Regulation of the land and naval Forces;

To provide for calling forth the Militia to execute the Laws of the Union, suppress Insurrections and repel Invasions;

To provide for organizing, arming, and disciplining, the Militia, and for governing such Part of them as may be employed in the Service of the United States, reserving to the States respectively, the Appointment of the Officers, and the Authority of training the Militia according to the discipline prescribed by Congress;

To exercise exclusive Legislation in all Cases whatsoever, over such District (not exceeding ten Miles square) as may, by Cession of particular States, and the Acceptance of Congress, become the Seat of the Government of the United States, and to exercise like Authority over all Places purchased by the Consent of the Legislature of the State in which the Same shall be, for the Erection of Forts, Magazines, Arsenals, dock-Yards, and other needful Buildings;—And

To make all Laws which shall be necessary and proper for carrying into Execution the foregoing Powers, and all other Powers vested by this Constitution in the Government of the United States, or in any Department or Officer thereof.

Section. 9. The Migration or Importation of such Persons as any of the States now existing shall think proper to admit, shall not be prohibited by the Congress prior to the Year one thousand eight hundred and eight, but a Tax or duty may be imposed on such Importation, not exceeding ten dollars for each Person.

The Privilege of the Writ of Habeas Corpus shall not be suspended, unless when in Cases of Rebellion or Invasion the public Safety may require it.

No Bill of Attainder or ex post facto Law shall be passed.

No Capitation, or other direct, Tax shall be laid, unless in Proportion to the Census or Enumeration herein before directed to be taken.

No Tax or Duty shall be laid on Articles exported from any State.

No Preference shall be given by any Regulation of Commerce or Revenue to the Ports of one State over those of another; nor shall Vessels bound to, or from, one State, be obliged to enter, clear, or pay Duties in another.

No Money shall be drawn from the Treasury, but in Consequence of Appropriations made by Law; and a regular Statement and Account of the Receipts and Expenditures of all public Money shall be published from time to time.

No Title of Nobility shall be granted by the United States: And no Person holding any Office of Profit or Trust under them, shall, without the Consent of the Congress, accept of any present, Emolument, Office, or Title, of any kind whatever, from any King, Prince, or foreign State.

Section. 10. No State shall enter into any Treaty, Alliance, or Confederation; grant Letters of Marque and Reprisal; coin Money; emit Bills of Credit; make any Thing but gold and silver Coin a Tender in Payment of Debts; pass any Bill of Attainder, ex post facto Law, or Law impairing the Obligation of Contracts, or grant any Title of Nobility.

No State shall, without the Consent of the Congress, lay any Imposts or Duties on Imports or Exports, except what may be absolutely necessary for executing it's inspection Laws; and the net Produce of all Duties and Imposts, laid by any State on Imports or Exports, shall be for the Use of the Treasury of the United States; and all such Laws shall be subject to the Revision and Controul of the Congress.

No State shall, without the Consent of Congress, lay any Duty of Tonnage, keep Troops, or Ships of War in time of Peace, enter into any Agreement or Compact with another State, or with a foreign Power, or engage in War, unless actually invaded, or in such imminent Danger as will not admit of delay.

ARTICLE. II.

Section. 1. The executive Power shall be vested in a President of the United States of America. He shall hold his Office during the Term of four Years, and, together with the Vice President, chosen for the same Term, be elected, as follows:

Each State shall appoint, in such Manner as the Legislature thereof may direct, a Number of Electors, equal to the whole Number of Senators and Representatives to which the State may be entitled in the Congress: but no Senator or Representative, or Person holding an Office of Trust or Profit under the United States, shall be appointed an Elector.

The Electors shall meet in their respective States, and vote by Ballot for two Persons, of whom one at least shall not be an Inhabitant of the same State with themselves. And they shall make a List of all the Persons voted for, and of the Number of Votes for each; which List they shall sign and certify, and transmit sealed to the Seat of the Government of the United States, directed to the President of the Senate. The President of the Senate shall, in the Presence of the Senate and House of Representatives, open all the Certificates, and the Votes shall then be counted. The Person having the greatest Number of Votes shall be the President, if such Number be a Majority of the whole Number of Electors appointed; and if there be more than one who have such Majority, and have an equal Number of Votes, then the House of Representatives shall immediately chuse by Ballot one of them for President; and if no Person have a Majority, then from the five highest on the List the said House shall in like Manner chuse the President. But in chusing the President, the Votes shall be taken by States, the Representation from each State having one Vote; a quorum for this Purpose shall consist of a Member or Members from two thirds of the States, and a Majority of all the States shall be necessary to a Choice. In every Case, after the Choice of the President, the Person having the greatest Number of Votes of the Electors shall be the Vice President. But if there should remain two or more who have equal Votes, the Senate shall chuse from them by Ballot the Vice President [Modified by Amendment XII].

The Congress may determine the Time of chusing the Electors, and the Day on which they shall give their Votes; which Day shall be the same throughout the United States.

No Person except a natural born Citizen, or a Citizen of the United States, at the time of the Adoption of this Constitution, shall be eligible to the Office of President; neither shall any Person be eligible to that Office who shall not have attained to the Age of thirty five Years, and been fourteen Years a Resident within the United States.

In Case of the Removal of the President from Office, or of his Death, Resignation, or Inability to discharge the Powers and Duties of the said Office, the Same shall devolve on the Vice President, and the Congress may by Law provide for the Case of Removal, Death, Resignation or Inability, both of the President and Vice President, declaring what Officer shall then act as President, and such Officer shall act accordingly, until the Disability be removed, or a President shall be elected [Modified by Amendment XXV].

The President shall, at stated Times, receive for his Services, a Compensation, which shall neither be increased nor diminished during the Period for which he shall have been elected, and he shall not receive within that Period any other Emolument from the United States, or any of them.

Before he enter on the Execution of his Office, he shall take the following Oath or Affirmation:—"I do solemnly swear (or affirm) that I will faithfully execute the Office of President of the United States, and will to the best of my Ability, preserve, protect and defend the Constitution of the United States."

Section. 2. The President shall be Commander in Chief of the Army and Navy of the United States, and of the Militia of the several States, when called into the actual Service of the United States; he may require the Opinion, in writing, of the principal Officer in each of the executive Departments, upon any Subject relating to the Duties of their respective Offices, and he shall have Power to grant Reprieves and Pardons for Offences against the United States, except in Cases of Impeachment.

He shall have Power, by and with the Advice and Consent of the Senate, to make Treaties, provided two thirds of the Senators present concur; and he shall nominate, and by and with the Advice and Consent of the Senate, shall appoint Ambassadors, other public Ministers and

Consuls, Judges of the supreme Court, and all other Officers of the United States, whose Appointments are not herein otherwise provided for, and which shall be established by Law: but the Congress may by Law vest the Appointment of such inferior Officers, as they think proper, in the President alone, in the Courts of Law, or in the Heads of Departments.

The President shall have Power to fill up all Vacancies that may happen during the Recess of the Senate, by granting Commissions which shall expire at the End of their next Session.

Section. 3. He shall from time to time give to the Congress Information of the State of the Union, and recommend to their Consideration such Measures as he shall judge necessary and expedient; he may, on extraordinary Occasions, convene both Houses, or either of them, and in Case of Disagreement between them, with Respect to the Time of Adjournment, he may adjourn them to such Time as he shall think proper; he shall receive Ambassadors and other public Ministers; he shall take Care that the Laws be faithfully executed, and shall Commission all the Officers of the United States.

Section. 4. The President, Vice President and all civil Officers of the United States, shall be removed from Office on Impeachment for, and Conviction of, Treason, Bribery, or other high Crimes and Misdemeanors.

ARTICLE. III.

Section. 1. The judicial Power of the United States shall be vested in one supreme Court, and in such inferior Courts as the Congress may from time to time ordain and establish. The Judges, both of the supreme and inferior Courts, shall hold their Offices during good Behaviour, and shall, at stated Times, receive for their Services a Compensation, which shall not be diminished during their Continuance in Office.

Section. 2. The judicial Power shall extend to all Cases, in Law and Equity, arising under this Constitution, the Laws of the United States, and Treaties made, or which shall be made, under their Authority;—to all Cases affecting Ambassadors, other public Ministers and Consuls;—to all Cases of admiralty and maritime Jurisdiction;—to Controversies to which the United States shall be a Party;—to Controversies between two or more States;—*between a State and Citizens of another State* [Modified by Amendment XI];—between Citizens of different States;—between Citizens of the same State claiming Lands under Grants of different States, and between a State, or the Citizens thereof, and foreign States, Citizens or Subjects.

In all Cases affecting Ambassadors, other public Ministers and Consuls, and those in which a State shall be Party, the supreme Court shall have original Jurisdiction. In all the other Cases before mentioned, the supreme Court shall have appellate Jurisdiction, both as to Law and Fact, with such Exceptions, and under such Regulations as the Congress shall make.

The Trial of all Crimes, except in Cases of Impeachment, shall be by Jury; and such Trial shall be held in the State where the said Crimes shall have been committed; but when not committed within any State, the Trial shall be at such Place or Places as the Congress may by Law have directed.

Section. 3. Treason against the United States shall consist only in levying War against them, or in adhering to their Enemies, giving them Aid and Comfort. No Person shall be convicted of Treason unless on the Testimony of two Witnesses to the same overt Act, or on Confession in open Court.

The Congress shall have Power to declare the Punishment of Treason, but no Attainder of Treason shall work Corruption of Blood, or Forfeiture except during the Life of the Person attainted.

ARTICLE. IV.

Section. 1. Full Faith and Credit shall be given in each State to the public Acts, Records, and judicial Proceedings of every other State. And the Congress may by general Laws prescribe the Manner in which such Acts, Records and Proceedings shall be proved, and the Effect thereof.

Section. 2. The Citizens of each State shall be entitled to all Privileges and Immunities of Citizens in the several States.

A Person charged in any State with Treason, Felony, or other Crime, who shall flee from Justice, and be found in another State, shall on Demand of the executive Authority of the State from which he fled, be delivered up, to be removed to the State having Jurisdiction of the Crime.

No Person held to Service or Labour in one State, under the Laws thereof, escaping into another, shall, in Consequence of any Law or Regulation therein, be discharged from such Service or Labour, but shall be delivered up on Claim of the Party to whom such Service or Labour may be due [Modified by Amendment XIII].

Section. 3. New States may be admitted by the Congress into this Union; but no new State shall be formed or erected within the Jurisdiction of any other State; nor any State be formed by the Junction of two or more States, or Parts of States, without the Consent of the Legislatures of the States concerned as well as of the Congress.

The Congress shall have Power to dispose of and make all needful Rules and Regulations respecting the Territory or other Property belonging to the United States; and nothing in this Constitution shall be so construed as to Prejudice any Claims of the United States, or of any particular State.

Section. 4. The United States shall guarantee to every State in this Union a Republican Form of Government, and shall protect each of them against Invasion; and on Application of the Legislature, or of the Executive (when the Legislature cannot be convened), against domestic Violence.

ARTICLE. V.

The Congress, whenever two thirds of both Houses shall deem it necessary, shall propose Amendments to this Constitution, or, on the Application of the Legislatures of two thirds of the several States, shall call a Convention for proposing Amendments, which, in either Case, shall be valid to all Intents and Purposes, as Part of this Constitution, when ratified by the

Legislatures of three fourths of the several States, or by Conventions in three fourths thereof, as the one or the other Mode of Ratification may be proposed by the Congress; Provided that no Amendment which may be made prior to the Year One thousand eight hundred and eight shall in any Manner affect the first and fourth Clauses in the Ninth Section of the first Article; *and that no State, without its Consent, shall be deprived of its equal Suffrage in the Senate* [Possibly abrogated by Amendment XVII].

ARTICLE. VI.

All Debts contracted and Engagements entered into, before the Adoption of this Constitution, shall be as valid against the United States under this Constitution, as under the Confederation.

This Constitution, and the Laws of the United States which shall be made in Pursuance thereof; and all Treaties made, or which shall be made, under the Authority of the United States, shall be the supreme Law of the Land; and the Judges in every State shall be bound thereby, any Thing in the Constitution or Laws of any State to the Contrary notwithstanding.

The Senators and Representatives before mentioned, and the Members of the several State Legislatures, and all executive and judicial Officers, both of the United States and of the several States, shall be bound by Oath or Affirmation, to support this Constitution; but no religious Test shall ever be required as a Qualification to any Office or public Trust under the United States.

ARTICLE. VII.

The Ratification of the Conventions of nine States, shall be sufficient for the Establishment of this Constitution between the States so ratifying the Same.

The Word, "the," being interlined between the seventh and eighth Lines of the first Page, The Word "Thirty" being partly written on an Erasure in the fifteenth Line of the first Page, The Words "is tried" being interlined between the thirty second and thirty third Lines of the first Page and the Word "the" being interlined between the forty third and forty fourth Lines of the second Page.

Attest William Jackson—Secretary

done in Convention by the Unanimous Consent of the States present the Seventeenth Day of September in the Year of our Lord one thousand seven hundred and Eighty seven and of the Independence of the United States of America the Twelfth In witness whereof We have hereunto subscribed our Names,

Go. Washington—Presidt.

and deputy from Virginia

New Hampshire:

John Langdon

Nicholas Gilman

Massachusetts:

Nathaniel Gorham

Rufus King

Connecticut:

Wm. Saml. Johnson

Roger Sherman

New York:

Alexander R. Hamilton

New Jersey:

Wil. Livingston

David Brearley

Wm. Paterson

Jona: Dayton

Pennsylvania:

B. Franklin
Thomas Mifflin
Robt. Morris
Geo. Clymer
Thos. Fitz Simons
Jared Ingersoll
James Wilson
Gouv Morris

Delaware:

Geo: Read
Gunning Bedford jun
John Dickinson
Richard Bassett
Jaco. Broom

Maryland:

James McHenry
Dan of St. Thos. Jenifer
Danl. Carroll

Virginia:

John Blair
James Madison Jr

North Carolina:

Wm. Blount
Richd. Dobbs Spaight
Hu Williamson

South Carolina:

J. Rutledge
Charles Cotesworth Pinckney
Charles Pinckney
Pierce Butler

Georgia:

William Few
Abr. Baldwin

In Convention Monday, September 17th, 1787.

Present

The States of

New Hampshire, Massachusetts, Connecticut, MR. Hamilton from New York, New Jersey, Pennsylvania, Delaware, Maryland, Virginia, North Carolina, South Carolina and Georgia.

Resolved,

That the preceding Constitution be laid before the United States in Congress assembled, and that it is the Opinion of this Convention, that it should afterwards be submitted to a Convention of Delegates, chosen in each State by the People thereof, under the Recommendation of its Legislature, for their Assent and Ratification; and that each Convention assenting to, and ratifying the Same, should give Notice thereof to the United States in Congress assembled. Resolved, That it is the Opinion of this Convention, that as soon as the Conventions of nine States shall have ratified this Constitution, the United States in Congress assembled should fix a Day on which Electors should be appointed by the States which have ratified the same, and a Day on which the Electors should assemble to vote for the President, and the Time and Place for commencing Proceedings under this Constitution. That after such Publication the Electors should be appointed, and the Senators and Representatives elected: That the Electors should meet on the Day fixed for the Election of the President, and should transmit their Votes certified, signed, sealed and directed, as the Constitution requires, to the Secretary of the United States in Congress assembled, that the Senators and Representatives should convene at the Time and Place assigned; that the Senators should appoint a President of the Senate, for the sole purpose of receiving, opening and counting the Votes for President; and, that after he shall be chosen, the Congress, together with the President, should, without Delay, proceed to execute this Constitution.

By the Unanimous Order of the Convention
Go. Washington—Presidt.
W. Jackson—Secretary.

NOTES

EPIGRAPH

1. Leon R. Kass, *The Beginning of Wisdom* (Chicago: University of Chicago Press, 2006), 7.
2. C. S. Lewis, *The Screwtape Letters* (New York: Simon and Schuster, 1996), 34.

A RISK WELL WORTH TAKING

1. Mary Poplin, *Finding Calcutta: What Mother Teresa Taught Me About Meaningful Work and Service* (Downers Grove, IL: InterVarsity, 2008).

CHAPTER 1: RESHAPING OUR NATIONAL IDENTITY

1. The Declaration of Independence, http://www.ushistory.org /declaration/document.
2. Niccolò Machiavelli, *The Prince*, 1515. Translated and edited by T. G. Bergin, *The Prince: Machiavelli* (Northbrook, IL: AHM, 1947), 52.
3. Frank Newport, "This Christmas, 78% of Americans Identify as Christian," Gallup Poll, December 24, 2009.
4. Jeffrey M. Jones, "Americans' Outlook for US Morality Remains Bleak," Gallup Poll, May 17, 2010, http://www.gallup.com/poll/128042 /americans-outlook-morality-remains-bleak.aspx.
5. Rasmussen Reports, "30% Say US Heading in the Right Direction," June 2, 2010, http://www.rasmussenreports.com/public_content /politics/mood_of_america/mood_of_america_archive /right_direction_or_wrong_track/may_2010/30_say_u_s_heading _in_right_direction2.

6. Dennis McCallum, *The Death of Truth: Responding to Multiculturalism, the Rejection of Reason, and the New Postmodern Diversity* (Minneapolis, MN: Bethany House, 1996).

7. Charles Colson coined the phrase "cultural enforcers" in his article "An Unexpected Totalitarianism: The Tyranny of Tolerance," *Breakpoint*, February 1, 2010.

8. Christopher Hedges, *Empire of Illusion: The End of Literacy and the Triumph of Spectacle* (New York: Nation Books, 2009), 90.

9. Hannah Arendt, *The Origins of Totalitarianism* (Berlin: Schocken, 1951); Colson, "An Unexpected Totalitarianism."

10. Matt Moynihan, interview with the author, March 13, 2010.

11. George Orwell, *Nineteen Eighty-Four* (London: Secker & Warburg, 1949), 6.

12. Ibid., 37.

13. Glenn Greenwald, "How Many Americans Are Targeted for Assassination?" *Salon*, June 6, 2010, http://www.salon.com/news /opinion/glenn_greenwald/2010/06/25/assassinations; Spencer S. Hsu, "Civil Rights Group Sue Treasury over Targeting of Terror Suspects for Killing," *Washington Post*, August 4, 2010, http://www.washingtonpost.com /wp-dyn/content/article/2010/08/03/AR2010080303847.html.

14. *Report of the Defense Science Board Summer 2008 Study on Capability Surprise, vol. II: Supporting Papers* (January 2010), http://www.acq.osd.mil/dsb /reports/ADA513074.pdf.

15. Sahil Kapur, "Pentagon Calls for Office of 'Strategic Deception,'" *The Raw Story*, January 27, 2010, at http://www.infowars.com/pentagon -calls-for-office-of-strategic-deception/.

16. Declan McCullagh, "Bill Would Give the President Emergency Control of Internet," *CNET News*, August 28, 2009, http://news.cnet.com/8301 -13578_3-10320096-38.html.

17. Grant Gross, "Obama 'Internet kill switch' plan approved by US Senate panel," *Tech World*, June 25, 2010, http://news.techworld.com/security /3228198/obama-internet-kill-switch-plan-approved-by-us-senate /?olo=rss.

18. Grant Gross, "ACLU Objects to Google Partnership with NSA," *PC World*, February 10, 2010, http://www.pcworld.com/businesscenter /article/189060/aclu_objects_to_reported_google_partnership_with _nsa.html.

19. Christopher Weber, "Google Street View Accused of Spying," Politics

Daily, July 9, 2010, http://www.politicsdaily.com/2010/07/09
/google-street-view-accused-of-spying-on-congress-members/.

20. "Google WiSpying Hit Congress; National Security Data Could Have
    Been Gathered," Inside Google, July 7, 2010, http://insidegoogle.com
    /2010/07/wispying-hit-congress-national-security-data-could-have
    -been-gathered/.

21. Ibid.

22. Ibid.

23. Ibid.

24. Jason Ryan, "During the Olympics, the Feds Will Be Reading Your
    Tweets—and the Blotter," ABC News: The Blotter from Brian Ross,
    February 13, 2010, http://abcnews.go.com/Blotter/olympics-feds
    -reading-tweets/story?id=9825070.

25. "Twitter Tapping," *New York Times*, December 12, 2009, editorial, http://
    www.nytimes.com/2009/12/13/opinion/13sun2.html?_r=2.

26. Saul Alinksy, *Rules for Radicals: A Pragmatic Primer for Realistic Radicals*
    (New York: Random House, 1971).

27. Ibid., Dedication.

28. Ibid., 1.

29. Ibid., 61.

30. Ibid., 103.

31. "Recommended Reading: Saul Alinsky, The American Organizer,"
    NEA, http://www.nea.org/tools/17231.htm.

32. The Declaration of Independence, preamble, http://www.ushistory.org
    /declaration/document.

33. Barack Obama, "10 Questions: Religion in America," June 28, 2006,
    http://www.youtube.com/watch?v=35sGJrWKcmY&feature=related.

34. "Obama Claims America One of the Largest Muslim Countries,"
    Politfact.com, June 4, 2009, http://www.politifact.com/truth-o-meter
    /statements/2009/jun/04/barack-obama/obama-claims-america
    -one-largest-muslim-countries/; Jeff Zeleny, "Obama Says US Can Be
    Seen as a Muslim Country, Too," *The Caucus* (blog), *New York Times*, June 2,
    2009, http://thecaucus.blogs.nytimes.com/2009/06/02/obama-signals
    -themes-of-mideast-speech.

35. President Barack Obama, interview with Canal Plus Television in Cairo,
    Egypt, June 1, 2009.

36. "Obama Claims America One of the Largest Muslim Countries,"
    Polifact.com.

37. Frank Newport, "This Christmas, 78% of Americans Identify as Christian," Gallup Poll, December 24, 2009.

38. Frank Newport, "One-Third of Americans Believe the Bible Is Literally True," Gallup Poll, May 25, 2007, http://www.gallup.com/poll/27682/onethird-americans-believe-bible-literally-true.aspx.

39. Catholic News Agency, "US Gives 23 Million to Push New Kenyan Constitution, Charges Rep. Smith," July 17, 2010, http://bit.ly/aSM0DX; Amanda Carey, "USAID report: US government using taxpayer money to support new Kenyan constitution that includes abortion provision," DailyCaller.com, July 14, 2010, http://dailycaller.com/2010/07/14/usaid-report-u-s-government-using-taxpayer-money-to-support-new-kenyan-constitution-that-includes-abortion-provision.

40. Monica Crowley, "American Exceptionalism," *Washington Times*, July 1, 2009, http://www.washingtontimes.com/news/2009/jul/1/american-exceptionalism.

41. Text of President Obama's Remarks to the UN General Assembly, *New York Times*, September 23, 2009, http://www.nytimes.com/2009/09/24/us/politics/24prexy.text.htm.

42. This novel can be read online at The Complete Works of George Orwell, http://www.george-orwell.org/1984.

CHAPTER 2: AMERICA'S RELIGIOUS ROOTS

1. Isaac Kramnick and R. Laurence Moore, *The Godless Constitution* (New York: Norton Press, 1996), 27.

2. Rick Scarborough, *Enough Is Enough: A Call to Christian Commitment* (Springdale, PA: Whitaker, 1996), 65.

3. US Constitution, art. 7.

4. Mayflower Compact (modern trans.), Pilgrim Hall Museum, Plymouth, MA, http://www.pilgrimhall.org/compact.htm.

5. Daniel J. Elazar, "Covenant as a Political Concept," *The Covenant Tradition in Politics*, vol. 1, chapt. 1, Jerusalem Center for Public Affairs, http://www.jcpa.org/dje/books/ct-vol1-ch1.htm.

6. Ibid.

7. Mayflower Compact (modern trans.), US Constitution Online, http://www.usconstitution.net/mayflower.html.

8. "John Winthrop Calls Massachusetts Bay Colony 'a City upon a Hill,'" excerpt from John Winthrop's "A Model of Christian Charity,"

Collections of the Massachusetts Historical Society 7 (1838), 31–48, http://www.
historytools.org/sources/winthrop-charity.pdf; emphasis added.

9. Gerald R. McDermott, "Jonathan Edwards and the National Covenant:
Was He Right?" in D. G. Hart, Sean Michael Lucas, and Stephen J.
Nichols, *The Legacy of Jonathan Edwards: American Religion and the Evangelical
Tradition* (Grand Rapids: Baker Academic, 2003), 147.

10. Ibid., 149.

11. Robert N. Bellah, "Civil Religion in America," *Daedalus* 96 (Winter
1967): 25.

12. Patrick Henry, address to the Virginia House of Burgesses, March 23, 1775,
http://en.wikisource.org/wiki/Give_me_liberty_or_give_me_death.

13. The Declaration of Independence, http://www.earlyamerica.com
/earlyamerica/freedom/doi/text.html.

14. C. S. Lewis, *Mere Christianity* (London: Collins, 1952), 6.

15. J. Budziszewski, *The Revenge of Conscience: Politics and the Fall of Man*
(Dallas: Spence Publishing, 1999).

16. Ibid., 35–36.

17. George Marsden, *Religion and American Culture* (Boston: Houghton Mifflin
Harcourt, 1990), 15–16.

18. Thomas Paine, *The Age of Reason*, http://www.positiveatheism.org/hist
/quotes/paine.htm.

19. Bruce Feiler, *America's Prophet: Moses and the American Story* (New York:
HarperCollins, 2009), 60.

20. Ibid., 64.

21. Ibid., 66.

22. Nathan Hatch, *The Democratization of Christianity* (New Haven: Yale
University Press, 1989).

23. Mark Noll and Nathan Hatch, *The Search for Christian America* (Wheaton,
IL: Good News Publishers, 1983), www.crossway.org.

24. Micheal Hickerson, "The Climate for Christians on Campus," *Mike
Hickerson.com* (blog), http://www.mikehickerson.com/teaching
/college101/the-climate-for-christians-on-campus/.

25. Kramnick and Moore, *The Godless Constitution*, 22.

26. Ibid., 44.

27. Ibid., 46–66.

28. US Constitution, amend. 1.

29. Joseph Story, "Commentaries on the Constitution 3:§§ 1865—73," The

Founders Constitution, document 69, http://press-pubs.uchicago.edu /founders/documents/amendI_religions69.html.

30. Bellah, "Civil Religion in America," 5.

31. Ibid., 7.

32. Philip Hamburger, *Separation of Church and State* (Cambridge, MA: Harvard University Press, 2004).

33. Public school prayer declared unconstitutional in *Engel v. Vitale*, 370 U.S. 421 (1962).

34. Bellah, "Civil Religion in America," 37.

35. Harriet Beecher Stowe, *Uncle Tom's Cabin*, 5th ed. (Dover, MD: Dover Publications, 2005).

36. Gunnar Myrdal, *An American Dilemma: The Negro Problem and Modern Democracy* (New York: Harper & Brothers, 1944).

37. C. Eric Lincoln, *Race, Religion and the Continuing American Dilemma* (New York: Hill and Wang, 1999), xix.

38. Carol Swain, *The New White Nationalism in America* (New York: Cambridge University Press, 2002), 448.

39. Keith B. Richburg, "American in Africa," *Washington Post*, March 26, 1995, W16.

40. Swain, *The New White Nationalism*, 448.

41. President Abraham Lincoln, "Proclamation Appointing a National Fast Day, March 30, 1863, http://showcase.netins.net/web/creative/lincoln /speeches/fast.htm.

42. President Abraham Lincoln, Second Inaugural Address, March 4, 1865, http://www.americanrhetoric.com/speeches/abrahamlincolnsecond inauguraladdress.htm.

43. Thomas Jefferson's letter to John Holmes in Thomas Jefferson Randolph, ed., *Memoirs, Correspondence, and Private Papers of Thomas Jefferson* 4 (1829): 323–33; "Thomas Jefferson: A Firebell in the Night," *Encyclopedia Britannica Profiles: The American Presidency*, http://www .britannica.com/presidents/article-9116898.

44. Stephen Keillor, *God's Judgments: Interpreting History and the Christian Faith* (Downers Grove, IL: InterVarsity, 2007).

45. Ibid., 7–10.

46. Ibid.

47. Ibid., 10.

48. U.S. National Debt Clock, http://www.brillig.com/debt_clock/.

49. Robert Spence, "Hillary Clinton: Chinese Human Rights Secondary to Economic Survival," Telegraph.co.uk, February 20, 2009, http://www.telegraph.co.uk/news/worldnews/asia/china/4735087/Hillary-Clinton-Chinese-human-rights-secondary-to-economic-survival.html.

50. Sheryl Gay Stolberg, "Diplomatic Dangers Lurk in State Dinner," *New York Times*, January 18, 2011.

51. "Foreign Investment Affects Americans' Lives Every Day," *USA Today*, February 22, 2006, http://www.usatoday.com/news/washington/2006-02-22-ports-foreign-investment_x.htm.

52. Ibid.

53. Peter Foster, "China's Human Rights Record Worse than a Year Ago," Telegraph.co.uk, December 10, 2009, http://www.telegraph.co.uk/news/worldnews/asia/china/6778859/Chinas-human-rights-record-worse-than-a-year-ago.html; "Iran's Human Rights Record Comes Under UN Spotlight," DW-World.de, May 2, 2010, http://www.dw-world.de/dw/article/0,,5247615,00.html.

54. William Koenig, *Eye to Eye: Facing the Consequences of Dividing Israel* (Alexandra, VA: About Him, 2004), 31; John P. McTernan, *As America Has Done to Israel* (New Kensington, PA: Whitaker House, 2008).

55. Richard John Neuhaus, *The Naked Public Square* (Grand Rapids: Eerdmans, 1984).

56. Hunter Baker, *The End of Secularism* (Wheaton: Crossway, 2009), 18.

57. Steven D. Smith, *The Disenchantment of Secular Discourse* (Princeton: Princeton University Press, 2010), 24.

CHAPTER 3: ABORTION'S FRAGILE FACADE

1. Mary Poplin, *Finding Calcutta: What Mother Teresa Taught Me About Meaningful Work and Service* (Downers Grove, IL: InterVarsity, 2008), 122.

2. Katherine Hancock Ragsdale, "Our Work Is Not Done," speech to Operation Save America, Birmingham, AL, July 21, 2007, http://pursuingholiness.com/wp-content/uploads/katherine-ragsdale_our-work-is-not-done.pdf.

3. Center for Bio-Ethical Reform. "Abortion Facts," http://www.abortionno.org/Resources/fastfacts.html.

4. Susan D. James, "Abortion Addict Confesses 15 Procedures in 16 Years," ABC News, September 21, 2009, http://abcnews.go.com/Health/ReproductiveHealth/abortion-addict-admits-multiple-abortions-suicide-attempts/story?id=8594347.

5. Ragsdale, "Our Work Is Not Done."

6. Marvin Olasky, "Lessons from the Past," *World,* January 17, 2009, http://www.worldmag.com/articles/14857.

7. John Winthrop, in a sermon included in Owen Collins, *Speeches That Changed the World* (Louisville, KY: Westminster John Knox, 1999), 63–65.

8. J. Budziszewski, *The Revenge of Conscience* (Dallas: Spence, 1999), 27–28.

9. American Pregnancy Association, "Types of Abortion Procedures," http://www.americanpregnancy.org/unplannedpregnancy /abortionprocedures.html.

10. Planned Parenthood, "The Abortion Pill (Medication)," http://www .plannedparenthood.org/health-topics/abortion/abortion-pill -medication-abortion-4354.asp.

11. Gardiner Harris, "F.D.A. Approves 5-Day Emergency Contraceptive," *New York Times*, August 13, 2010, http://www.nytimes.com/2010/08/14 /health/policy/14pill.html.

12. Jeanne Monahan, "Ella and Abortion," *National Review Online*, October 5, 2010, http://www.nationalreview.com/corner/248875 /ella-and-abortion-jeanne-monahan.

13. Carey Goldberg, "Shots Assist in Aborting Fetuses: Legal Injections Offer Legal Shield," *Boston Globe*, May 10, 2007.

14. Lisa Harris, "Second Trimester Abortion Provision: Breaking the Code of Silence and Changing the Discourse, Reproductive Health Matters Supplement," *Reproductive Health Matters* 16, no. 31 (May 2008), http:// lib.tcu.edu/staff/bellinger/abortion/Harris.pdf.

15. Ibid.

16. *Born-Alive Infants Protection Act*, Public Law 107–207, *U.S. Statues at Large* 926 (August 5, 2002).

17. Gianna Jessen, "Abortion Survivor in Australia," http://www .streetdirectory.com/etoday/pregnancy/abortion.

18. Jill Stanek, Testimony on H.R. 4292, the "Born Alive Infant Protection Act of 2000, July 12, 2001," Testimony before Illinois Health and Human Services Committee, March 12, 2003, http://www.jillstanek .com/Testimony,%20IL%20Senate%20Health%20&%20Human %20Services,%203-12-03.pdf.

19. Barack Obama, Town Hall Meeting in Johnstown, Pennsylvania, March 29, 2008.

20. *Roe v. Wade*, 410 US 113 (1973).

21. Robert Bork, *Slouching Towards Gomorrah* (New York: Regan, 1996), 103.
22. Erika Bachiochi, *The Cost of "Choice": Women Evaluate the Impact of Abortion* (San Francisco: Encounter, 2004), 4.
23. *Doe v. Bolton*, 410 US 179 (1973).
24. Ibid., 179–92.
25. Bachiochi, *The Cost of "Choice,"* 4.
26. Robert P. George, "Gay Marriage, Democracy, and the Courts," *Wall Street Journal*, August 3, 2009.
27. Ibid.
28. Anne Hendershott, *The Politics of Abortion* (New York: Encounter, 2006), 3.
29. *Planned Parenthood v. Casey*, 505 US 833 (1992).
30. Ibid., 864–69.
31. Ibid., 855–56.
32. *Sternberg v. Carhart*, 530 US 914 (2000).
33. *Gonzales v. Carhart*, 550 US 124 (2007).
34. Chris Guthrie, "Carhart, Constitutional Rights, and the Psychology of Regret," *Southern California Review* 81, no. 5 (July 2005): 877.
35. Betty Friedan, *The Feminist Mystique* (New York: W. W. Norton & Co, 1963).
36. Bernard Nathanson, "National Abortion Rights Action League Founder Reminisces," *Pro-Life Infonet* (2598): December 24, 2002, citing WorldNetDaily, December 20, 2002, http://www.pregnantpause.org /abort/remember-naral.htm.
37. Bachiochi, *The Cost of "Choice,"* xiv.
38. Placenta previa is "a medical condition where the placenta covers the cervix, making a cesarean section medically necessary to deliver the child" (Bachiochi, *The Cost of "Choice,"* 67).
39. Bachiochi, *The Cost of "Choice,"* 67.
40. Ibid., 73.
41. Ibid., 83–84.
42. Ibid., 86.
43. "Is Abortion Linked to Breast Cancer?" American Cancer Society, http://www.cancer.org/Cancer/BreastCancer/MoreInformation/ is-abortion-linked-to-breast-cancer.
44. Bachiochi, *The Cost of "Choice,"* 67.
45. Ibid., 67–70.
46. Ibid., 69.
47. Ibid., 87–100.

48. Climategate Document Database, http://www.climate-gate.org.
49. "University of East Anglia emails: the most contentious quotes," *Telegraph*, November 23, 2009, http://www.telegraph.co.uk/earth /environment/globalwarming/6636563/University-of-East-Anglia -emails-the-most-contentious-quotes.html.
50. "Facts on Induced Abortion," Alan Guttmacher Institute, http://www .alanguttmacher.org/pubs/fb_induced_abortion.html.
51. Ibid.
52. Lila Rose, "Abortions earmarked by race," Live Action, http:// liveaction.org/planned-parenthood-racism-project.
53. "Houston We Have a Problem," Bound4Life, 2009, http://bound4life .com/houston.
54. Leslie Fulbright, "Berkeley Pastor Calls for Blacks to Fight Abortion," *SFGate.com*, January 7, 2008, http://articles.sfgate.com/2008-01-07 /bay-area/17152058_1_abortion-clinics-black-women.
55. Carol M. Swain and Gerald McDermott, "Working against the good of the public," *Roanoke Times and World News*, April 18, 2008, http://www .carolmswain.net/articles/againstthegood.html.
56. National Council for Research on Women, "Member Organization: Planned Parenthood Federation of America," http://www.ncrw.org /member-organizations/planned-parenthood-federation-america.
57. "Federal Funds: Fiscal Years 2002–2009 Obligations, Disbursements, and Expenditures for Selected Organizations Involved in Health-Related Activities," Government Accounting Office, May 28, 2010, http://gao. gov/products/GAO-10-533R.
58. Rita Diller, "Diller: Planned Parenthood's Missing Millions: New GAO Report Reveals Disturbing Financial Discrepancies," *Washington Times*, June 18, 2010, at http://plannedparenthoodhouston.com/DILLER %206_18_2010.htm.
59. Swain and McDermott, "Working against the good of the public."
60. Joseph Abrams, "Planned Parenthood Director Quits After Watching Abortion on Ultrasound," FoxNews.com, November 2, 2009, http:// www.foxnews.com/story/0,2933,571215,00.html.
61. Ibid.
62. Samantha Singson, "Pro-Life Nations Beat Pro-Abortion Ones on Maternal Mortality, New Report Shows," LifeNews.com, December 11, 2009, http://lifenews.com/intl408.html.

63. Margaret Sanger, "In Her Own Words," http://www.dianedew.com /sanger.htm.

64. Margaret Sanger, *The Pivot of Civilization* (New York: Brentano, 1922).

65. Adolf Hitler, *Mein Kampf [My Struggle]*, 2 vols. (Munich: Franz Eher, 1925–1926).

66. Benjamin Wiker, *10 Books That Screwed Up the World* (Washington, D.C.: Regnery, 2008), 8.

67. Margaret Sanger, letter to Clarence Gamble, December 10, 1939, in Sanger manuscripts, Sophia Smith Collection, Smith College, Northampton, Massachusetts.

68. Planned Parenthood, "About Us: Who We Are, The Reverend Martin Luther King Jr.," http://www.plannedparenthood.org/about-us/who -we-are/reverend-martin-luther-king-jr-4728.htm.

69. "The Planned Parenthood Racism Project: Abortions earmarked by race," Live Action, 2009, http://liveaction.org/planned-parenthood -racism-project; "Live Birth Abortions" http://impiousdigest.com /Livebirth.htm.

70. Robie Harris, *It's Perfectly Normal* (Cambridge, MA: Candlewick Press, 1996); http://www.prolifewaco.org/documents/Normal4pages.pdf.

71. "Healthy, Happy, and Hot: A Young Person's Guide to Their Rights, Sexuality, and Living with HIV," http://www.ippf.org/NR/rdonlyres /B4462DDE-487D-4194-B0E0-193A04095819/0/HappyHealthyHot.pdf.

72. Ibid.

73. Ibid.

74. Ken Blackwell, "How to Really Reform the UN," *The American Thinker*, October 16, 2010, http://www.americanthinker.com/2010/10 /how_to_really_reform_the_un.html.

75. Lila Rose, "Mona Lisa Project, Memphis, Tennessee," http://liveaction .org/mona-lisa/memphis-tn.

76. Lydia Saad, "More Americans 'Pro-Life" than "Pro-Choice" for First Time," Gallup, May 7–10, 2009, http://www.gallup.com/poll/118399 /More-Americans-Pro-Life-Than-Pro-Choice-First-Time.aspx.

77. Ibid.

78. Ibid.

79. Ibid.

80. Lucy Laing, "We're Twinseparable! Happy with his brother, the boy who refused to die," *Daily Mail Online*, November 3, 2007, http://www

.dailymail.co.uk/news/article-491443/Were-twinseparable-Happy
-brother-boy-refused-die.html; Emma Morton and Kate Wighton,
"Career Woman has 15 Abortions in 17 Years," *Sun Online*, October 15,
2009, http://www.thesun.co.uk/sol/homepage/woman/health
/health/2682798/Woman-has-15-abortions-in-17-years.html.

81. Patricia Bauer, "Vanderbilt Enrolls Students with Intellectual
Disabilities, *Disability News*, October 13, 2010, http://www
.patriciaebauer.com/2010/10/13/vanderbilt-program-2-30223.

82. Lynn Vincent, "The Harvest of Abortion." *World*, October 23,
1999; Kelly Patricia O'Meara, "Harvesting Body Parts," *New World
Communications*, December 22, 2004.

83. Robert George and Christopher Tollefsen, *Embryo: A Defense of Human Life*
(New York: Doubleday, 2008), 50.

84. J. Budziszewski, *The Revenge of Conscience* (Dallas: Spence, 1999), 24.

85. Robert P. George, *In Defense of Natural Law* (New York: Oxford University
Press, 1999), 205–13; Anne Morse, "Conservative Heavyweight: The
Remarkable Mind of Robert P. George," *Crisis* (September 2003):
36–42.

86. Budziszewski, *The Revenge of Conscience*, 27.

87. Ibid., 26.

88. Mary Poplin, *Finding Calcutta: What Mother Teresa Taught Me About
Meaningful Work and Service* (Downers Grove, IL: InterVarsity, 2008), 120.

89. Ibid., 121.

90. Paul A. Murtaugh and Michael G. Schlax, "Reproduction and Carbon
Legacies of Individuals," *Global Environmental Change* 19, no. 1 (2009): 14–20.

91. Brendan O'Neill, "OPT: Save the Planet by Preventing African Births,"
National Review Online, December 4, 2009; see also Paul R. Ehrlich, Anne
Ehrlich, and John Holdren, *Ecoscience: Population, Resources, Environment*
(New York: W. H. Freeman, 1978).

92. "Your Questions Answered," Pop*Offsets*, http://www.popoffsets.com
/faq.php.

93. Ibid.

94. Wei Xing Zhu, Li Lu, and Therese Hesketh, "China's excess males,
sex selective abortion, and one child policy: analysis of data from 2005
national intercensus survey," *BMJ*, 338 (April 2009): 1211.

95. "The Kenyan Connection: Obama Administration Efforts in Africa
May Violate Federal Law," editorial, *Washington Times*, July 16, 2010,

http://www.washingtontimes.com/news/2010/jul/16/the
-kenya-connection.

96. Marvin Olasky, "Lessons from the Past," *World*, January 17, 2009,
     http://www.worldmag.com/articles/14857.

97. Greg Hasek, personal communication with author, July 19, 2010.

98. Ibid.

99. Ibid.

100. Phil Holsinger, personal communication with author, August 8, 2010.

101. "Religion and Ethics—Abortion and Hinduism," BBC, August 25,
     2009, http://www.bbc.co.uk/religion/religions/hinduism/hinduethics
     /abortion_1.shtml.

102. Abul Fadl Mohsin Ebrahim, *Abortion, Birth Control and Surrogate Parenting:
     An Islamic Perspective* (Indianapolis: American Trust Publications, 1989),
     90, http://caae.phil.cmu.edu/cavalier/Forum/abortion/background
     /islam1.html.

103. Qur'an 5:32, quoted in Ebrahim, *Abortion, Birth Control and Surrogate
     Parenting*, 102.

104. Gerald McDermott, unpublished lecture quoted with permission from
     the author.

105. Michael Gorman, *Abortion and the Early Church* (Downers Grove, IL:
     InterVarsity, 1982), 9; James Hoffmeier, *Abortion: A Christian Understanding*
     (Grand Rapids: Baker, 1987), 53.

106. Poplin, *Finding Calcutta*, 122.

107. Ibid.

108. Ibid., 118–19.

109. Ibid., 119.

110. ProlifeAmerica.com, http://www.prolifeamerica.com/right-to-life_pro
     -life_organizations.cfm.

CHAPTER 4: FAMILY MATTERS

1. Thornton Wilder, *The Skin of Our Teeth* (New York: HarperCollins, 1942),
    92–93. It became a Pulitzer Prize–winning play that opened on October
    15, 1942, at the Shubert Theatre in New Haven, Connecticut.

2. Betty Friedan, *The Feminine Mystique* (New York: W. W. Norton, 1963,
    reprint 2001), 57.

3. Maggie Gallagher, *The Abolition of Marriage: How We Destroy Lasting Love*
    (Washington, D.C.: Regnery, 1996), 5.

4. Ibid.

5. I have chosen the names Quigley and Brenda and the home location of Fort Wayne, Texas, to protect the privacy of the Moynihans.

6. Quigley Moynihan, "The Ultimate Quigley Talk," letter written for his children and grandchildren and shared with the author on March 22, 2010.

7. Ibid.

8. Ibid.

9. Bob Drogin and Kathleen Hennessey, "Al and Tipper Gore announce separation," *Los Angeles Times,* June 2, 2010, http://articles.latimes.com/2010/jun/02/nation/la-na-gore-separation-20100602.

10. Linda Chavez, "Until Death Do Us Apart," TownHall.com, June 4, 2010, http://townhall.com/columnists/LindaChavez/2010/06/04/until_death_do_us_part.

11. Ibid.

12. *Catholic Encyclopedia* (New York: Robert Appleton, 1912), s.v. "matrimony."

13. Medina Estévez, *Male and Female He Created Them: On Marriage and the Family* (San Francisco: Ignatius, 2003), 19–20.

14. Pope John Paul II, "Man Enters the World as a Subject of Truth and Love," address, Paul VI Hall for the General Audience, Rome, Italy, February 20, 1980, http://www.ewtn.com/library/papaldoc/jp2tb18.htm.

15. *Catholic Encyclopedia*, s.v. "matrimony."

16. Rev. Jeffrey Keefe, O.F.M., "Why the Church Is Granting More Annulments," AmericanCatholic.org. http://www.americancatholic.org/newsletters/cu/ac1080.asp; emphasis added. Used by permission of St. Anthony Messenger Press, 28 W. Liberty St., Cincinnati, OH 45202. 800-488-0488. www.americancatholic.org. © 1980. All rights reserved.

17. Ibid.

18. "Why Can't Women Have Multiple Husbands?" Islamic Centre.org, http://www.islamiccentre.org/index.php?option=com_content&view=article&id=445:why-cant-women-have-multiple-husbands-&catid=40:marriage-faqs&Itemid=88.

19. Elizabeth Fox-Genovese, *Marriage: The Dream That Refuses to Die* (Wilmington, DE: Intercollegiate Studies Institute, 2008), 7–8.

20. Gallagher, *Abolition of Marriage*, 9.

21. Jason M. Fields and Kristin E. Smith, "Poverty, Family Structure, and Child Well-Being," US Bureau of the Census, April 1998, working paper no. 23, http://www.census.gov/population/www/documentation/twps0023/twps0023.html.

22. Jennifer Marshall, "Marriage Shows the Way Out of Poverty," The Heritage Foundation, October 4, 2010, http://www.heritage.org/Research/Commentary/2010/10/Marriage-Shows-the-Way-Out-of-Poverty.

23. Irwin McClanahan, Sara S. Robbins, Philip K. Garfinkel, eds., *Child Support and Child Well-Being* (Lanham, MD: University Press of America, 1997).

24. David J. Eggebeen and Daniel T. Lichter, "Race, Family Structure, and Changing Poverty Among American Children," *American Sociological Review* 56, no.6 (1991): 80117.

25. David Popenoe, *War Over the Family* (New Brunswick, NJ: Transaction, 2008).

26. William G. Axinn and Arland Thornton, "The Relationship Between Cohabitation and Divorce: Selectivity or Causal Influence?" *Demography* 29, no. 3 (August 1992): 357–74; M. D. Bramlett and W. D. Mosher, "Cohabitation, Marriage, Divorce, and Remarriage in the United States," National Center for Health Statistics, *Vital Health Stat* 23 (22): 2002.

27. Larry L. Bumpass and James A. Sweet, "National Rates of Cohabitation," *Demography*, 26, no. 4 (November 1989): 615–25; Betsey Stevenson and Justin Wolfers, "Marriage and Divorce: Changes and Their Driving Forces," *Journal of Economic Perspectives, American Economic Association* 21, no. 2 (Spring): 27–52.

28. Linda J. Waite and Maggie Gallagher, *The Case for Marriage: Why Married People Are Happier, Healthier, and Better Off Financially* (New York: Doubleday, 2000), 37.

29. Elizabeth H. Baker, Laura Ann Sanchez, Steven L. Nock, and James D. Wright, "Covenant Marriage and the Sanctification of Gendered Marital Roles," *Journal of Family Issues* 30, no. 2 (2009): 147–78.

30. Jennifer Baker as quoted in "Fact Sheet: Marriages and Divorces in America," Real Relational Solutions, http://www.terryreal.com/press/pdfs/marriage_divorce_in_america-FS.pdf.

31. Honorable Anne Kass (retired judge Second Judical District), Albuquerque, NM, "Second Marriage Can Be as Difficult as the First

One," DivorceRecovery101.com, http://www.divorcerecovery101.com
/kass81.html.

32. "Fact Sheet: Marriages and Divorces in America."

33. Douglas Allen and Maggie Gallagher, "Does Divorce Law Affect the
Divorce Rate? A Review of Empirical Research, 1995–2006," IMAPP
Research Brief, *Institute for Marriage and the Family* 1, no. 1 (2007), 1.

34. Ibid., 2.

35. Ibid., 1.

36. Gallagher, *The Abolition of Marriage*, 247–65.

37. George Barna December 21, 1999, survey data cited in "U.S. Divorce
Rates for Various Faith Groups, Age Groups, and Geographical Areas,"
Ontario Consultants for Religious Tolerance.org, http://www
.religioustolerance.org/chr_dira.htm.

38. National Center for Policy Analysis, "Bible Belt Leads US in Divorces,"
Daily Policy Digest, November 19, 1999, http://www.ncpa.org/sub/dpd
/index.php?Article_ID=10961.

39. George Barna, "New Marriage and Divorce Rates Released," March 31,
2008, http://www.barna.org/barna-update/article/15-familykids
/42-new-marriage-and-divorce-statistics-released.

40. Ibid.

41. Ibid.

42. W. Bradford Wilcox and Steven L. Nock, "What's Love Got to Do with
It? Equality, Equity, Commitment and Women's Marital Quality," *Social
Forces* 84, no. 3 (March 2006): 1339.

43. W. Bradford Wilcox, *Soft Patriarchs, New Men: How Christianity Shapes
Fathers and Husbands* (Chicago: University of Chicago Press, 2004).

44. W. Bradford Wilcox, "Religion and the Domestication of Men," *Contexts*,
Fall 2006, 42.

45. Wilcox, "Religion and the Domestication of Men," 44; W. Bradford
Wilcox and Nicholas Wolfinger, "Living and Loving 'Decent': Religion
and Relationship Quality Among Urban Parents," *Social Science Research*
37 (2008): 828–43.

46. C. S. Lewis, *Mere Christianity* (New York: Harper One, 1952), 112.

47. Robert P. George, "Gay Marriage, Democracy, and the Courts," *Wall
Street Journal*, August 3, 2009, http://online.wsj.com/article/SB10001424
0529702046190045743220842795484334.html.

48. Ibid.

49. *Goodridge v. Dept. of Public Health*, 798 N.E.2d 941 (Mass. 2003).
50. Fox-Genovese, *Marriage*, 43–44.
51. *Encyclopedia.com*, s.v. "rational basis test," http://www.encyclopedia.com /doc/1G2-3437703651.html.
52. *Lawrence v. Texas*, 539 US 558 (2003).
53. Fox-Genovese, *Marriage*, 43–44.
54. Christine Vestal, "California Gay Marriage Ruling Sparks a New Debate," Stateline.org, http://www.stateline.org/live/details/story ?contentId=310206.
55. Ian Urbina, "Gay Marriage Is Legal in the Capital," *New York Times*, March 3, 2010, http://www.nytimes.com/2010/03/04/us/04marriage.html.
56. Hannah Wilkens, "D.C. Mayor to Sign Gay Marriage Bill at Church," Gay Vantage, December 17, 2009, http://www.gayvantage.com/gay -agenda/gay-marriage/d-c-mayor-to-sign-gay-marriage-bill-at-a-church -8177717/.
57. Vestal, "California Gay Marriage Ruling."
58. *Perry v. Schwarzenegger*, 704 F. Supp. 2d 921 (N.D. Cal. 2010).
59. Joe Eskenazi, "Prop. 8 Ruling: Judge Vaughn Walker's Most Scathing Language," *SF Weekly* (blog), August 4, 2010, http://blogs.sfweekly.com /thesnitch/2010/08/prop_8_ruling_judge_vaughn_wal.php.
60. Ibid.
61. Peter Henderson and Dan Levine, "California Gay Marriage Case Hangs on a Technicality," Reuters, August 17, 2010, http://www.reuters .com/article/idUSTRE67G4Y820100817.
62. *Defense of Marriage Act*, Public Law 104-199, *U.S. Statutes at Large* 110 (1997), 2419.
63. "Powers Reserved to the States," *Defense of Marriage Act*, Public Law 104- 199, *U.S. Statutes at Large* 110 (1997), 2419.
64. "Definition of Marriage," *Defense of Marriage Act*, Public Law 104-199, *U.S. Statutes at Large* 110 (1997), 2419.
65. Ibid.
66. Vestal, "California Gay Marriage Ruling."
67. Robert Benne and Gerald McDermott, "Speaking Out: Why Gay Marriages Would Be Harmful," *Christianity Today*, February 1, 2004, http://www.christianitytoday.com/ct/2004/februaryweb-only/2-16 -41.0.html?start=2.

68. Gerald McDermott, "The Problem with Gay Marriage," debate at Antrim Chapel, Roanoke College, March 18, 2004.

69. Benne and McDermott, "Speaking Out."

70. Andrew Sullivan, *Virtually Normal: An Argument About Homosexuality* (New York: Vintage, 1996).

71. Benne and McDermott, "Speaking Out."

72. Paul Cameron and Kirk Cameron, "Homosexual Parents," *Adolescence* 31, no. 24 (Winter 1996): 757–75; Judith Stacey and Timothy Biblarz, "(How) Does the Sexual Orientation of Parents Matter," *American Sociological Review* 66, no. 2 (April 2001): 159–83; Gary Remafedi, James Farrow, and Robert W. Deisher, "Risk Factors for Attempted Suicide in Gay and Bisexual Youth," *Pediatrics* 87, no. 6 (June 1991): 869–75.

73. *Loving v. Virginia*, 388 US 1 (1967).

74. George, "Gay Marriage, Democracy, and the Courts."

75. *Hernandez v. Robles*, 7 NY3d 338 (NY 2006) http://www.courts.state .ny.us/reporter/3dseries/2006/2006_05239.htm.

76. Lawrence D. Jones, "The American Bar Association Adopts Gay Marriage Resolution," *Christian Post*, August 13, 2010, http://www .christianpost.com/article/20100813/american-bar-association -backs-same-sex-marriage/.

77. William N. Eskridge, *The Case for Same Sex Marriage: From Sexual Liberty to Civilized Commitment* (New York: Free Press, 1996).

78. George, "Gay Marriage, Democracy, and the Courts."

79. Ibid.

80. Lydia Saad, "American Acceptance of Gay Relations," Gallup, May 25, 2010, http://www.gallup.com/poll/135764/Americans-Acceptance-Gay -Relations-Crosses-Threshold.aspx.

81. "Americans Still Opposed to Gay Marriage," *Public Policy Polling* (blog), August 13, 2010, http://publicpolicypolling.blogspot.com/2010/08 /americans-still-opposed-to-gay-marriage.html.

82. Matthew J. Franck and Gwen Brown, "Same-Sex Marriage and Public Opinion: Spirals, Frames, and the Seinfeld Effect," *Public Discourse*, Witherspoon Institute, August 30, 2010, http://www.thepublicdiscourse .com/2010/08/1551.

83. Pew Research Center, "Public Opinion on Gay Marriage: Opponents Consistently Outnumber Opponents," *Pew Research Center's Forum on Religion and Public Life*, July 9, 2009, http://pewforum.org/Gay-Marriage

-and-Homosexuality/Public-Opinion-on-Gay-Marriage-Opponents
-Consistently-Outnumber-Supporters.aspx.

84. Jeni Loftus, "America's Liberalization in Attitudes Towards
Homosexuality, 1973–1998," *American Sociological Review* 66, no. 5
(October 2001): 762–82.

85. Lewis, *Mere Christianity*, 112.

86. Pew Research Center, "Religious Groups' Official Positions on Same
Sex Marriage," *Pew Research Center's Forum on Religion and Public Life*, July
27, 2010, http://pewforum.org/Gay-Marriage-and-Homosexuality
/Religious-Groups-Official-Positions-on-Same-Sex-Marriage.aspx.

87. Ibid.

88. Laurie Goodstein, "Lutherans Offer Warm Welcome to Gay Pastors,"
New York Times, July 25, 2010, http://www.nytimes.com/2010/07/26
/us/26lutheran.html.

89. Jeff Martin, "Lutherans Opposed to Gay Clergy form New US
Denomination," *USA Today*, August 27, 2010, http://www.usatoday.com
/news/religion/2010-08-28-Lutheran27_ST_N.htm.

90. Jan Hoffman, "Can a Boy Wear a Skirt to School?" *New York Times*,
November 8, 2009, http://www.nytimes.com/2009/11/08/fashion
/08cross.html.

91. Robie Harris, *It's Perfectly Normal* (Cambridge, MA: Candlewick Press,
1996); http://www.prolifewaco.org/documents/Normal4pages.pdf.

92. Kathryn Jean Lopez, "The Cookie Crumbles: The Girl Scouts Go PC,"
National Review, October 23, 2000, http://old.nationalreview.com
/23oct00/lopez102300.shtml.

93. Nancy Manahan, *On My Honor: Lesbians Reflect on Their Scouting Experience*
(Northboro, MA: Madwoman, 1997).

94. Lopez, "The Cookie Crumbles."

95. Chris McGreal, "Sexual Abuse Scandal Rocks Boy Scouts of America
After $18.5m Payout," *Guardian*, April 29, 2010, http://www.guardian
.co.uk/world/2010/apr/29/boy-scouts-sexual-abuse-dykes.

96. Anne Hendershott, *The Politics of Abortion* (New York: Encounter, 2006),
80–92.

97. Paula Martinac, "Do We Condone Pedophilia?" PlanetOut.com,
February 27, 2002, as cited in Peter Sprigg, "The Top Ten Myths About
Homosexuality," (Washington D.C.: Family Research Council, 2010).

98. Ibid.

99. Edward O. Laumann, John H. Gagnon, Robert T. Michael, and Stuart Michaels, *The Social Organization of Sexuality: Sexual Practices in the United States* (Chicago: University of Chicago Press, 1994), 293.

100. William F. Jasper, "Obama's Safe Schools Czar," *New American*, November 24, 2009, http://www.thenewamerican.com/index.php /culture/education/2386-obamas-safe-schools-czar-kevin-jennings.

101. Ibid.

102. Michael O'Brien, "53 Republicans Demand the Firing of 'Safe Schools Czar' Kevin Jennings," *The Hill* (blog), October 15, 2009, http://thehill .com/blogs/blog-briefing-room/news/63249-53-republicans-demand -firing-of-safe-schools-czar.

103. Jack Date, "Duke U. Official Caught in Alleged Child Sex Sting," ABC News, June 26, 2009, http://abcnews.go.com/News/story?id=7942546 &page=1.

104. Nicholas Sabloff, "Frank Lombard, Duke Univ. Official, Charged in Child Sex Case," Huffington Post, June 27, 2009, http://www .huffingtonpost.com/2009/06/27/frank-lombard-duke-univ-o_n _221900.html.

105. J. Budziszewski, *The Revenge of Conscience*, 20.

106. Popenoe, *War Over the Family*, 4.

107. US Census Bureau, "Current Population Survey (CPS)—Definitions and Explanations," http://www.census.gov/population/www/cps /cpsdef.html.

108. Paul Boghossian, "What Is Social Construction?" in *Times Literary Supplement*, February 2001, http://as.nyu.edu/docs/IO/1153 /socialconstruction.pdf.

109. Ibid.

110. Linda Gordon, "Functions of the Family," *WOMEN: A Journal of Liberation*, Fall 1969.

111. Sheila Cronan, "Marriage," in Anne Koedt, Ellen Levine, and Anita Rapone, eds., *Radical Feminism* (New York: HarperCollins, 1973), 219.

112. Rebecca Walker as cited in Bridget Bland, "Alice Walker's Estranged Daughter Makes Startling Revelations About 'Color Purple' Author," EntertainmentWire.com, September 17, 2010, http://www.bvnewswire .com/2010/09/17/alice-walkers-rebecca-walker-startling-revelations.

113. Phyllis Schlafly, *Feminist Fantasies* (Dallas: Spence, 2003), 207.

114. Pamela Johnston Conover and Virginia Gray, *Feminism and the New Right: Conflict Over the American Family* (New York: Praeger, 1983), 70.

115. Louise B. Silverstein and Carl F. Auerbach, "Deconstructing the Essential Father," *American Psychologist* 54, no. 6 (June 1999): 397–407.

116. Ibid., 397.

117. Ibid., 400–7.

118. Robert Nolin, "State Agency Won't Fight to Keep Florida's Ban on Gay Adoptions, *Sun Sentinel,* October 12, 2010.

119. Media Matters, "Tony Perkins' fearmongering about same-sex parenting is refuted by medical consensus," August 8, 2010, http://mediamatters .org/research/201008080013.

120. Sara McLanahan and Gary Sandefur, *Growing Up with a Single Parent: What Hurts, What Helps* (Cambridge: Harvard University Press, 1994), 1.

121. National Marriage Project at Rutgers University, "The State of Our Unions: The Social Health of Marriage in America," July 2005, http:// www.virginia.edu/marriageproject/pdfs/SOOU2005.pdf.

122. Noval Glenn and Thomas Sylvester with Alex Roberts, "The Shift and the Denial: Scholarly Attitudes Toward Family Change, 1977-2002," Center for Marriage and Families, *Research Brief* 8 (February 2008).

123. Kyle Pruett, *Fatherneed* (New York: Broadway, 2001), 204.

124. Bruce J. Ellis, "Does Father Absence Place Daughters at Risk for Early Sexual Activity and Teenage Pregnancy?" *Child Development* 74, no. 3 (May/June 2003): 801–21; David Popenoe, *Life Without Father* (Cambridge, MA: Harvard University Press, 1999).

125. Brenda Hunter, *The Power of Mother Love: Transforming Both Mother and Child* (Colorado Springs: WaterBrook, 1997); Eleanor MacCoby, *The Two Sexes: Growing Up Apart, Coming Together* (Cambridge, MA: Harvard University Press, 1998).

126. Albert Mohler, "Should Spanking Be Banned? Parental Authority Under Assault," Christianity.com, http://www.christianity.com /Christian%20Living/Just%20for%20Families/1269621/page2/print/.

127. Benjamin Spock and Stephen J. Parker, *Dr. Spock's Baby and Child Care*, 7th ed. (New York: Simon & Schuster, 1998), 437–38.

128. Daniel Costello, "Spanking Makes a Comeback: Tired of Spoiling the Child, Parents Stop Sparing the Rod; Dr. Dobson vs. Dr. Spock," *Wall Street Journal,* June 9, 2000, W1.

129. Quigley Moynihan, personal communication with author, March 2010.

130. Associated Press, "More Texas Parents Opt for Home Schooling," WFAA.com, August 23, 2010, http://www.wfaa.com/news/texas-news /More-Texas-parents-opt-for-home-schooling-101292714.html.

131. Valonda Calloway, "Wake Judge Orders Home Schoolers into Public Schools," March 12, 2009, http://www.wral.com/news/local/story /4727161/; Associated Press, "Home-Schooler Ordered to Attend Public Schools," *Washington Times*, September 4, 2009, http://www .washingtontimes.com/news/2009/sep/04/home-schooled-christian -girl-ordered-to-join-publi/print.

132. Phyllis Schlafly, "The Awesome Power of Family Courts," *Phyllis Schlafly Report* 43, no. 11 (June 2010): 1.

133. Daniel Patrick Moynihan, "The Negro Family: The Case for National Action," Office of Policy Planning and Research, United States Department of Labor (March 1965), http://www.blackpast.org/?q =primary/moynihan-report-1965.

134. Elizabeth Wright, "The Moynihan Report: 30 Years Later and Counting," *Issues and Views* (blog), Winter 1995.

135. V. Dion Haynes, "Blacks Hit Hard by Economy's Punch: 34.5 Percent of Young African American Men Are Unemployed," *Washington Post*, November 11, 2009, http://www.washingtonpost.com/wp-dyn/content /article/2009/11/23/AR2009112304092.html.

136. Joy Jones, "Marriage Is for White People," *Washington Post*, March 26, 2006, http://www.washingtonpost.com/wp-dyn/content/article/2006 /03/25/AR2006032500029.html.

137. Daniel Lichter, Diane K. McLaughlin, George Kephart, and David J. Landry, "Race and the Retreat from Marriage: A Shortage of Marriageable Men?" *American Sociological Review* 57, no. 6 (December 1992): 781–99.

138. Erma Jean Lawson and Tanya L. Sharpe, "Black Men and Divorces: Implications for Culturally Competent Practice, *Minority Health Today*, 2000, 1.

139. William J. Sabol and Heather Couture, Bureau of Justice Statistics, "Prison Inmates at Midyear 2007" (Washington, DC: US Department of Justice, June 2008), NCJ.221944, 7.

140. Bureau of Justice Statistics, "Homicide Trends," http://bjs.ojp.usdoj.gov /content/homicide/race.cfm.

141. Patrick Fagan, "The US Index of Belonging and Rejection," *Research*

Synthesis, Marriage and Family Research Institute, Family Research Council (December 2010): 3.

142. Centers for Disease Control and Prevention, "HIV in the United States," fact sheet, July 2010, http://www.cdc.gov/hiv/resources/factsheets /us.htm.

143. Ibid.

144. Jose Antonio Vargas and Darryl Fears, "At Least 3 Percent of D.C. Residents Have HIV or AIDS, City Study Finds; Rate Up 22% from 2006," *Washington Post,* March 15, 2009, http://www.washingtonpost .com/wp-dyn/content/article/2009/03/14/AR2009031402176.html.

145. Ibid.

146. Ibid.

147. Benoit Denizet-Lewis, "Double Lives on the Down Low," *New York Times Magazine,* August 3, 2003, 28–33.

148. Ibid.

149. Jessie Heath and Kathy Goggin, "Attitudes Towards Male Homosexuality, Bisexuality, and the Down Low Lifestyle: Demographic Differences and HIV Implications," *Journal of Bisexuality* 9, no 1 (January 2009): 17–31. Copyright Taylor and Francis, 325 Chestnut St., Suite 800, Philadelphia, PA 19106. 215-625-8900, ext. 293. www.taylorandfrancis.com.

150. Ibid., 17–18.

151. Richard J. Wolitski, Kenneth T. Jones, Jill L. Wasserman, and Jennifer C. Smith, "Self Identification as 'Down Low' Among Men Who Have Sex with Men (MSM) from 12 US Cities,' *AIDS Behavior* 10, no. 5 (2006): 519.

152. Ibid., 519–20.

153. Keith Boykin, *Beyond the Down Low: Sex, Lies, and Denial in Black America* (New York: Carroll and Graf, 2005), 28–29.

154. Patrik Jonsson, "Bishop Eddie Long Case: Will It Alter Black Church's View of Gays?" *Christian Science Monitor,* September 22, 2010, http://www .csmonitor.com/USA/2010/0922/Bishop-Eddie-Long-case-Will-it -alter-black-church-s-view-of-gays.

155. Pew Research Center, "Majority Continues to Support Civil Unions," *Pew Research Center's Forum on Religion & Public Life,* October 9, 2009, http://pewforum.org/Gay-Marriage-and-Homosexuality/Majority -Continues-To-Support-Civil-Unions.aspx#1.

156. Krissah Thompson, "The NAACP Reaches Out to Gays," *Washington Post,* September 23, 2010, http://www.washingtonpost.com/wp-dyn /content/article/2010/09/22/AR2010092205697.html.

157. Charles Murray, *Losing Ground: American Social Policy, 1950–1980* (New York: Basic Books, 1984).

158. Thomas Sowell, *Barbarians Inside the Gates: And Other Controversial Essays* (Stanford, CA: Hoover Institution Press, 1999), 182–83.

159. Glenn Loury, "A Professor Under Reconstruction," in Kelly Monroe, ed., *Finding God at Harvard: Spiritual Journeys of Thinking Christians* (Grand Rapids: Zondervan, 1996), 69.

160. W. Bradford Wilcox and Nicholas Wolfinger, "Then Comes Marriage? Religion, race, and marriage in urban America," *Social Science Research* 36, no. 2 (2007), 569–89.

161. Horace Cayton and St. Clair Drake, *Black Metropolis: A Study of Negro Life in a Northern City* (New York: Harcourt, Brace, and Company, 1945), 612, 615.

162. Patrick F. Fagan, "Religious Practice and Educational Attainment," unpublished paper, Family Research Council, Washington, D.C.

163. For instance, see Richard B. Freeman, "Who Escapes? The Relation of Church-Going and Other Background Factors to the Socio-Economic Performance of Black Male Youths from Inner-City Poverty Tracts," *Working Paper Series* no. 1656 (Cambridge, MA: National Bureau of Economic Research, 1985); Patrick F. Fagan, "Why Religion Matters: The Impact of Religious Practice on Social Stability," *Backgrounder* no. 1064 (Washington, D.C.: Heritage Foundation, 1996); David B. Larson, and Byron R. Johnson, "Religion: The Forgotten Factor in Cutting Youth Crime and Saving At-Risk Urban Youth," report 98-102, (New York: Manhattan Institute, 1998).

164. Richard M. Weaver, *Ideas Have Consequences* (1948; Chicago: University of Chicago Press, 1984), 3.

165. The Manhattan Declaration, http://www.manhattandeclaration.org /the-declaration/read.aspx.

CHAPTER 5: IMMIGRATION, THE RULE OF LAW, AND NATIONAL SOVEREIGNTY

1. President Theodore Roosevelt, "Letter to the President of the American Defense Society," January 3, 1919, in Joseph Bucklin Bishop, ed., *Theodore Roosevelt and His Time Shown in His Own Letters* (New York: Scribners, 1920), 2:474, available at http://www.theodoreroosevelt.org/tr%20web %20book/tr_cd_to_html280.html.

2. C-SPAN coverage of House Judiciary Committee, Subcommittee on

Immigration, Citizenship, Refugees, Border Security, & International Law, *panel on Immigrant Farm Workers*, September 24, 2010, http://www.c-spanvideo.org/program/295639-1.

3. Lou Dobbs, *War on the Middle Class: How Government, Big Business, and Special Interest Groups Are Waging War on the American Dream and How to Fight Back* (New York: Viking, 2006).

4. Kay B. Day, "Did Democrat Invite Colbert to Distract from Dr. Swain's Damaging Testimony on Immigration?" *US Report*, September 26, 2010, http://www.theusreport.com/the-us-report/2010/9/26/did-democrat-invite-colbert-to-distract-from-dr-swains-damag.html.

5. Ibid.

6. Philip Martin, "Farm Labor Shortages: How Real? What Response?" Center for Immigration Studies, *Backgrounder Report*, November 2007.

7. The data for the U-6 calculations came from Stephen Camarota's "From Bad to Worse: Unemployment Among Less Educated US Born Workers, 2007–2010," Center for Immigration Studies, *Backgrounder Report*, August 2010.

8. Mark Krikorian, *How Obama Is Transforming America Through Immigration* (New York: Encounter, 2010), 10.

9. Ibid., 7.

10. Westat Evaluation of the E-Verify Program: USCIS Synopsis of Key Findings and Program Implications (January 2010). The report estimated the program's total "accuracy" and "inaccuracy" rates (i.e., how consistent were the responses with the person's actual work authorization status) for the first time, finding that 96 percent of all E-Verify initial responses were consistent with the person's work authorization status, and that the remaining 4.1 percent inaccuracy rate was primarily due to identity fraud. Looking just at the group of authorized workers, Westat found that more than 99 percent of that subset of E-Verify cases are initially found to be employment authorized—a resounding affirmation of the accuracy and efficiency of the system. See http://www.uscis.gov/USCIS/Native%20Docs/Westat%20Evaluation%20of%20the%20E-Verify%20Program.pdf.

11. *Aliens and Nationality: Immigration and Nationality, U.S. Code* 8 (year), §§ 1101, available at Cornell Law School Legal Information Institute, http://www.law.cornell.edu/uscode/html/uscode08/usc_sec_08_00001101----000-.html.

12. Jeffrey Passel, "The Size and Characteristics of the Unauthorized Migrant Population in the U.S.," *Pew Hispanic*, http://pewhispanic.org /files/reports/61.pdf.

13. Griselda Nevarez, "Many illegal immigrants enter on visas," Cronkite News Service, May 10, 2010, http://ktar.com/?sid=1292983&nid=6.

14. Heather McDonald, "Say No to Amnesty," Forbes.Com, June 28, 2010, http://www.manhattan-institute.org/html/mac_donald.htm/.

15. Ibid.

16. Douglas Massey, "Borderline Madness: America's Counterproductive Immigration Policy" in Carol M. Swain, ed., *Debating Immigration* (New York: Cambridge University Press, 2007), 129–38.

17. The Mexica Movement, http://www.mexica-movement.org/.

18. "Hispanic Group Boycotts Disney 'White Supremacist,'" WorldNetDaily, July 15, 2006, http://www.wnd.com/?pageId=37030.

19. Carol M. Swain, "Mission Creep and the Southern Poverty Law Center's Misguided Focus," Huffington Post, August 10, 2009, http:// www.huffingtonpost.com/carol-m-swain/mission-creep-and-the -sou_b_255029.html.

20. Heidi Beirich and Mark Potok, "Broken Record," *Intelligence Report*, no. 120 (Winter 2005), http://www.splcenter.org/get-informed/intelligence -report/browse-all-issues/2005/winter/broken-record.

21. Swain, "Mission Creep."

22. James Taranto, "In Defense of Carol Swain," *Wall Street Journal*, October 26, 2009, http://online.wsj.com/article/SB1000142405274870433590457 4496250622719022.html.

23. The 2010 retraction and apology appears online at the beginning of David Holthouse, "State of Denial: Turkey Spends Millions to Cover Up Armenian Genocide," *Intelligence Report*, no. 130 (Summer 2008), http:// www.splcenter.org/get-informed/intelligence-report/browse-all-issues /2008/summer/state-of-denial; Turkish Coalition of America, "Free Inquiry Triumphs, Professor Guenter Lewy's Reputation Restored: Southern Poverty Law Center Retracts False Statements That Professor Lewy's Scholarship Challenging the Armenian Thesis Was Compromised," *TCS News and Issues*, September 30, 2010, http://www .turkishcoalition.org/ProfessorGuenterLewysReputationRestored.html.

24. Office of Intelligence and Analysis Assessment, "Rightwing Extremism: Current Economic and Political Climate Fueling Resurgence in

Radicalization and Recruitment, The Department of Homeland Security," April 7, 2009, 4–6.

25. N. C. Aizenman and Spencer S. Hsu, "Activist's Arrest Highlights Key Immigrant Issue," *Washington Post*, October 21, 2007, http://www .washingtonpost.com/wp-dyn/content/article/2007/08/20 /AR2007082001675.html.

26. Timothy Thomas Jr., "You Are No Rosa Parks," *Chicago Sun-Times*, August 21, 2006.

27. Harry R. Jackson Jr. and Tony Perkins, *Personal Faith and Public Policy* (Lake Mary, FL: Frontline, 2008), 82.

28. "Illegal Alien Activist Elvira Arellano Hides Out in Church to Avoid Deportation," *Diggers Realm* (blog), August 16, 2006, http://www .diggersrealm.com/mt/archives/001790.html.

29. *Dred Scott v. Sandford*, 60 US 393 (1857). "Dred Scott: The Supreme Court Decision," *PBS: Africans in America*, http://www.pbs.org/wgbh/aia/part4 /4h2933t.html.

30. Peter Schuck, "Birthright of a Nation," *New York Times*, August 13, 2010, http://www.nytimes.com/2010/08/14/opinion/14schuck.html.

31. Elizabeth Cohen, "*Jus Tempus* in the Magna Carta: The Sovereignty of Time" in *Modern Politics and Citizenship* (July 2010): 463–66. See Elizabeth Cohen, "Carved from the Inside Out; Immigration and America's Public Philosophy of Citizenship," in Carol M. Swain, ed., *Debating Immigration* (New York: Cambridge University Press, 2007), 32–45.

32. *United States v. Wong Kim Ark*, 169 US 649 (1898), 42 L. Ed. 890 (1898).

33. Chinese Exclusion Act, 22 Stat. 58 (1882). For more information, see Sucheng Chan, ed., *Entry Denied: Exclusion and the Chinese Community in America, 1882–1943* (Philadelphia: Temple University Press, 1991).

34. *Elkins v. Wilkins*, 112 US 94, 5. S. Ct. 41, 28 L. Ed. 643 (1884).

35. Peter H. Schuck and Rogers M. Smith, *Citizens Without Consent: Illegal Aliens in the American Polity* (New Haven, CT: Yale University Press, 1985), 5.

36. Gerald L. Neuman, congressional testimony for the panel, "Societal and Legal Issues Surrounding Children Born in the United States to Illegal Alien Parents," Joint Hearing Before the Subcommittee on Immigration and Claims and the Subcommittee on the Constitution of the House Committee on the Judiciary, 104th Cong. 1st Sess., (December 13, 1995) 105–9.

37. Peter Schuck, "Birthright of a Nation."

38. Ibid.

39. Ibid.

40. See Schuck and Smith, *Citizens Without Consent*.

41. Jon Feere, "Birthright Citizenship in the United States: A Global Comparison," *Backgrounder Report* (Washington, D.C.: Center for Immigration Studies, August 2010).

42. Ibid.

43. Richard Posner, "The Controversy Over Birthright Citizenship—Posner," Posner/Becker Blog, http://www.becker-posner-blog.com/.

44. Schuck and Smith, *Citizens Without Consent*, 9–42; Dan Stein and John Bauer, "Interpreting the 14th Amendment: Automatic Citizenship for Children of Illegal Immigrants," *Stanford L. & Policy Rev.* 127, no. 130 (1996), 7; Feere, "Birthright Citizenship in the United States."

45. John McCaslin, "Inside the Beltway: Rotund Tourists," *Washington Times*, August 27, 2002, A7.

46. Keith Richburg, "For Many Pregnant Chinese, a US Passport for Baby Remains a Powerful Lure," *Washington Post*, July 18, 2010, http://www.washingtonpost.com/wp-dyn/content/article/2010/07/17/AR2010071701402.html.

47. "New York Hotel Pioneers Birth Tourism," *Muslim Observer*, June 24, 2010, http://muslimmedianetwork.com/mmn/?p=6400.

48. Marianna Alvarado, "Hospital Lures Mexican Moms; Tucson Medical Center 'Birth Package' Raises Questions," *Arizona Daily Star*, June 28, 2009, http://www.wincoast.com/forum/archive/index.php/t-90605.html.

49. For more details, see Schuck and Smith, *Citizens Without Consent*.

50. Congressional Budget Office, "The Impact of Illegal Immigration on the States," http://www.cbo.gov/ftpdocs/87xx/doc8711/12-6-Immigration.pdf.

51. James Orlando, "Summary of Arizona Immigration Legislation and Legislation in Other States," http://www.cga.ct.gov/2010/rpt/2010-R-0213.htm.

52. Ibid.

53. Randal C. Archibold, "Judge Blocks Arizona's Immigration Law," *New York Times*, July 29, 2010, http://www.nytimes.com/2010/07/29/us/29arizona.html.

54. Patrick Goodenough, "Obama Administration Submits Arizona

Immigration Law to U.N. Review, Reviving Questions About US Engagement with Human Rights Council," August 31, 2010, CNSNews.com, http://www.cnsnews.com/news/article/71922.

55. Stephen Dinan and Kara Rowland, "Justice: Sanctuary Cities Safe from Law," *Washington Times*, July 14, 2010, http://www.washingtontimes.com/news/2010/jul/14/justice-sanctuary-cities-are-no-arizona/.

56. Krikorian, *Transforming America through Immigration*, 1–40.

57. Susan Carroll, "Immigration cases being tossed by the hundreds: Docket review pulls curtain back on procedure by Homeland Security," *Houston Chronicle*, October 16, 2010, http://www.chron.com/disp/story.mpl/metropolitan/7249505.html.

58. Randal Archibal, "Mexican Drug Cartel Violence Spills Over, Alarming U.S," *New York Times*, March 23, 2009, http://www.nytimes.com/2009/03/23/us/23border.html.

59. Peter Schuck, "The Disconnect Between Public Attitudes and Policy Outcomes in Immigration," in Carol M. Swain, ed., *Debating Immigration* (New York: Cambridge University Press, 2007), 17–31.

60. Brad Hirschfield, "Welcoming Bible's 'Stranger' May Not Include Illegal Aliens," *Washington Post*, May 25, 2010, http://onfaith.washingtonpost.com/onfaith/panelists/brad_hirschfield/2010/05/welcoming_bibles_stranger_may_not_include_illegal_aliens.html.

61. John Pomfret, "Cardinal Puts Church in Fight for Immigration," *Washington Post*, April 2, 2006, http://www.washingtonpost.com/wp-dyn/content/article/2006/04/01/AR2006040101206.html.

62. Carol Zimmerman, "Drop in number of US Catholics offset by new immigrants, study says," Catholic News Service, February 27, 2008, http://www.catholicnews.com/data/stories/cns/0801087.htm.

63. Parts of this section were published in Carol M. Swain, "A Judeo-Christian Approach to Immigration Reform," *Review of Faith and International Affairs* 8, no. 2 (June 2011): 3–14.

64. National Council of La Raza is an advocacy group for Hispanics that wields considerable influence in the nation. *La Raza* is a Spanish expression for "the race."

65. Westoff, "Immigration and Future Population Change in America"; Heather McDonald, "Say No to Amnesty," *Forbes*, June 28, 2010, http://www.forbes.com/forbes/2010/0628/special-report-immigration-laws-deportation-mexico-say-no-to-reform.html.

66. J. S. Passel, "The Size and Characteristics of the Unauthorized Migrant Population in the US," Pew Hispanic Center Research Report, March 7, 2006, http://pewhispanic.org/files/reports/61.pdf.

67. Operation Paperclip, "Welcome to Operation Paperclip," http://www.operationpaperclip.info/.

68. Capitol Immigration Law Group, "Report Highlights E-Verify Accuracy Problems," February 25, 2010, http://www.cilawgroup.com/news/2010/02/25/report-highlights-e-verify-accuracy-problems/.

69. Peter Schuck, "Birthright of a Nation."

70. Thomas Hobbes, *The Leviathan* (1651; London: C. J. Clay and Sons, 1904), 84.

71. Brian Z. Tamanaha, *On the Rule of Law: History, Politics, Theory* (New York: Cambridge University Press, 2004), 4–5.

72. Ibid.

73. James C. McKinley Jr., "A Mexican Manual for Illegal Migrants Upsets Some in US," *New York Times,* January 6, 2005, http://cryptome.quintessenz.org/mirror/mx/mx-migrants.htm.

74. Leo Shane III, "INS Plans to Deport Wife of GI in Iraq," Military.com, June 25, 2009, http://www.military.com/news/article/ins-plans-to-deport-wife-of-gi-in-iraq.html.

75. Deborah Davis, "Illegal Immigrants: Uncle Sam Wants You," *In These Times,* July 25, 2007, http://www.inthesetimes.com/article/3271; Julia Preston, "US Military Will Offer a Path to Citizenship," *New York Times,* February 15, 2009, http://www.nytimes.com/2009/02/15/us/15immig.html.

76. David McClemore, "Immigrant Soldiers Serve the US," *Dallas Morning News,* November 28, 2006.

77. Jerry Markon, Shaiq Hussain, and William Wan, "5 US Men Had Months of Contact with Taliban Officials," *Washington Post,* December 12, 2009, http://www.washingtonpost.com/wp-dyn/content/article/2009/12/11/AR2009121101337.html.

78. "Five Muslim Soldiers Arrested over Fort Jackson Poison Probe," *New York Post,* February 19, 2010, http://www.nypost.com/p/news/national/five_muslim_soldiers_arrested_over_zYTtFXIBnCecWcbGNobUEJ.

79. Pew Center Report, "Muslim Americans: Middle Class and Mostly Mainstream," http://pewresearch.org/assets/pdf/muslim-americans.pdf.

80. Ronald Kessler, *The Terrorist Watch: Inside the Desperate Race to Stop the Next Attack* (New York: Three Rivers Press, 2007).

81. Arnaud Borchgrave, "Al Qaeda's US Network," *Washington Times*, August 12, 2004, http://www.washingtontimes.com/news/2004 /aug/12/20040812-094056-4667r/.

82. Evan Perez and Keith Johnson, "Hasan, Radical Cleric Had Contact," *Wall Street Journal*, November 11, 2009, http://online.wsj.com/article /SB125778227582138829.html; Markon, Hussain, and Wan, "5 US Men Had Contact."

83. Kelly P. Kissel, "Suspect Says Shootings at Arkansas Recruiting Center Were Justified," CNS News, June 10, 2009, http://www.cnsnews.com /news/article/49374.

84. Tim Reid, "Sentenced to die, US Muslim soldier who killed comrades," *Sunday Times*, April 30, 2005, http://www.timesonline.co.uk/tol/news /world/iraq/article386812.ece.

85. Sarah Netter, "Devout Muslim Soldier Hopes to Avoid Deployment to Afghanistan," ABC News, August 31, 2010, http://abcnews.go.com/US /muslim-soldier-hoping-avoid-deployment-faith-conflicts-service/story ?id=11514381.

86. Islam Online Net, http://www.islamonline.net/servlet/Satellite?cid= 1119503544440&pagename=IslamOnline-English-Ask_Scholar %2FFatwaE%2FFatwaEAskTheScholar (this link is now inactive; information archived by author).

87. Kissel, "Suspect Says Shootings at Arkansas Recruiting Center Justified."

88. "Lieberman: Fort Hood could be terror attack," JTA, November 9, 2009, http://jta.org/news/article/2009/11/09/1009015/ft-hood -alleged-shooter-has-palestinian-roots-relatives.

89. "Islamic flag over the White House," *Washington Times*, editorial, October 4, 2010, http://www.washingtontimes.com/news/2010/oct/4 /islamic-flag-over-the-white-house/.

90. *Word Net Web*, s.v. "shariah," wordnetweb.princeton.edu/perl/webwn.

91. "US Military Burning Christian Bibles in Afghanistan," http://www .youtube.com/watch?v=xsToSlpa8jA.

92. Hanna Rosin, "Wiccan Controversy Tests Military Religious Tolerance," June 8, 1999, *Washington Post*, http://www.washingtonpost .com/wp-srv/national/daily/june99/wicca08.htm.

93. Andy McCarthy, "Why Does Interpol Need Immunity from American Law?" *National Review*, December 23, 2009, http://www.nationalreview

.com/corner/191918/why-does-interpol-need-immunity-american-law
/andy-mccarthy.

94. Matthew Spalding, *We Still Hold These Truths: Rediscovering Our Principles, Reclaiming Our Future* (Wilmington, DE: Intercollegiate, 2009), 163.

95. Ibid.

96. Ambassador John R. Bolton, *How Barack Obama Is Endangering Our National Sovereignty* (New York: Encounter, 2010), 11.

97. Arthur M. Schlesinger Jr., *The Disuniting of America: Reflections on a Multicultural Society* (New York: Norton, 1992), 13.

98. Dennis McCallum, ed., *The Death of Truth: Responding to Multiculturalism, the Rejection of Reason, and the New Postmodern Diversity* (Minneapolis: Bethany House, 1996), 283.

99. President Theodore Roosevelt, "Letter to the President of the American Defense Society."

CHAPTER 6: MOVING BEYOND RACE AND RACISM

1. John Turbyfill, personal communication with author, 2010.

2. Matthew Moynihan, e-mail to author, November 4, 2010.

3. Hope Yen, "Black-White Marriages Triple over Last Three Decades," theGrio, May 26, 2010, http://www.thegrio.com/news/interracial -marriage-more-likely-between-black-and-white.php.

4. Moynihan, e-mail to author, November 4, 2010.

5. Mary Kate Cary, "Republican Minorities Made Historic Gains in 2010 Elections," November 5, 2010, http://politics.usnews.com/opinion /blogs/mary-kate-cary/2010/11/05/republican-minorities-made -historic-gains-in-2010-elections.

6. Ibid.

7. Margaret Sanger, *The Pivot of Civilization* (New York: Brentano, 1922).

8. Madison Grant, *The Passing of the Great Race; Or, the Racial Basis of European History* (New York: Scribner, 1916).

9. Lothrop Stoddard, *The Rising Tide of Color Against White World-Supremacy* (New York: Scribner, 1920).

10. *Immigration Act of 1924*, Public Law 68-139, *U.S. Statutes at Large* 153 (1924): 43.

11. Max Ingman, "Mitochrondria," Actionbioscience.org, http://www .actionbioscience.org/evolution/ingman.html.

12. Stephen Oppenheimer, *The Real Eve: Modern Man's Journey out of Africa* (New York: Basic, 2004); Mark Schoofs, "The Myth of Race: What DNA Says About Human Ancestry—and Bigotry," *Village Voice*, part 3, excerpted at http://web.mit.edu/racescience/in_media/what_dna _says_about_human/index.html; Human Genome Project Information, http://www.ornl.gov/sci/techresources/Human_Genome/project/info .shtml.

13. Viktor E. Frankl, *Man's Search for Meaning* (1959; repr., Boston: Beacon, 2006), 86.

14. For brief discussions of what the Bible has to say about slavery, civil rights, abortion, and homosexuality, see Jim Hill and Rand Cheadle, *The Bible Tells Me So: Uses and Abuses of Holy Scripture* (New York: Bantam, 1996).

15. Arthur Schlesinger Jr., *The Disuniting of America* (Knoxville, TN: Whittle Direct Books, 1991), 48.

16. Paragraphs from this section draw heavily from pages 37–41 of Carol M. Swain, *The New White Nationalism in America: Its Challenge to Integration* (New York: Cambridge University Press, 2002).

17. Karl Marx and Friedrich Engels, *The Communist Manifesto* (1848; New York: Signet Classics, 1998).

18. Adolf Hitler, *Mein Kampf [My Struggle]*, trans. Ralph Manheim (1925–1926; Boston: Mariner, 1998).

19. Mao Tse-Tung, *Quotations from Chairman Mao Tse-tung* (1964; China: China Books and Periodicals, 1990).

20. Andrew Macdonald, *The Turner Diaries*, 2nd ed. (Hillsboro, WV: National Vanguard Press, 1980).

21. Robert L. Snow, *The Militia Threat: Terrorists Among Us* (New York: Plenum Trade, 1999), 95.

22. "'Turner Diaries' introduced in McVeigh trial," CNN, April 28, 1997, http://edition.cnn.com/US/9704/28/okc/.

23. Macdonald, *The Turner Diaries*, 79.

24. Swain, *New White Nationalism in America*, 40.

25. Ibid.

26. Ibid.

27. Khalid Abdul Muhammad, speech at Kean College, Union, New Jersey, November 29, 1993; expletives deleted.

28. Malik Zulu Shabazz, quoted in "Glenn Beck: Black Panthers Respond to 'Kill Cracker Babies' Comment," *The Glenn Beck Show*, July 9, 2010, http://www.glennbeck.com/content/articles/article/198/42766/; expletives deleted.

29. Darren W. Davis and Ronald E. Brown, "The Antipathy of Black Nationalism: Behavioral and Attitudinal Implications of an African American Ideology," *American Journal of Political Science* 46, no. 2 (April 2002): 241.

30. Ibid.

31. Scott Glover, "Huge Sweeps Target Latino Gangs That Allegedly Attacked Blacks," *LA Times*, May 21, 2009, http://latimesblogs.latimes.com/lanow/2009/05/huge-gang-sweeps-targets-latino-gangs-that-allegedly-targeted-blacks.html.

32. Tanya K. Hernandez, "Latino Anti-Black Violence in Los Angeles: Not 'Made in the USA,'" *Harvard Journal of African American Public Policy* 13 (Summer 2007): 37.

33. Ibid., 38.

34. Nicolas Vaca, *The Presumed Alliance: The Unspoken Conflict Between Latinos and Blacks and What It Means for America* (New York: Rayo, 2004), ix.

35. Ibid.

36. Eric Hoffer, *The True Believer: Thoughts on the Nature of Mass Movements* (New York: Harper & Row, 1951).

37. Swain, *New White Nationalism in America*, 128–29.

38. Ibid, 137. For more information see Carol M. Swain, ed., *Race Versus Class: The New Affirmative Action Debate* (Lanham, MD: University Press of America, 1995).

39. US Constitution, amend. 14, sec. 1.

40. Civil Rights Act of 1964, Public Law 78, *U.S. Statutes at Large* 241, *U.S. Code* 42 (1964), §§ 2000a.

41. Ibid., §. 2000e.

42. Daniel Seligman, "Affirmative Action Is Here to Stay," *Fortune*, April 19, 1982; Jennifer Hochschild, "Affirmative Action as Culture War," in Michele Lamont, ed., *The Culture Territories of Race: Black and White Boundaries* (Chicago: University of Chicago Press, 1999); William G. Bowen and Derek Bok, *The Shape of the River: Long-Term Consequences of Considering Race in College and University Admissions* (Princeton: Princeton University Press, 1998).

43. Michael Kinsley, "The Spoils of Victimhood," *New Yorker*, March 27, 1995, 69.

44. *Grutter v. Bollinger*, 539 US 306 (2003).

45. Mark J. Richards, "Affirmative Action," *Free Speech Politics* (blog), http://freespeechpolitics.blogspot.com/2007/04/affirmative-action.html.

46. Swain, *New White Nationalism in America*, 434.

47. David K. Shipler, *A Country of Strangers: Blacks and Whites in America* (New York: Knopf, 1997), 460–61.

48. Seymour M. Lipset, *American Exceptionalism: A Double-Edged Sword* (New York: Norton, 1997), 132.

CHAPTER 7: RACIAL POLITICS: PRESIDENT OBAMA AND ME

1. Barack Obama, speech at Democratic National Convention, Boston, Massachusetts, July 27, 2004. Transcript available at http://www.washingtonpost.com/wp-dyn/articles/A19751-2004Jul27.html.

2. Niccolo Machiavelli, *The Prince*, trans. and ed. by Thomas G. Bergin (Northbrook, IL: AHM Publishing Corporation, 1947), 51.

3. Carol M. Swain, "Is America Ready for a Black President? America Is Ready, but It Won't Be a Veteran of the Civil Rights Movement," *Ebony* 62, no. 3 (January 2007), 141, at Carol M. Swain website, http://www.carolmswain.com/articles/isamericaready.html; emphasis added.

4. YouTube Video of Peggy Joseph, http://www.youtube.com/watch?v=P36x8rTb3jI.

5. Candidate Barack Obama, speech, Sarasota, Florida, October 30, 2008, http://www.barackobama.com/2008/10/30/remarks_of_senator_barack_obam_151.php.

6. Michelle Malkin, "And the Winner Is . . . Peggy the Moocher," November 8, 2008, *Michelle Malkin* (blog), http://michellemalkin.com/2008/11/05/and-the-real-winner-ispeggy-the-moocher/.

7. Dewey M. Clayton, *The Presidential Campaign of Barack Obama: A Critical Analysis of a Racially Transcendent Strategy* (New York: Routledge, 2010), xiii.

8. Claire Morgenstern, "Election 2008: The Second-Largest Youth Voter Turnout in American History," *Tartan*, November 10, 2008, http://www.thetartan.org/2008/11/10/news/elections.

9. Mark Hugo Lopez and Paul Taylor, "Dissecting the 2008 Electorate: Most Diverse in US History," Pew Center for Research, April 30, 2009, http://pewresearch.org/pubs/1209/racial-ethnic-voters-presidential-election.

10. Pew Research Center, "A Look at Religious Voters in the 2008 Election," *Pew Forum on Religion and Public Life*, February 2, 2009, http://pewresearch.org/pubs/1112/religion-vote-2008-election.

11. Alexander Mas and Enrico Moretti, "Racial Bias in the 2008 Presidential Elections," *American Economic Review of Papers and Proceedings* 99 (May 2002): 323–29.

12. Lydia Saad, "Obama and Bush: A Contrast in Popularity," Gallup, November 10, 2008, http://www.gallup.com/poll/111838/obama-bush-contrast-popularity.aspx.

13. Bernard Goldberg, *A Slobbering Love Affair: Starring Barack Obama* (Washington, D.C.: Regnery, 2009), 4.

14. Christopher Hedges, *Empire of Illusion: The End of Literacy and the Triumph of Spectacle* (New York: Nation Books, 2009), 51.

15. Ibid.

16. Jeffrey M. Jones, "Obama Quarterly Approval Average Slips Nine Points to 53%," Gallup, October 21, 2009, http://www.gallup.com/poll/123806/Obama-Quarterly-Approval-Average-Slips-Nine-Points.aspx.

17. Ben Evans, "CBC Demands Obama Address Recession Fallout for Black Community," CNS News, December 10, 2009, http://www.cnsnews.com/news/article/58361#; Tolu Olorunda, "The State of Black America vs. Tavis Smiley vs. Rev. Al Sharpton," *Daily Voice*, February 10, 2010, http://thedailyvoice.com/voice/2010/02/the-state-of-black-america-vs-002564.php.

18. Cornel West, quoted in Boyce Watkins, "Cornel West Questions Barack Obama's Commitment to Black People," *Black Voices*, February 25, 2010, http://www.bvblackspin.com/2010/02/25/cornel-west-barack-obama/.

19. Christian E. Weller, "Economic Snapshot for 2009," Center for American Progress, http://www.americanprogress.org/issues/2009/01/econ_snapshot_0109.html.

20. Karen Travers, "Obama Administration's report on Stimulus Act After Year One," ABC News, February 16, 2010, http://blogs.abcnews.com/politicalpunch/2010/02/obama-administrations-report-on-stimulus

-act-after-year-one.html; James Surowiecki, "Second Helpings," *New Yorker*, September 20, 2010, http://www.newyorker.com/talk /financial/2010/09/20/100920ta_talk_surowiecki.

21. Michelle Malkin, *Culture of Corruption: Obama and His Team of Tax Cheats, Crooks, and Cronies* (Washington, D.C.: Regnery, 2009).

22. Sean Hannity, *Conservative Victory: Defeating Obama's Radical Agenda* (New York: Harper Collins, 2010); Dick Morris and Eileen McCann, *Catastrophe: How Obama, Congress, and the Special Interests Are Transforming . . . a Slump into a Crash, Freedom into Socialism, and a Disaster into a Catastrophe . . . How to Fight Back* (New York: HarperCollins, 2009).

23. Hannity, *Conservative Victory*, 193–94.

24. Pew Forum on Religion and Public Life, "Growing Number of Americans Say Obama Is a Muslim," Pew Research Center, August 18, 2010, http://www.pewforum.org/Politics-and-Elections/Growing -Number-of-Americans-Say-Obama-is-a-Muslim.aspx.

25. Paul Harris, "Obama Under Fire Over Support for Mosque Near Ground Zero," *Guardian.co.uk: Observer*, August 15, 2010, http://www .guardian.co.uk/world/2010/aug/15/obama-under-fire-mosque-support. © Guardian News & Media Ltd 2010.

26. Jordan Fabian, "Poll: Public Strongly Opposes Ground Zero Mosque," The Hill, August 11, 2010, http://thehill.com/blogs/blog-briefing-room /news/113747-poll-public-strongly-opposes-ground-zero-mosque.

27. Jerome R. Corsi, "Congress report concedes Obama eligibility unvetted: 'There is no specific federal agency' to review candidates for federal office," WorldNetDaily, November 8, 2010, http://www.wnd.com /?pageId=225561.

28. Excerpt from Congressional Research Services Memo drafted by Jack Maskell, a legislative attorney. The memo entitled "Qualifications for the Office of President of the United States and Legal Challenges to the Eligibility of a Candidate," is dated April 3, 2009. It was distributed to several congressional offices, and later someone posted it on the Internet. http://www.scribd.com/doc/41131059/Members-of-Congress-Memo -What-to-Tell-Your-Constituents-in-Answer-to-Obama-Eligibility -Questions.

29. Emer de Vattel, *The Law of Nations* (Northampton, MA: Thomas M. Pomroy, 1805), 162.

30. Sharon Rondeau, "Army Flight Surgeon Facing Court Martial for

Refusal to Obey Orders," *Post & E-Mail*, April 13, 2010, http://www
.thepostemail.com/2010/04/13/army-seizes-computer-and-revokes
-pentagon-access-for-challenger-to-obamas-eligibility/; J. B. Williams,
"Military Veterans Unify—Placing Obama Eligibility on Front Burner,"
Michigan News, October 4, 2010, http://www.freerepublic.com/focus
/f-bloggers/2601021/posts.

31. "Obama Born in Kenya? His Grandmother Says Yes," IsraelNationalNews
.com, October 12, 2008, http://www.israelnationalnews.com/blogs
/message.aspx/3074.

32. Amanda Paulson, "Why Hawaii Gov. Neil Abercrombie Is Taking on
the Birthers," *Christian Science Monitor*, December 28, 2010, http://
www.csmonitor.com/USA/Politics/The-Vote/2010/1228/Why-Hawaii
-Gov.-Neil-Abercrombie-is-taking-on-anti-Obama-birthers.

33. Jack Cashill, "Friend Says Abercrombie Told Him, 'There Is No Birth
Certificate!'" American Thinker, January 20, 2011, http://www
.americanthinker.com/blog/2011/01/friend_says_abercrombie_to
_him.html; Robert Paul Reyes, "Gov. Neil Abercrombie Has Utterly
Failed to Prove Obama Was Born in Hawaii, *Hawaii Reporter*, January
20, 2011, http://www.hawaiireporter.com/gov-neil-abercrombie-has
-utterly-failed-to-prove-obama-was-born-in-hawaii.

34. Mark Niesse, "Hawaii Bars Release of Obama's Birth Info," Yahoo
News, January 22, 2011, http://news.yahoo.com/s/ap/20110122/ap_on
_re_us/us_obama_birth_certificate; "Birthers Claim Gibbs Lied When
He Said Obama's Birth Certificate Is Posted on the Internet," PolitiFact,
July 28, 2009, http://www.politifact.com/truth-o-meter/statements
/2009/jul/28/worldnetdaily/birthers-claim-gibbs-lied-when
-he-said-obamas-birt.

35. CNN Poll, "Quarter Doubt Obama Was Born in the United States,"
August 4, 2010, http://politicalticker.blogs.cnn.com/2010/08/04
/cnn-poll-quarter-doubt-president-was-born-in-u-s/.

36. Jeffrey M. Jones, "Obama Approval Rating Continues to Hover Around
50%," Gallup Poll, February 22, 2010, http://www.gallup.com/poll
/126149/Obama-Approval-Rating-Continues-Hover-Around.aspx.

37. "Obama Job Approval," Gallup Poll, http://www.gallup.com/poll
/113980/Gallup-Daily-Obama-Job-Approval.aspx.

38. "Obama Approval Averages 45% in September," Gallup Poll, http://
www.gallup.com/poll/143354/Obama-Approval-Averages-September
.aspx?utm_source=alert&utm_medium=email&utm_campaign
=syndication&utm_content=morelink&utm_term=Politics.

39. *Ricci v. DeStefano*, 129 S. Ct. 2658, 2671, 174 L. Ed. 2d 490 (2009).

40. Denise Lavoie, "Cop Who Arrested Black Scholar Is Profiling Expert," Breitbart.com, July 23, 2009, http://www.breitbart.com/article.php ?id=D99KBEAO1.

41. Carol M. Swain, "'Whites Are People Too': Why Some White People Are Stating the Obvious," Huffington Post, August 20, 2009, http:// www.huffingtonpost.com/carol-m-swain/whites-are-people-too-why _b_263720.html.

42. Carol M. Swain and Russell Nieli, *Contemporary Voices of White Nationalism* (New York: Cambridge University Press, 2003).

43. President Barack Obama as quoted by Suzanne Gamboa, "Obama Turns to 'Piolin' to Rev Up Latino Vote," APNews, October 25, 2010, http://townhall.com/news/politics-elections/2010/10/25/Obama_turns _to_poilin_to_rev_up_latino_vote.

44. Eugene Robinson, "Don't Make Obama Look Bad, Now," *St. Louis American*, October 21, 2010, http://www.stlamerican.com/news /columnists/article-bc97b6fc-dcb7-11df-9bf4-001cc4c03286.html.

45. Rasmussen Report, "Right Direction or Wrong Track? 31 Percent Say US Heading in Right Direction," November 3, 2010, http://www .rasmussenreports.com/public_content/politics/mood_of_america /right_direction_or_wrong_track.

46. Norimitsu Onishi, "Obama Visits a Nation That Once Knew Him as Barry," *New York Times*, November 8, 2010, http://www.nytimes .com/2010/11/09/world/asia/09indo.html?pagewanted=1&_r=1; Matt DeLong, "Obama's Indonesian Gay Nanny and Other Things from His Past," *Washington Post*, November 8, 2010, http://voices.washingtonpost .com/44/2010/11/obamas-indonesian-transvestite.html.

47. Chip Reid and Robert Hendin, "In Indonesia: A Glimpse into Obama's Childhood," CBS News, November 9, 2010, http://www.cbsnews.com /8301-503544_162-20022313-503544.html.

48. Ibid.

49. This statement appears on page 142 of the 1996 paperback version of *Dreams from My Father*, originally published in 1995 by Times Books, a division of Random House; in 1996 by Kodansha Globe; and 2004 by Three Rivers Press. The statement does not appear on page 142 of the Three Rivers Press version released in 2004.

50. Barack Obama, *The Audacity of Hope: Thoughts on Reclaiming the American Dream* (New York: Crown, 2006), 274.

51. Daniel Pipes, "Barack Obama's Muslim Childhood," *FrontpageMagazine .com*, April 29, 2008, http://www.danielpipes.org/5544/barack -obamas-muslim-childhood.

52. Aswini Anburajan, "Obama Asked About His Connection to Islam," MSN.com, December 22, 2007, http://firstread.msnbc.msn.com /_news/2007/12/22/4436605-obama-asked-about-connection-to-islam.

53. Madeline Brooks, "Obama's Unique Form of 'Christianity: 'No Baptism or Renunciation of Islam Required," Canada Free Press, August 21, 2010, http://www.canadafreepress.com/index.php/article/26810; Jodi Kantor, "Barack Obama's Search for Faith," *New York Times*, April 4, 2007, http://www.nytimes.com/2007/04/30/world/americas/30iht -30obama.5501905.html?pagewanted=3&_r=1.

54. Kantor, "Barack Obama's Search for Faith."

55. Barack Obama, speech at Democratic National Convention, Boston, Massachusetts, July 27, 2004, http://www.washingtonpost.com/wp-dyn /articles/A19751-2004Jul27.html.

56. Barack Obama, *Dreams from My Father: A Story of Race and Inheritance* (New York: Times Books, 1995; Kodansha Globe, 1996; Two Rivers Press, 2004); Obama, *The Audacity of Hope*.

57. *Free Dictionary*, s.v. "standing," http://legal-dictionary.thefreedictionary .com/standing.

58. Daniel P. Tokaji, "The Justiciability of Eligibility: May Courts Decide Who Can Be President?" *Michigan Law Review First Impressions* 107 (2008): 31, http://www.michiganlawreview.org/articles/the-justiciability-of -eligibility-may-courts-decide-who-can-be-president.

59. Nikita Khrushchev, speech in Yugoslavia, August 24, 1963, http://www .quotationspage.com/quotes/Nikita_Khrushchev/; Nikita Khrushchev, quoted in "We Will Bury You," *Time*, November 26, 1956, http://www .time.com/time/magazine/article/0,9171,867329,00.html?artID =867329?contType=article?chn=us.

60. I have shared this information in the preface of *The New White Nationalism in America*, xviii.

CHAPTER 8: RECLAIMING AMERICA'S FAITH AND PROMISE

1. Richard J. Neuhaus, *The Naked Public Square* (Grand Rapids: Eerdmans, 1984), ix.

2. William J. Bennett, foreword in Matthew Spaulding, *We Still Hold These Truths* (Wilmington, DE: Intercollegiate, 2009), xiii.

3. Luke Timothy Johnson, quoted in Richard John Neuhaus, "The Future of Sex and Marriage," *First Things*, January 4, 2008, 943; emphasis added.

4. Tullian Tchividjian, *Unfashionable* (Colorado Springs: Multnomah, 2009).

5. Ibid., 19; emphasis in original.

6. Ibid.

7. Ibid., 65.

8. Ibid., 64.

9. Robert Benne, *Introduction to the Christian Life* (Minneapolis: Fortress, 1988), 9.

10. Pastor Joe Wright, opening prayer for the Kansas State House, January 23, 1996. Used by permission.

11. *The New King James Study Bible* (Nashville: Thomas Nelson, 1988).

12. *New Living Translation* (Carol Stream, IL: Tyndale, 2007).

13. "How to Contact Your Senator," http://www.senate.gov/reference /common/faq/How_to_contact_senators.htm; "Comments for the House of Representatives," http://www.house.gov/house/house _comments.shtml.

APPENDIX B: THE DECLARATION OF INDEPENDENCE

1. "The Unanimous Declaration of the Thirteen United States of America," July 4, 1776, available at US History.org, http://www .ushistory.org/declaration/document.

APPENDIX C: THE BILL OF RIGHTS

1. *The Laws of the United States in Three Volumes* (Philadelphia: Richard Folwell, 1796).

APPENDIX D: THE CONSTITUTION OF THE UNITED STATES OF AMERICA (1787)

1. US Constitution, available at Constitution Society, http://www.constitution.org/constit_.htm.

INDEX

ABOUT THE AUTHOR

CAROL M. SWAIN IS AN AWARD-WINNING AUTHOR AND WIDELY RECOGNIZED expert on race relations, immigration, black leadership, and evangelical politics. Her opinion pieces have been published in the *New York Times*, *Washington Post*, *Wall Street Journal*, *Washington Times*, and *USA Today*. She is a regular contributor to Fox News' *Hannity* "Great American Panel" segment, and she has been a regular contributor to CNN's *Lou Dobbs Tonight*. Professor Swain has appeared on BBC Radio, NPR, CNN, *Fox News Live*, *News Hour with Jim Lehrer* on PBS, *Washington Journal*, and ABC's Headline News, among other media. Before joining Vanderbilt in 1999, Professor Swain was a tenured associate professor of politics and public policy at Princeton University's Woodrow Wilson School of Public and International Affairs. She is a foundation member of the Virginia Chapter of Phi Beta Kappa.

Website: www.CarolMSwain.com
Twitter: www.twitter.com/carolmswain
Facebook: www.facebook.com/carolmswain

LEARN MORE

GET INVOLVED

JOIN THE EFFORT TO RECLAIM AMERICA

The CAROL SWAIN FOUNDATION
is a non-profit 501c (3), designed to educate
the public about the cultural, economic,
political, and social issues of our day.

P.O. Box 40032
Nashville, TN 37204-0032

WWW.CAROLMSWAIN.COM